# Walking in
# Italy

## by Gillian & John Souter

Interlink Books
An imprint of Interlink Publishing Group, Inc.
New York • Northampton

This edition first published 2002 by

**INTERLINK BOOKS**
An imprint of Interlink Publishing Group, Inc.
99 Seventh Avenue • Brooklyn, NY 11215 and
46 Crosby Street • Northampton, MA 01060
**www.interlinkbooks.com**

**Library of Congress Cataloging-in
Publication Data**

Souter, Gillian.
Walking in Italy by Gillian & John Souter.
p. cm.
Includes bibliographical references and index.
ISBN 1-56656-453-0
1. Walking--Italy--Guidebooks. 2. Italy--
Guidebooks. I. Souter,
John, 1956- II. Title.
DG416 .S64 2002
914.504'93--dc21

2001007391

Printed and bound in Singapore

To request our complete 40-page full-color catalog,
please call us toll free at **1-800-238-LINK,** visit our
web site at **www.interlinkbooks.com**, or write to
**Interlink Publishing**
46 Crosby Street, Northampton, MA 01060
E-mail: info@interlinkbooks.com

# CONTENTS

Introduction  4

# INTRODUCTION

The Italians have a fine tradition known as the *passeggiata*: a leisurely evening stroll along the street, taking the opportunity to greet friends and neighbours. It's more of a social exercise than a physical one—most will just take a short walk or *due passi*—and its purpose is not sight-seeing, though the route of the promenade will no doubt take in the most attractive piazza or the seafront, or the grandest street. It is just one of the pleasures of life in Italy.

Those of us merely visiting the country need to take a more rigorous approach to viewing our surroundings. Italy is a small country but it boasts a vast array of beautiful landscapes and an astounding number of treasures tucked away in city and town. For those who enjoy a longer walk—*quattro passi* or more—there is enough to fill many holidays. We have written this book to help you make the most of your few weeks, whether it be your first visit or your fifth.

This book is designed for people who have a love of landscape and, when in cities, an interest in things historic and cultural. It's also for those who like to travel slowly, if they have the option. That doesn't mean loitering by the pool; it means enjoying as much as you can of a particular place and getting a sense of it as somewhere people live and have lived.

Walking holidays in Italy are becoming a more popular travel option with each year and an array of tour companies provide packaged walking trips, guided or self-guided, to the better-known destinations. Of course, such tours have their place, but they can be inflexible and dauntingly expensive. The prospect of walking independently in a foreign country can be equally daunting: where and when to walk; which village to use as a base and how to get there; which walks to try; how to get to the trail head; what map to buy... Our aim is to ease you into the great delights of independent walking by providing answers to such questions and to give you a book full of inspirational walking ideas. We have personally 'road-tested' all the main walks and most of the supplementary walks that appear at the end of each chapter. Likewise, one of us took the photographs en route, so they're a real reflection of what there is to see when you head off along the track.

Many of Italy's finest treasures—its hill-towns, sanctuaries, castles, ancient ruins—exist in an organic relationship with the landscape. We long ago realised that the effect of these places when encountered on foot (as they were meant to be reached) is far more profound than that created when alighting from a bus and joining a tour group. For some reason, it took us longer to realise that the same holds true in cities, probably because it's harder to block out the modern incursions and see the building as it was designed to be seen.

Out of these musings came the idea for this book; as far as we know, it's unique in its coverage of both city and country walks.

< A stroll in the Foro Romano

0 km    100    200

CITY WALKS
AND COUNTRY
WALKING AREAS

LAGO di COMO
(Lake Como)

The DOLOMITI
(Dolomites)

GRAN
PARADISO

Venezia
(Venice)

Bergamo

Verona

Padova
(Padua)

Torino
(Turin)

Ferrara

Genova
(Genoa)

Bologna

Ravenna

The
CINQUE
TERRE

Lucca

Firenze
(Florence)

Pisa

CHIANTI

Heart of
TOSCANA
(Tuscany)

Siena

Perugia

UMBRIAN
Hilltowns

The MAIELLA

Roma
(Rome)

Napoli
(Naples)

SARDEGNA
(Sardinia)

SARDEGNAN
Wilds

COSTIERA
AMALFITANA
(Amalfi Coast)

Cagliari

Palermo

Taormina

N

SICILIA
(Sicily)

Temples of
SICILIA

Siracusa
(Syracuse)

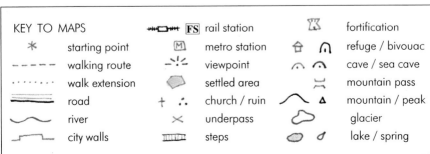

KEY TO MAPS

* starting point

– – – – walking route

· · · · · walk extension

road

river

city walls

**FS** rail station

M metro station

viewpoint

settled area

church / ruin

underpass

steps

fortification

refuge / bivouac

cave / sea cave

mountain pass

mountain / peak

glacier

lake / spring

## GRADING THE WALKS

One person's short jaunt is another's wearisome slog. We're assuming a reasonable level of fitness and the stamina to walk for some hours, but we've tried to include itineraries of varying lengths so you can choose what suits you. Our estimate of walking times includes rest and food breaks. We haven't given times for the city walks as these will depend greatly on how long you spend at each point of interest. Much of Italy is mountainous or at least hilly; walks in such areas will almost inevitably involve ascents and descents! Needless to say, the fitter you are, the more you'll enjoy it, so do some walking beforehand.

Our grading scheme is necessarily subjective and gradings assume decent weather and that the path remains in its current condition. Our gradings take into account the route length and distance, height gained and lost, navigational difficulty and the roughness of the path.

## PATH WAYMARKING

Hiking or trekking is not such a popular activity among the Italian population. The country does, however, have a club of

A typical CAI waymark

A city waymark

committed mountain walkers, known as the Club Alpino Italiano or CAI. This group, which has branches in most cities, has collectively waymarked many existing paths—old mule paths, drove tracks or pilgrimage routes—so that they can be more easily followed by walkers.

The standard CAI waymark is a red-and-white stripe, usually painted on a tree or a boulder. You will become quite adept at sighting these. Sometimes the dauber seems to run out of paint just when you need a guiding sign! In some areas, such as national parks, local authorities have marked walking tracks using their own system. Where our route follows a waymarked path, we tend to give fewer directions.

## WHERE TO GO

This book offers a selection of places in Italy that are ideal for walking, organised roughly north to south. If you think this is your one and only chance to visit Italy, you'll no doubt want to visit the major centres of Roma, Firenze and Venezia.

A less frenetic holiday would combine a few cities interspersed with nearby country areas. For example, a few leisurely days spent walking in Chianti's delightful vineyards or in the hills around San Gimignano would prove a welcome antidote to the cultural overload of Firenze and Siena. Or, perhaps you could enjoy the charms of Amalfi's dramatic coastline after visiting chaotic Napoli.

We have used the Italian version of placenames, which may be a little disconcerting at first. However, it will be good preparation for reading signs and timetables and it won't take long for you to adjust.

When planning your trip, you might be guided by the season, particularly for a walking holiday. Some regions are more popular than others; if you want to avoid other people then take a risk and head for somewhere you've not heard much about.

## THE TOWNS

We have included most of the larger cities and towns plus a handful of the smaller gems. There are some notable omissions: Milano, Bari, Trieste and Orvieto are just some. Some cities' attractions are not easily negotiated on foot, while limited space has precluded the inclusion of others.

## THE COUNTRY

Our most difficult and subjective decisions revolved around which parts of Italy's wonderfully varied countryside to include. The renown of Chianti, the Cinque Terre, the Amalfi coastline and Lago di Como made them automatic inclusions. We have generally favoured Italy's mountains and hills over its coastline; unfortunately, large stretches of waterfront have been marred by concrete promenades, holiday parks and multistorey buildings. Most mountain areas have fared much better, protected by topography and statute. Here, we've favoured walks in national parks or reserves.

We've selected rural areas that can be reached by public transport and that can accommodate tourists. There are countless others, some of which have been mentioned briefly in the back of the book.

Marmots are common in Alpine areas

One of the bonuses of country walking is the opportunity to see wildlife, though sadly, Italian hunters have seen to it that this is a slim chance, outside of national parks. Most likely, you'll spy some soaring birds of prey, seen both in wild and farmed countryside. Wild boars are quite common in Italian woodland, though you're more likely to hear them or to see only the signs of their scrabbling in the earth; their destructive habits make them an enemy of Italian farmers. In high regions above the treeline, you may be fortunate enough to witness marmots, chamois and even ibex.

Wildflowers are relatively thicker on the ground and spring and early summer are the best times to see them. The vegetation of the Mediterranean areas is quite different to the Alpine flora and you can also expect to enjoy flowers in cultivated areas, where poppies and other seasonal flowers carpet olive groves and meadows.

## WHEN TO GO WHERE

Italy is a long and mountainous country and its climate is accordingly quite varied. The south has a Mediterranean climate, with hot, dry summers and mild, wet winters. Mid-country, apart from the Appennini, is somewhat milder, with cold winters. The

Female ibex, spotted on a misty day

mountainous north has short, cool summers and long months of winter snow. This is a great simplification, but it gives you a rough guide for your travel plans.

Country walking is more constrained by season and climate than is walking in towns and cities but, whatever the time of year, you will be able to find walks in this book to suit.

July and August, the hottest months, are also the most touristed. Italians flee the stifling cities for their summer holidays during the first three weeks of August; we would advise against walking in August, except in mountain areas.

June to September is the best time for walking in mountain areas. Wildflowers are at their best in June and early July. Services—buses, *rifugi*, chairlifts, etc.—can be severely reduced either side of mid-June and mid-September. Adjusted summer time (which runs to the end of October) gives you an extra hour for walking. Avoid low-altitude walks—with the possible exception of the Cinque Terre—during summer. This applies especially to Sardegna and Sicilia.

Away from the mountains, spring and autumn are ideal walking seasons. Winter is no barrier to city walking, but be prepared for near-freezing temperatures in the north.

Fire salamanders appear after rain

## HOW TO TRAVEL

We confess to a strong public transport bias. Italy has a good and inexpensive rail system that, in combination with local bus services, will take you almost everywhere. Reliance on public transport is environmentally-friendly, less stressful and means that you don't have a rental car sitting idly while you walk. Private cars are effectively banned from driving in the centre of many popular towns. However, if you do use public transport, you need to read any timetables carefully (note that *feriale* means working days, including Saturday) and keep in mind that travel on Sundays can be problematic.

The state rail system is known as FS for Ferrovie dello Stato. Their website (www.fs-on-line.com) can be extremely useful for planning your itinerary. The local tourist websites given at the start of each chapter will often provide some bus information, and you could email them if you have a particular transport query. It's worth noting that the rail station is often at the edge of a town or, in the case of a hilltown, often a bus trip downhill from the town centre.

We have never driven a car in Italy but, observing from our vantage point on buses, you will need skill and bravado!

## WHERE TO STAY

Most Italian cities and towns offer a good range of accommodation, from the humblest family-run *pensione* to more opulent hotels; a star rating indicates the relative sophistication. You might also consider one of the many youth hostels (by no means restricted to youth) or *agriturismo*, farm-stays that are proliferating in parts of Italy. In a country hotel, you might have the option of half-pension (*mezzo pensione*), where dinner and breakfast are provided. This is usually a sound investment, particularly if you come back weary from a full day of walking, and we have had some memorable culinary experiences this way.

Rifugio Sella, Gran Paradiso

In country chapters, we have suggested a base town convenient for all the walks. Use of a car will increase your options. All of the routes are day walks, though on occasion we suggest how to extend them with an overnight stay. In remote areas, you might be tempted to organise a night in a CAI or private *rifugio*, one of the mountain huts run on simple lines but often extremely hospitable and beautifully situated.

In general, whether or not you book ahead should depend on the season, your itinerary and level of flexibility. Key cities—Venezia, Firenze, Pisa, Siena, for example—can be overrun with visitors throughout the summer months, making early reservations highly desirable.

Information on hotels is available in the countless guide books currently published; select one that is pitched at your comfort level and budget. Alternatively, some of the tourist office websites we've mentioned list hotels and prices, particularly in rural regions. Avoid the sites of commercial agencies, as these only tend to list more expensive hotels. The tourist office for each town will also be able to assist and can usually find you a bed if you arrive with nothing reserved.

## WHAT TO TAKE

As a rule, we pack lightly and wash often. Modern fabrics that dry quickly are a great boon to the walker-traveller. Trousers with zip-off legs are versatile in changeable weather and for visiting churches! Take a good pair of walking boots that you have already worn in, plus a light pair of comfortable but tidy shoes. Thin lining socks, worn in conjunction with a pair of thick socks, can increase comfort and reduce washing. You'll also need a good waterproof jacket, sunscreen and sunglasses.

Aluminium water bottles are lightweight but much more sturdy than a plastic mineral water bottle. A penknife is indispensable for picnics; pack it in your main luggage on flights. A torch can be quite useful for investigating caves and unlit churches and for the occasional tunnel. A compass is handy, not only if you lose your way, but for identifying major landmarks. A compact pair of binoculars is good both for watching distant wildlife and for inspecting high frescoes and mosaics. We carry several things that we hope never to use: a basic first-aid kit, a whistle and blister plasters.

Carry water, even in towns

Depending on the season and your destination, you might need gloves, a warm hat, warm polypropolene garments, or conversely, a sunhat, shorts and swimwear. Collapsible walking poles are a good investment if, like us, you plan to keep walking into old age. They are particularly useful for saving your knees on steep descents and ascents, and for crossing streams, loose scree or muddy patches.

We each take a day-pack as our hand luggage on flights and then carry these on our walks. We opt to use a medium-sized backpack as our main luggage so that we can walk the distance from the bus/train to our accommodation. Combination packs (two different packs that join) are a good option if you need to purchase luggage.

## USING THIS BOOK

This is a walking book, rather than a general guide. It contains no accommodation or dining recommendations, nor does it provide detailed information on transport, entertainment and so on. Most readers will probably want to supplement this book with either a general guide book on Italy, or with something more specialised on a particular region or city.

The schematic maps in this book are a good starting point and for city walks should prove sufficient for your needs, but we do recommend buying a good topographical map in country areas. These can sometimes be bought in advance at a map shop in your own country or online. Alternatively, you should be able to buy a map from the local bookshop or *libreria* when you arrive in a particular region. A key to the maps in this book appears on page 5.

## OTHER TRAVEL INFORMATION

Italy's overblown bureaucracy has provided a confusing array of information offices for tourists. In cities and larger towns, there will usually be an Azienda Promozione Touristica (APT). It has information about

Stop by the market for picnic fare

both the province and the town, and can be good for transport information from there to the major cities.

Most towns will have a local office where you can get information on local buses, accommodation and up-to-date opening times of attractions. These are known by the acronyms IAT and AAST. There are also other agencies and all these distinctions can be confusing to the traveller. We have listed whichever office is central and most helpful. The tourist office will often have a free town map and possibly some notes on other walks nearby.

## WARNINGS & TIPS

Here are a few suggestions to make your trip safer and more enjoyable.

In cities and towns, opening hours can be a source of frustration. The hours of galleries, museums and other attractions are usually much shorter in the winter months. We've tried to give details at the back of the chapter (in order of appearance in the walk) but they can change. All but the major churches close for several hours at lunchtime and you can't visit if there is a service in progress, or if you're 'improperly' dressed. We haven't always listed church opening hours, as they're not always publicised.

On country walks, always pack an emergency food supply, some chocolate at least, even if you expect to buy lunch en route. Take plenty of water and refill your bottles at every opportunity. Be careful of poisonous vipers in summer and of men (always men) with guns during the hunting season, which runs from October to March. Don't start a mountain walk in uncertain weather conditions and don't be too proud to turn back if you're having any difficulty. If walking in a remote area, let your host know where you're heading each morning.

On slopes, don't short cut the track as this causes erosion. Where a path passes through farmland, respect the owner's rights by obeying signs, closing gates and not damaging crops. In national parks and reserves, it goes without saying that wildflowers are protected.

Italian is an easy language to dabble in and people will appreciate your attempts, no matter how clumsy. Few Italians speak much English—the young know more than most—and while a command of the language is not essential for travel, a smattering of words and phrases is certainly useful and will make your trip more enjoyable.

We like to stay in smaller towns if possible, perhaps visiting larger cities on a day trip. Sometimes we'll visit a town or compact city in transit, leaving our luggage at the rail station and walking around unencumbered, then collecting it and heading on to our destination.

Everyone develops his or her own pace and style of travel, the idiosyncrasies of which make it such a fascinating experience. We hope you can adapt the information in this book to your own needs and likes, and enjoy more fully what Italy has to offer!

# GRAN PARADISO

Stunning Alpine mountain views, fresh air, close sightings of rare ibex, a good local cuisine: all these are to be had in Italy's oldest national park, along with some excellent walking on well-marked trails.

At 4061 m in height, Gran Paradiso is Italy's highest wholly-owned mountain; a few higher peaks are shared with France and Switzerland. It lends its name to Italy's first national park, established in 1922 as an extension of a Royal Hunting Reserve donated to the state by King Vittorio Emanuele III. This 70,000-hectare park is twinned with France's Vanoise national park, which it borders.

The Parco Nazionale del Gran Paradiso is aptly named; it's an Alpine paradise for walkers and lovers of wildlife, in particular the once-near-extinct ibex that the park was created to protect. Geographically, the park is formed by a series of mountain ridges separating deep parallel valleys, north–south tributaries of the Val d'Aosta and Val di Cogne. Geologically, much of the rock is gneiss, a coarse metamorphic rock, with patches of greenstone and outcrops of granite and diorite and, in the

NOTES

Suggested base: Cogne

Getting there: rail/bus from Torino or Milano to Aosta, then bus to Cogne

Tourist Office: P. Emile Chanoux 11012 Cogne, Tel: 0165 74040 Fax: 0165 749125  www.cogne.org email: apt@cogne.org

Map: Eurocart Gran Paradiso 1:50000

Best timing: June-September

Val di Cogne, seams of iron minerals that were mined until 1972.

With many peaks over 3000 m, the park boasts 57 glaciers so there's an abundance of ice-related phenomena—exquisite U-shaped valleys, glacial moraines and ice-polished rock slabs—as well as a profusion of icy mountain streams, cascades and glacier-fed tarns. There's ample opportunity to observe Alpine fauna at close quarters, including chamois and marmots and ibex. Rarer, but possible, are sightings of the bearded vulture, golden eagle, white hare and the once-endangered lynx. Don't forget your binoculars!

The region's human inhabitants have the rich cultural heritage of a mountain frontier zone. This area is more French than Italian, having been part of the French-speaking Duchy of Savoy from the 11th century, more or less continuously until Italian unification in 1861. French is still spoken by some, taught in school and appears in bilingual signage. The charming, chalet-like farmhouses have lauze roofing and ground floor byres with

Vallone di Grauson >

the living quarters above. Sympathetic tourism has replaced mining in the Val di Cogne. In the side valleys, where herders traditionally led a self-sufficient existence, the population has been in steady decline and you'll walk through abandoned hamlets and past ruined shepherds' huts in the high *alpe* or meadows.

There's a fine Valdostane gastronomy and excellent wines for you to enjoy. Many specialities are based on farm-made Fontina cheese, including the delicious bread-based *zuppa Valdostane* and the local *polenta alla Valdostana*. You may acquire a taste for *genepy*, a digestif made from an infusion of wormwood, and you should take some spicy *tegole* biscuits on the trail.

Our walks are around the pretty town of Cogne, just north of the park's boundary and at the confluence of four spectacular valleys. Useful buses connect Cogne to trail heads at nearby villages for a short summer season. The usual mountain-walking precautions apply here as well as

a cautionary note about waymarking: confusingly, major routes are waymarked with yellow paint; the classic red-and-white stripes tend to be deployed here for lesser forest rambles.

For those who wish to admire the scenery without too much effort, we've described a number of valley walks at the end of the chapter. The main walks are more demanding but offer huge rewards. Walks 1 and 3 explore the upper reaches of the Valnontey on opposite sides and provide an excellent opportunity to get close to the park's prolific wildlife. The second walk, leading up the lesser-known Vallone di Grauson to a hidden tarn, is equally scenic. The valley's isolation and the quaint legacy of abandoned *alpe* buildings provides an insight into the hardships of traditional mountain life. Together, these itineraries should whet your appetite for a region with limitless walking opportunities.

A coy chamois

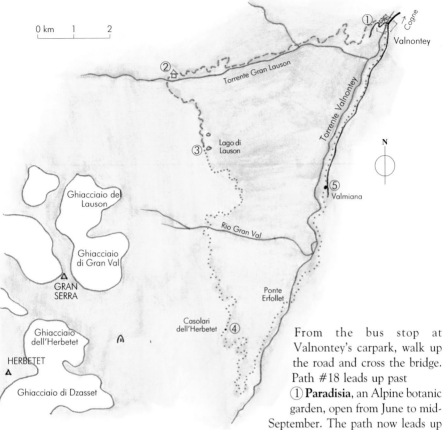

0 km    1    2

Torrente Gran Lauson

Torrente Valnontey

Cogne

Valnontey

① 

② 

③ Lago di Lauson

⑤ Valmiana

N

Rio Gran Val

Ghiacciaio del Lauson

Ghiacciaio di Gran Val

GRAN SERRA

Ghiacciaio dell'Herbetet

HERBETET

Ghiacciaio di Dzasset

Casolari dell'Herbetet ④

Ponte Erfollet

## WALK 1: LAGO DI LAUSON

*The ascent from Valnontey village to Rifugio Sella is the park's most popular walk and a great opportunity to see wildlife. You soon reach a high tarn, from where you can retrace your steps or continue on the longer but dramatic loop via Casolari dell'Herbetet.*

| | |
|---|---|
| Distance | 12 km (7.5 miles) or 19 km (12 miles) for longer variant |
| Time | 5 hours (or 9 hours for variant) |
| Difficulty | moderate |
| Start/Finish | Valnontey village |
| Transport | bus from Cogne and return (in summer only) |

Rifugio Sella offers accommodation and meals from Easter to the end of September. You might want to stay there overnight and walk the extension via Casolari dell' Herbetet the next day.

From the bus stop at Valnontey's carpark, walk up the road and cross the bridge. Path #18 leads up past ① **Paradisia**, an Alpine botanic garden, open from June to mid-September. The path now leads up along a mule track by a high waterfall on Torrente Gran Lauson. After about 50 minutes of winding up through larch woods, a short detour leads to Ponte Puccini. Your path continues to climb and, 1.5 hours or so from Valnontey, reaches a bench. You'll likely see chamois grazing on the slope across the stream.

Continue the steady climb, now above the trees, keeping an eye open for marmots, ibex and chamois. To your left, across the valley, are the picturesque huts of Le Pascieu. Some distance further up, you pass a turn-off for Alpe Lauson and then ② the **Lauson royal lodge**, built for King Vittorio Emanuele II to accommodate his frequent hunting expeditions. A short way beyond this, at 2584 m, are the buildings of the *rifugio*, named in memory of Vittorio Sella, an alpinist who pioneered mountain photography. The bar/restaurant in its

A male ibex below Rifugio Sella

second building serves a great bowl of soup.

Beyond the *rifugio*, pick up #23 trail to cross the river and follow the broad hunting path that winds gently up to a height of 2656 m. Here you'll find the pretty
③ **Lago di Lauson**, often visited by chamois and ibex. In good weather, you'll have a wonderful view from here of the mountains across the Valnontey, notably Torre del Gran San Pietro at 3692 m. From the lake, you can return by the same route via Rifugio Sella (though if you cross the river on the side track to Alpe Lauson you can descend on that side and regain the main track at the Ponte Puccini) then continue down to Valnontey; this is the quick option.

The alternative route involves an exposed stretch, unsuitable in low cloud or for those unsteady on their feet, and a descent near the head of the valley, followed by a long walk down the valley to Valnontey village. To proceed this way, keep on past the lake.

The path narrows and there is a 30-minute stretch of scrambling over exposed rocks on the Bec du Vallon, which you should cross with care. The path traverses a valley, crossing the Rio Gran Val below the Gran Val and Lauson glaciers. Cairns guide you over loose rocks and then you climb to a ledge with a stunning panorama of the surrounding mountains and their glaciers.

A short descent brings you to
④ **Casolari dell'Herbetet** at 2435 m. The old farm huts are now the property of the national park, but their position offers further sweeping views.

Continue on path #23 as it zigzags, wider now, rapidly downhill. This was a royal game track and it is an amazing piece of work. On the descent you pass a plaque to a young park ranger who was shot by poachers in 1981. The path turns south and enters woodland, eventually crossing two new bridges at the valley floor. At a junction, keep left on the good path, now following red stripes. You pass several huge boulders, one the size of a hut, and then cross the Ponte Erfollet at 1830 m, then a second bridge immediately afterwards. Ignore several path junctions and join a broad track, passing through the hamlet of
⑤ **Valmiana**, where a tall cross stands. Some distance on, you reach a wonderful house, built up against a large boulder, with another used as a terrace. Keep on the track down the valley until you reach Valnontey.

Lago di Lauson >

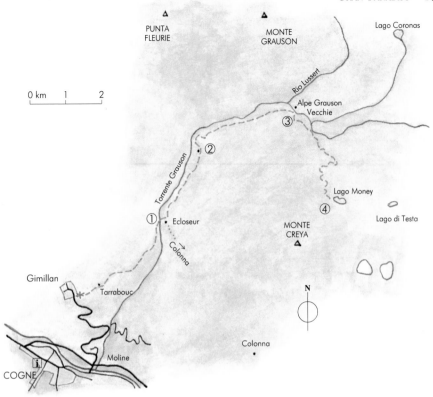

PUNTA
FLEURIE

MONTE
GRAUSON

Lago Coronas

Rio Lussert

0 km   1   2

Alpe Grauson
Vecchie

③

②

Torrente Grauson

Lago Money

④

①   Ecloseur

MONTE
CREYA

Lago di Testa

Colonna

Gimillan

N

Tarrabouc

Colonna

Moline

COGNE

## WALK 2: VALLONE DI GRAUSON

*This rarely walked route north of Cogne is through a remote but spectacular valley, accessible only by mule path. Our destination is the isolated tarn of Lago Money.*

| | |
|---|---|
| Distance | 14 km (8.7 miles) |
| Time | 5.5 hours |
| Difficulty | moderate |
| Start/Finish | Gimillan |
| Transport | bus from Cogne and return (summer only) |

Buy lunch supplies from Cogne. As you walk up through the village of Gimillan from its bus stop, a set of yellow signs directs you right, between houses. Cross a road and take the #8/8a footpath uphill over rich pasture. At a path junction, veer left on the path signed to Lago Money. As you gain height you can see further east up the Vallone di Urtier, beyond an ugly chain of communication pylons. You pass a white shrine

and then the path draws closer to the river, Torrente Grauson. Near the farm huts of ① **Ecloseur,** you cross the river on a bridge. Climb up the other bank, skirting flood-eroded gullies, and then continue up the valley towards a waterfall. This disappears from view as you ascend ② **a series of steps** to its side. The valley narrows into a gorge at this point and you walk high above the river through a lovely stretch of larches. A thin cascade ribbons down the opposite side of the gorge. The path climbs a rise to reach ③ **a large metal cross,** from where there are great views both up and down the valley. There is a path junction here: ignore the level path to the scattered stone huts of Alpe Grauson Vecchie. Instead, take the narrow #8a footpath right, which steadily climbs the slope. Marmots live around here, as their burrows and shrieks attest. You gain

Abandoned huts, Alpe Grauson Vecchie

rocks. The trail becomes less clear as you cross stony, cairn-marked ground to reach the hidden

④ **Lago Money**, a small hanging tarn at 2553 m. Above it loom, from right to left, Monte Creya, Testa di Money and Punta Coupe, with small patches of glacial ice on their slopes. Across the valley stands shapely Monte Grauson at 3240 m and, to its left, Punta Garin at 3448 m. To the right of Monte Grauson is a pass leading to a *bivacco* or bivouac shelter and, beyond it, the several large tarns of Laghi di Lussert. Lago Money makes a perfect picnic spot; a couple of large glacial boulders offer shelter if there is a chill wind blowing.

On the return to Gimillan you are treated to a quite different series of views as you head back down the valley, including the splendid vista southwest beyond Cogne to the glaciers of the Valnontey. To vary the walk and extend it by a couple of hours, you could pick up path #7 at Ecloseur and visit the old Colonna iron mines, before descending on path #5 to Moline and then to Cogne.

a good view over the abandoned huts clustered in the valley below.

Now comes a steady 300-metre climb, waymarked in yellow. High up, a surprising number of Alpine flowers thrive among the

Alpine seclusion, Lago Money

# WALK 3: ALPE MONEY

*Another walk in the beautiful Valnontey, taking you up to high pasture, with a ringside view of a spectacular cirque of mountains and glaciers.*

| | |
|---|---|
| Distance | 15 km (9 miles) |
| Time | 6.5 to 7 hours |
| Difficulty | moderate–strenuous |
| Start/Finish | Valnontey village |
| Transport | bus from Cogne and return |

This walk up Valnontey's eastern slopes crosses several mountain streams, possibly difficult after heavy rain or during the spring thaw. The terrain is also rough in places so walkers should take care. Carry lunch supplies with you.

From Valnontey's carpark and bus stop, head up through the village, keeping left of the river. Follow the track up the valley, passing an amazing rock-house and then through the hamlet of Valmiana.

About 45 minutes from the start, take the #23 footpath off left up steps; the broad track currently ends at the river some 20 m later, so you'll soon know if you've gone too far. Ten minutes further on, just after ① **a park notice-board**, is a path junction: take path #20 for Alpe Money. This narrow path climbs steeply through the woods. On a ledge backed by cliffs and alpenrose, you emerge to gain a wonderful view of the

Gran Paradiso

the same height across the valley, the huts of Casolari dell'Herbetet (see Walk 1) are visible on a shelf of the triangular Herbetet, which rises to 3778 m. Southwest is Gran Paradiso, at 4061 m, the highest mountain wholly in Italy. Below it spills the massive Ghiacciaio della Tribolazione and adjoining glaciers. Left are Testa di Valnontey (3562 m) and Roccia Viva (3650 m). Collectively, they make a daunting sight.

From the huts, you continue on path #20, which climbs briefly at one point but then it's a slow descent over more rough terrain. Watch for stone cairns when the waymarking is not obvious. There is a swift, steep descent down the spine of a spur and then more stream crossings. After 2 hours or so from Alpe Money, you cross the main torrent on a footbridge. Follow yellow waymarks downstream and then head through scrub to

③ **the path junction** where path #23 from the Herbetet huts comes in; from here the walking is much easier. Continue on down the valley to cross the river once more on the Ponte Erfollet. Stay on this (right) side of the river as you retrace your steps through Valmiana. Downstream, cross over

④ **a bridge** with a sign promoting farm produce and turn immediately right. Turn right again at a track and follow this to a stream, then turn right onto a footpath that leads into the village of Valnontey.

waterfall on the Rio Gran Val across the valley. The path continues to climb the mountainside and then crosses the rough ground of glacial moraine, as well as several streams. The views get ever more dramatic!

The waymarking becomes less obvious as you cross huge sheets of rock, scoured smooth by glaciers. The ground here can be slippery with ice. Soon, you reach the pasture terrace of

② **Alpe Money** and its several huts in varying condition. There are plenty of spots here to sit and enjoy lunch or just to rest and enjoy the panorama. West, at about

The hamlet of Valmiana >

< Alpe Money

Cogne's *Battailles des Reines*,
an ancient and annual contest
between pregnant cows of the district

## EASY WALKS IN THE REGION

### Cogne to Valnontey and return

Leave Cogne's Piazza Chanoux south along Via Gran Paradis, passing an expanse of meadowland. Where the road's footpath ends, cross the road and turn left onto an uphill lane. This forks: turn right and follow the track as it heads through woods, parallel to the road. Eventually it crosses under the road and leads you beside the river into the village of Valnontey, which has drinking water, a bar and a seasonal shop. It is also home to **Paradisia**, an alpine botanical garden (open June to mid-September) on the western side of the river.

You can continue walking the track beyond the village, passing through the pretty hamlet of Valmiana, to gain views of the cirque of peaks and glaciers at the head of the valley. On your return, cross the bridge where a sign offers farm produce and keep by the river as it heads down valley. You can stay on the left side of the river all the way down the valley, crossing it shortly before reaching Cogne. *Allow 2 to 3 hours.*

Autumn foliage in the Valnontey

## Cogne to Gimillan and Epinel

Gimillan sits prettily on a ledge just above Cogne and though not far, it takes almost an hour to walk up to it. Leave Cogne's Piazza Chanoux along Via Mines de Cogne and cross the Moline bridge; by the narrow road directly opposite, take the #8 footpath left up steps. Turn left onto the road and pick up another short cut where the road bends, at one point crossing someone's garden. Gimillan has a fountain, a seasonal shop and charming houses boasting well-tended flower boxes.

Beside Gimillan's church, turn left then quickly right along a lane to the communications tower. Beyond this, pick up a good track (path #3/4) leading west, which descends gradually with a wonderful view back over Cogne. Enter pleasant forest and descend to cross a stream. A short way on, cross under an old rail line and fork left to pass below the abandoned Castello Tarambel. Pass new housing and then turn left to weave down through Epinel to the road. The stop for the bus to Cogne is by a bar in the *piazzetta*. *Allow 2 hours.*

Cogne from near Gimillan

## Cogne to Cascate di Lillaz and return

A level walk to the village of Lillaz leads you to the base of its tiered waterfalls. Leave Cogne's Piazza Chanoux along Via Mines de Cogne and soon veer right on the broad riverside path to Lillaz.

This traffic-free track passes through pleasant forest and crosses the exposed area of a landslide, a sign of the major floods of October 2000 that seriously changed the landscape. Cross the Torrente Urtier on a bridge and walk up the road past the hamlet of Champlong to the upper carpark at Lillaz.

A 'cascate' signpost directs you to cross the river and weave between the houses of the village to a picnic area. From here the path follows the Urtier upstream to the lower falls and then steeply up the slope to the middle and upper falls. There are many viewpoints to enjoy before you retrace your steps to Cogne. *Allow 3 hours.*

One fall of the Cascate di Lillaz

# TORINO

NOTES
Population: 903,000
Getting there: bus from Caselle airport
15 km (9 miles) north; rail from
Milano or Genova
Tourist Office: Piazza Castello, 161
Tel: 011 535181 Fax: 011 530070
email: info@turismotorino.org
www.turismotorino.org
Markets: daily, Piazza della Repubblica
Note: many monuments close Monday

Famous for its shroud, Torino or Turin remains off the beaten tourist track. For those who aren't normally swayed by the baroque sensibility, Torino is a pleasant surprise. Here, broad avenues and large piazzas give the buildings ample space to exert their pomp and grandeur. Elaborate churches and imposing palazzi are set in a harmonious scene, endowing the city with an air of orderly sophistication that you won't find elsewhere in Italy. This may be one place to hide your boots away!

Torino is a meeting point in the Piemonte region, both of rivers—the Dora Riparia and the mighty Po—and of transalpine routes from France and Switzerland. A Celtic tribe, the Taurini, settled here and the Romans turned it into a military base. From the 11th century, it was in the hands of the Dukes of Savoy, who ruled absolutely for centuries. After a relatively brief recess, imposed by the Napoleonic occupation, the Savoys were restored to the throne and supported the cause of the Risorgimento leader Camillo Cavour. As a reward, the dynasty ruled as Italy's royal family until the country became a republic in 1946.

When the capital transferred from Torino to Roma, the far-sighted Torinese created industry to fill the void. Textile makers prospered here, but the greatest success was the motor industry, notably the giant Fiat company. On factory floors, the labour movement also flourished and Torino is an interesting political mix.

From the early 18th century, the Savoys lavished attention on the city as the capital of Piemonte. Town planning gave the city the grid pattern that makes it so easy to navigate today, and architects such as Guarini and Juvarra were set to work creating opulent palazzi and splendid churches. Guarino Guarini was a monk who used his great mathematical ability to create brilliant spatial effects. Filippo Juvarra, a Sicilian who trained in Roma, designed many lavish Torinese buildings, including the amazing Basilica di Superga.

Countless porticoes in the city offer pedestrians shelter from sun and rain. If your grand tour of the city is hampered by bad weather, there are some fine museums to explore. Allow time to enjoy Torino's rich culinary tradition; Piemonte is famous for the *tartufo bianco* or white truffle and this is where chocolate-making was perfected. Excellent vintage wines are created nearby and the city is the coffee-roasting capital of Italy. Tempted?

Piazza Castello

Fontana, Giardini Reale >

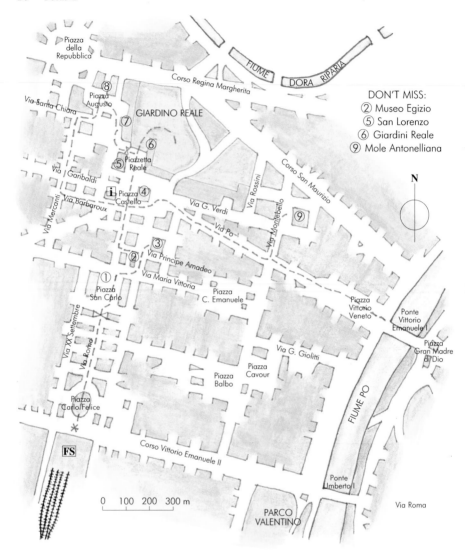

Piazza
della
Repubblica

Corso Regina Margherita

FIUME DORA RIPARIA

Via Santa Chiara

⑧ Piazza
Augusto

⑦

GIARDINO REALE

DON'T MISS:
② Museo Egizio
⑤ San Lorenzo
⑥ Giardini Reale
⑨ Mole Antonelliana

Via Garibaldi

⑥

⑤ Piazzetta
Reale

Corso San Maurizio

Via Mercanti

Via Barbaroux

ℹ️ Piazza ④
Castello

Via G. Verdi

Via Rossini

Via Montebello

⑨

N

Via Po

③

Via Principe Amadeo

②

Via Maria Vittoria

① Piazza
San Carlo

Piazza
C. Emanuele

Piazza
Vittorio
Veneto

Ponte
Vittorio
Emanuele I

Piazza
Gran Madre
di Dio

Via XX Settembre

Via Roma

Via G. Giolitti

Piazza
Cavour

Piazza
Balbo

FIUME PO

Piazza
Carlo Felice

✱

FS

Corso Vittorio Emanuele II

Ponte
Umberto I

Via Roma

PARCO
VALENTINO

0  100 200 300 m

# A WALK IN TORINO

*Pomp and circumstance are the keynotes of this walk: expect to be looking upwards a lot.*

Our route starts at the city's rail station, Stazione Porta Nuova, which bears a distinctive arched façade.

Cross Corso Vittorio Emanuele II (there's an underpass but it has a seedy air to it!) and walk through the gardens of Piazza Carlo Felice then up Via Roma. This broad, porticoed street is the spine of the city, lined with shops boasting label names. It leads to ① **Piazza San Carlo**, a graceful public space that is unfortunately used for parking cars. The characteristic porticoes house some renowned cafés. Two baroque churches, San Carlo and Santa Cristina, stand symmetrically at one end. The façade of the latter was designed by Filippo Juvarra. The 1838 equestrian statue in the centre depicts an earlier Savoy duke, Emanuele Filiberto, savouring a 1574 military triumph.

At the top of the piazza, turn right along Via Maria Vittoria and first left into Via dell'Accademia delle Scienze to the palazzo housing two excellent museums. First is the unexpected
②**Museo Egizio**. This is one of the world's most important collections of Egyptian antiquities, put together in the late 18th century. There are two floors of the most amazing pieces, including the well-furnished tomb of an Egyptian architect and his wife.

Upstairs, you'll find the **Galleria Sabauda**, the House of Savoy's main art collection, arranged in five sections. Dutch and Flemish works augment a comprehensive collection of Italian paintings from the 15th to 17th centuries.

Turn left out of the museums and cross the road to
③ **Palazzo Carignano**, a baroque masterpiece designed by Guarini and completed in 1685; its undulating brick façade makes it arguably Torino's finest building. This was the birthplace of united Italy's first king and, briefly, the house of its first parliament. Today, it contains the **Museo Nazionale del Risorgimento Italiano**, a collection of arms and documents relating to the uprisings and Unification.

Palazzo Madama's older core

Return along Via Principe Amadeo and then turn right to continue up Via Roma. This soon brings you to the vast Piazza Castello, with a tourist office under the left-hand portico. In the centre of the piazza is
④ **Palazzo Madama**, a building with a strange history. Its nucleus is the Porta Decumana, which was built as part of the city's Roman ramparts. Around this core, a massive brick medieval castle was constructed. The stone façade is pure baroque, the work of Filippo Juvarra from 1718–21. The palazzo is so named because the Madama Reale, widow of one Savoy king and mother of the next, lived here. The interior has recently been restored and contains the **Museo Civico d'Arte Antica**, a collection of mostly decorative medieval and Renaissance arts.

Beside this palazzo, in a wing of the Palazzo Reale, is the **Armeria Reale**, which displays an excellent array of arms. Across the piazza, somewhat tucked away, is the 17th-century church of
⑤ **San Lorenzo**. Created by Guarini as the royal chapel, this is filled with multicoloured

San Lorenzo's dome

marble, frescoes and stucco statuettes, topped by a masterful, swirling dome.

Walk through the Piazzetta Reale and enter the gates of

⑥ the **Palazzo Reale** for a tour of the sumptuously over-decorated apartments. Alternatively, you can simply walk through the courtyard and into the lovely **Giardini Reale**. These gardens were laid out by Louis le Nôtre, more famous for his work at Versailles. Around to the right you'll find the cavorting figures of the Fontana della Nereide e dei Tritoni.

Leave the palazzo and turn right to walk through an arcade and then up the steps of the late 15th-century duomo or

⑦ **Cattedrale di San Giovanni**, home of Torino's most famous prize, the *sindone* or Holy Shroud of Turin. The long cloth, which bears the imprint of a crucified man complete with wounds and bruises, has been revered for centuries. Following carbon dating, it's now generally agreed to be medieval and therefore not Christ's shroud. It is kept safely out of sight, but a large image is on display. Guarini designed the chapel

that usually houses the shroud. Above the duomo door, as you exit, is a highly valued oil reproduction of Leonardo's *Last Supper*.

Turn right out of the duomo to walk around the jumbled ruins of a Roman theatre. Across Via XX Settembre is a somewhat more impressive sign of the Roman era, the massive

⑧ **Porta Palatina**, a red-brick construction with two 16-sided towers on either side of an archway.

Cross the piazza and turn right into Via Santa Chiara then left into the narrow Via Conte Verde. Cross Via Garibaldi, a pleasant pedestrian-only street of shops, and continue on Via Mercanti, a charming lane lined with interesting food shops. Turn left into Via Barbaroux and cross the busy Via XX Settembre to regain Piazza Castello.

Walk around Palazzo Madama to view the older structure behind the façade and head down the left side of Via Po. This porticoed street is lined with cafés and interesting, slightly down-at-heel shops. In the second block, you pass the Palazzo dell' Università, built in 1712, with bookstalls nearby. Turn off left, down Via Montebello,

The view over the Fiume Po

to visit Torino's 'Eiffel Tower', the ⑨ **Mole Antonelliana**, a highly distinctive feature of the skyline. Designed in the late 19th century as a synagogue by the eccentric architect Antonelli, it grew to more than three times its intended height, to become the world's tallest building, towering 167 m into the air. It now houses a very visual museum of cinema. A glass elevator takes you to the top of the dome (85 m) for a fleeting glimpse of the curious interior and for a panorama over the city.

Back track and continue down Via Po to pass the museum of decorative arts, though you should peek into its pretty courtyard. Beyond the long Piazza Vittorio Veneto, which serves as another carpark, you'll reach the banks of the Fiume Po near Ponte Vittorio Emanuele I. The church directly across the river is **Gran Madre de Dio**; the hill to its right, Monte dei Cappuccini, offers a fine view back.

Here ends our walk, leaving you well-placed to continue on the first excursion below, or to saunter back along Via Po to revisit one of the museums.

OTHER EXCURSIONS

**Parco del Valentino** stretches along the banks of the Po, a short walk south from where our main itinerary ends. As well as its expansive landscaped gardens, the park contains such oddities as the Borgo e Rocca Medioevale, a bizarre village and castle built in 1884. You'll also see the more authentic

The Mole Antonelliana

Castello Valentino, another former home of the Savoy dynasty.

The **Basilica di Superga**, an extraordinary baroque confection, stands on a high hill with panoramic views over the Po valley. This circular basilica was built in thanks for deliverance from French forces in 1706; it is another of Juvarra's designs, in neoclassical style. To reach the Superga, catch a bus from the rail station, or tram #15 from Via XX Settembre to Stazione ·Ferrovia Superga and a *funivia* up the hill.

OPENING HOURS

| | |
|---|---|
| Museo Egizio | Tue-Fri & Sun 8.30-7.30; Sat 9am-11pm |
| Galleria Sabauda | Tue-Fri & Sun 8.30-7.30; Sat 9am-11pm |
| Museo del Risorgimento | Tue-Sun 9-7 |
| Palazzo Madama | Tue-Fri 10-8; Sat 10am-11pm; Sun 10-8 |
| Palazzo Reale | Tue-Fri & Sun 8.30-7.30; Sun 8.30am-11pm |
| Cattedrale di San Giovanni | daily 8.30-noon, 4-7 |
| Mole Antonelliana | Tue-Fri 10-8; Sat 10am-11pm; Sun 10-8 |
| Rocca Medioevale | Tue-Sun 9-7 |
| Basilica di Superga | daily 9.30-noon, 3-6 |

# — LAGO DI COMO —

Henry James sensibly wrote 'One can't describe the beauty of the Italian lakes, nor would one try if one could.' Lombardia's 'Lake District' has been given a lot of advance publicity. The Roman poet Catullus wrote lyrically of Lago di Garda and both Plinys, Elder and Younger, wrote of the beauty of Lago di Como where they were born. A few thousand years later, the 19th-century Romantics—both poets and composers—romanced this lake, making it world famous.

For the walker, Lago di Como, the most famous of the five great lakes, has the most varied scenery. It is a glacially scoured valley, framed to the north by the snow-capped Alpi, with the peaks of Monti Grigne towering above its eastern shore. In places, wooded hillsides or fabulous villas in luxuriant terraced gardens spill down to the water's edge. There are also the bucolic charms of its hidden side valleys and high pastures, where farm life goes on much as it always has, oblivious

NOTES

Suggested base:  Menaggio
Getting there:  rail from Milano to
  Como and then bus to Menaggio
Tourist Office:  P. Garibaldi 4  22017
  Menaggio, Tel/Fax: 0344 32924
  email: infomenaggio@tiscalinet.it
  www.menaggio.com
Map:  Kompass #91 1:50000
Best timing:  May-July; Sept-Oct

to the imperatives of modern tourism.

The lake's central zone, where it forks into two branches, is the finest. The wedge of land between branches has, at its tip, Bellagio, the 'pearl of the lake'. Almost as lovely is Menaggio, midway along the western shore, which we've chosen as a base. The village is backed by a horseshoe sweep of mountains and has spectacular views east across the lake to Varenna and south to Bellagio and beyond. Menaggio also has good bus and ferry connections, of which we've made full use.

Until recent times much of the lake's hinterland could only be reached on foot or by mule, so there's no shortage of walking trails. Our first walk leads past rural hamlets and high pasture to a 16th-century sanctuary overlooking the lake. Walk 2 involves a ferry ride to charming Varenna; from there you'll climb to a panorama above Castello di Vezio before descending inland to the sleepy town of Esino Lario. Lastly we've described a true summit walk to Monte Grona that, though rated as strenuous, is short enough to do at a leisurely place. The summit view is, James would have it, indescribable.

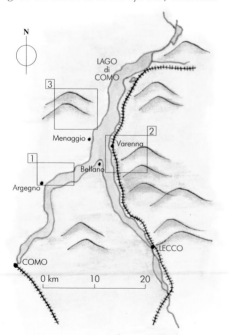

The view from
Madonna del
Soccorso >

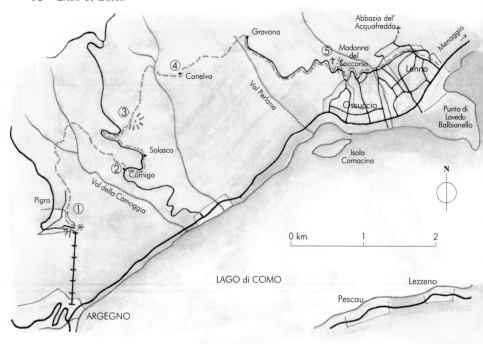

## WALK 1: PIGRA TO LENNO

*This bucolic ramble makes use of a* funivia *to gain height and then meanders through high meadows with lake views before descending via a 16th-century sanctuary.*

| | |
|---|---|
| Distance | 11 km (7 miles) |
| Time | 4.5 to 5 hours |
| Difficulty | easy–moderate |
| Start | Pigra |
| Finish | Lenno |
| Transport | bus to Argegno and *funivia* to Pigra; return bus from Lenno |

There is a bar at Pigra and a trattoria at Madonna del Soccorso but nothing in between, so you might want lunch supplies to enjoy en route. Catch a C10 bus from Menaggio and get off at the stop near the funivia station, before Argegno's centre. Take the *funivia* (every half hour, 8-12 and 2-sunset) for the dramatic ride up to
① **Pigra**, a small town on a ledge at 860 m. Walk straight up the hill and follow the sign for the *biblioteca* (library), where you take the street uphill to a public wash house.

Turn right and pass a large hall bearing the name 'Antica Societa Operaia'.

The road becomes a track, signed for Corniga, and you pass right of a small chapel. The track loops down through woods and into the Valle delle Camogge. Pass a water trough and at a fork, take the track right, signed to Corniga. The track narrows and crosses a partially underground stream then rises to the small settlement of Serta. The path then heads southeast to
② **Corniga**, a charming hamlet of stone houses. Pass left of Corniga's small church of Sant'Anna (built in 1631) on a mule track leading steeply uphill. This passes through the few houses of Solasco and continues to wind uphill. Almost 1 km from Solasco, at a point where the lane veers left uphill, pick up the footpath straight ahead to a farm building. Here the path contours across delightful
③ **high pasture** on a balcony over the lake, with a stunning panorama over the south-west leg of Lago di Como. From here, the walking becomes easier as you contour at about 1050 m, heading north. The path

crosses the pretty stream of Pesetta and then passes below a house in the hamlet of
④ **Canelva**. Turn left, uphill, on a grassy path between houses and, after 30 m or so, turn right on a footpath heading northeast. Pass through a gate and along a fence, then by a stone wall to reach the farm buildings of Colombera. The track now leads down to a water fountain shortly before the hamlet of Gravona.

Turn right onto a lane heading steeply downhill. This drops steadily, passing the occasional farm building to a path junction at about 530 m. The path coming in from the left leads up the Val Perlana to the 11th-century Romanesque monastery of San Benedetto, visible from the junction. Keep right and, after a further steep descent, you arrive at the welcome shade of the
⑤ **Santuario della Madonna del Soccorso**, with its lovely position above the lake. The 16th-century church was built to house a statue of the Virgin, found by a deaf-mute shepherd girl who was miraculously cured. A trattoria is tucked behind the church.

Descend on the Viale delle Cappelle, a cobblestone path lined with 14 chapels, featuring sculpted dioramas. From the bottom chapel continue east on Via San Rocco to cross the Torrente Perlana. Continue on Viale Libronica and, at a bend, turn right into Via Don Cadenazzi, then

Corniga houses

immediately left. Pass in front of a church and then pick up the narrow Via al Soccorso down to the right. This leads down to the main road at Lenno, where you'll find the bus stop a few steps to the right.

If you have a wait for the next bus, you might cross the main road (there is an underpass nearby) and view Lenno's 11th-century baptistry in the *piazzetta* by the church of San Stefano.

The view from
the *alpe* >

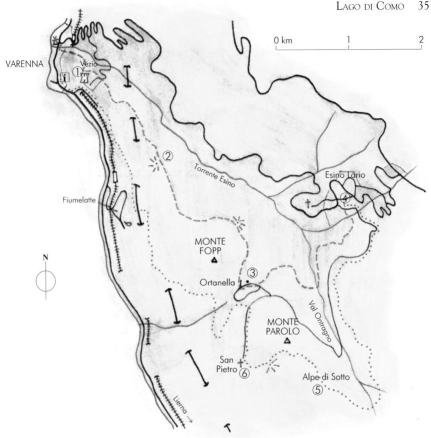

# WALK 2: ABOVE VARENNA

*Across the lake from Menaggio is Varenna and the vast Parco delle Grigne. This route climbs to a perched castle and then over the meadows of Ortanella to the town of Esino Lario. Those who want to extend the walk can return via the Valle Ontragno.*

| | |
|---|---|
| Distance | 9 km (5.6 miles) |
| Time | 4.5 hours (or 9 with extension) |
| Difficulty | moderate |
| Start | Varenna |
| Finish | Esino Lario |
| Transport | ferry to and from Varenna; bus from Esino to Varenna |

From Menaggio there are frequent ferries across Lago di Como to the charming lakeside village of Varenna. South of the

*< Lakeside, Argegno*

ferry wharf is Varenna's centre, which boasts a huddle of 17th-century buildings, the medieval church of San Giorgio, and the 11th-century Oratorio di San Giovanni, worth a visit on your return from the walk. Before you start off, check the timetable for the return bus from Esino Lario.

From the ferry, walk up to the main road and turn right then soon left at Hotel Montecodeno and up Via delle Croce. Soon turn left onto Via Per Vezio and take this walled lane uphill. It narrows and then you cross a track and take a stepped lane up, right of the track.

Pass a public wash house, still used, to reach the hamlet of **Vezio** at its Piazza Belvedere. Turn right and right again, following signs to the castello and passing the church and walled cemetery. A path

The view over Varenna

leads to the strategically sited ① **Castello di Vezio**, now in ruins. Local history would have it that this stronghold was founded by the Lombard Queen Theodolinda. It remains an atmospheric site.

Return to Piazza Belvedere and turn right then left to reach the road. Turn uphill on the road a short way then climb right on a concrete lane daubed with orange paint and continue past a sign 'Sentiero Monte Fopp – Ortanella'. This stony path (the 'Sentiero del Viandante') winds uphill through lush woodland; you might see brightly spotted fire salamanders if the ground is damp.

Pass a shrine and yellow arrows pointing to Esino. At one of these, by a broken orange sign, take a right-hand track up to a viewpoint over Varenna and Vezio's *castello*. A short distance further on, at ② **a wooden cross** on a spur, you gain an even better panorama, across the lake to Menaggio and the mountains beyond.

The path continues from the cross, through chestnut woods to pass a stone hut. From here, the path becomes a stony track

A farmhouse, Val d'Esino >

winding uphill, then joins a broader track. Continue ahead, gently downhill, as it contours around Monte Fopp with inland views over the valley to Esino Lario. You soon reach the emerald green meadows of ③ **Ortanella**, a farming community on the saddle between Monte Fopp and Monte Parolo. This would make a delightful spot for a picnic lunch. Turn left onto a road and follow it through the hamlet. Pass an inn on your right and, before a house with bright red shutters, take a track left. At a fountain by a mill wheel, turn left onto a rough path which drops steeply down a gully. This soon improves, and joins a broader track downhill. Turn right onto another track. Continue on, passing between farm houses and abandoned buildings, to cross the Torrente Ontragno and follow along a lane.

At a pair of shrines, ignore the concrete road left and keep straight ahead on the path, crossing several streams and then climbing into Esino Lario Inferiore near the old church of ④ **San Giovanni Battistero**. Wind uphill on alleys to reach the Varenna road, where you'll find the bus stop. If there is time before the bus arrives, head up to the church of **San Vittore**, sited dramatically on a spur.

This walk can be extended by heading further south and then looping back to Varenna. You will need an extra 4.5 hours for this. Return to the door of San Giovanni in the lower town and walk right of the church and then right again. Continue on this lane to leave the village, cross two streams and pass a shrine to San Grato.

Shortly after this, head left uphill on a track signed to Alpe di Lierna. Keep on this cobbled mule track, passing picturesque farm buildings and climbing, gently at first then more steeply through tall forest. After a long steady incline, you reach signposts; keep on path #21 to Alpe di Esino at this and the next sign. Cross the head of the valley and head across pasture between ⑤ **new CAI buildings** at Alpe di Sotto. Keep straight on as you join path #71 which comes in from the left. You regain a view of the lake at a high pass below Monte Parolo and then descend steeply on the now narrow path. Above, to your left, are the dramatic crags of Monti Cucco and Pelágia.

Turn right at a junction on the path marked to San Pietro and Ortanella to soon reach the church of ⑥ **San Pietro**. From here, follow the lane

Crags above Lierna

north for 750 m or so and pick up the path #74 diverging left. This soon descends steeply and, at a path junction, you turn right onto the 'S.V.' path. This climbs initially then descends, steeply at first, traversing the lake side of Monte Fopp to reach remnant fortifications at Il Baluardo near the Fiumelatte, Italy's shortest river, measuring only 250 m from source to the lake. It is a karstic river which flows only from March to October. Some 2 km further on, you arrive at the centre of Varenna.

Varenna's small harbour

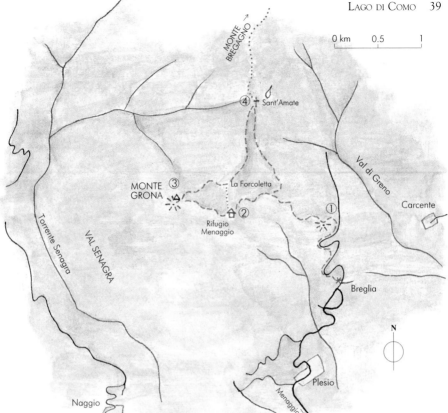

# WALK 3: MONTE GRONA

*From the peak of Monte Grona you can view three lakes—Como, Piano and Lugano—in the same panorama. This popular ascent via Rifugio Menaggio requires some exertion and is only for sure-footed walkers.*

| | |
|---|---|
| Distance | 10 km (6 miles) |
| Time | 5.5 hours |
| Difficulty | strenuous |
| Start/Finish | Breglia |
| Transport | bus from Menaggio & return |

The *rifugio* (open daily in summer and on weekends in other seasons) serves meals; otherwise you'll need to buy provisions before you leave Menaggio. Carry water. Catch a C13 bus to Breglia, 6 km from Menaggio and the last stop on the route.

From the bus stop, pick up the lane

< Lago di Como from Monte Grona

leading uphill to Monti di Breglia and the *rifugio*. Waymarked footpaths short cut loops of the road as it winds steadily uphill. Keep following signs for Rifugio Menaggio. At a picnic area you leave the track and pick up a footpath up to the left. Take the 'sentiero alto' through stands of birches and low broom up to

① **a path junction** where you keep left (right leads to S.Amate). The path now levels and contours around to

② **Rifugio Menaggio**, sited on a spur below Monte Grona and a good spot to enjoy the panorama over lunch. There is a water fountain outside the *rifugio*.

Once refreshed, walk around the *rifugio* and pick up the path to Monte Grona signed 'Direttisimo'. (The alternative, Via Normale, is easier but doesn't offer such dramatic views. The Via Ferrata is only for equipped mountaineers.) The Via Ferrata

The lonely Sant'Amate

wild goat you can revel in the view from ③ the **peak of Monte Grona** (1736 m). North is the rounded peak of Monte Bregagno (2107 m) then, northeast across Lago di Como, is Monte Legnone (2529 m). Southeast, beyond Varenna, is Monte Grigne (2410 m). Between the lakes of Como and Lugano lies the diminutive Lago di Piano.

Clamber down off the summit and descend on the Via Normale to the path junction at La Forcoletta on the ridge. Keep left and follow the path along the treeless ridge to the lonely ④ **Cappella di Sant'Amate**, which possibly dates back to 1500. Below, beyond the high pasture, is the wooded Val Senagra. Beyond the chapel is the grassy path for the summit of Monte Bregagno, a return trip of around 3 hours.

From Sant'Amate, follow the sign down-hill to Breglia. After a steep section, you turn left to rejoin the *rifugio* track you were on earlier. Now retrace your steps back to the bus stop at Breglia for a bus back to Menaggio.

forks off left; keep right and climb steeply (and carefully) on the narrow path past spectacular crags and matching views. Near the top, join the Via Normale for the final ascent with a fixed wire for assistance. Once you've grown used to the heady scent of

A ferry leaves Menaggio

Lakeside, Menaggio >

# OTHER WALKS IN THE REGION

## Menaggio
For a stroll around the village of Menaggio itself, ask at the tourist office for its historical itinerary of the town. *Allow 1.5 hours.*

## Lake views
Catch a C12 bus from Menaggio for the uphill ride to the district of Croce. From the Hotel Adler, continue on the main road for 30 m then cross and head towards the golf course. Follow the signs of the Via dei Monti Lariani (path #2) which then leads past the church of Madonna di Paullo and then steeply up through chestnut woods and pastures to Bocchetta di Nava (850 m). Near the last building you leave the Via dei Monti Lariani and take the left turn, signed to Griánte. Keep left at the next two junctions to reach the main road by the Griánte bus stop, where you can catch a bus back to Menaggio. *Allow 3.5 hours.*

## Val Senagra
The first half of this forest walk coincides with the Sentiero delle 4 Valli, a 50-km trail linking the lakes of Como and Lugano. Catch a C13 bus from Menaggio to Breglia, then head uphill on the track to Rifugio Menaggio. After 500 m, turn left onto the path signed 'Sentiero delle 4 Valli' and keep straight on at the next path junction.

Follow the waymarks (#3 with a diagonal line through it) through forest and past farm buildings. The waymarks divert around new properties, then continue along a better track through forest and into woodland. After crossing a stream, you reach a long meadow below the restored Alpe Varò. Head up left into woods. Further on, you cross the Torrente Senagra and climb to a jeep track, where you turn left. At a junction

after 1.2 km you part ways with #3 and, instead, keep left. The track descends for a stretch, then traverses a gully. At another junction, keep left, to eventually reach the picturesque hamlet of Naggio, where there is a bus stop. *Allow 5 to 6 hours.*

## Dorsale del Triangolo Lariano
The Triangolo Lariano is the land between the two legs of Lago di Como. The way-marked path #1 follows a series of mule paths and cart tracks along the spine or *dorsale* of the triangle. The two-day walk starts at Brunate, reached by funicular from Como, and continues for 30 km to Bellagio. The ideal stopover point is Pian del Tivano, which is accessible by bus from Bellagio and Como and which neatly divides the distance in two. The tourist office in Menaggio has an excellent pamphlet on the walk, which includes accommodation details.

A full day walk can be arranged as follows. Catch a ferry from Menaggio to Bellagio and then a bus up to Pian del Tivano. Walk 800 m further up the road and turn left on a farm lane, heading northeast. Follow this (#37) through several *alpi* or alpine farms to join the main path (#1) at Alpe Spessola. There are wonderful views as you descend by meadows and woodland to the hamlet of Guggiate, following red-and-white waymarks. From here, you walk north along the lakeside road to the ferry point. *Allow 5 to 6 hours for walking.*

# BERGAMO

Most Italian cities have their 'old town': usually a small core of buildings huddled together for protection from the onslaught of modern architecture. Bergamo is different; its old town is perched on the hills of the Valtelline, high above the Lombardia plain where the town's newer district—the Città Bassa—is spread out in neoclassical style. Bergamo Alta is a cluster of gems, with Piazza Vecchia as its centrepiece.

This strategic hilltop attracted Ligurian settlers as early as 1200 BC. Celts, Goths and Romans all occupied Bergamo, though little remains of their stay. The city prospered under Lombard rule and was an independent *comune* from the 11th to the 13th centuries. Bartolomeo Colleoni, the mercenary leader, had political control over it in the 15th century and then ceded Bergamo to the Venetian Republic, which ruled the city for over 350 years. The Venetians built mansions and

> ### NOTES
> Population: 117,000
> Getting there: rail from Milano; bus from Milano, Como and other cities
> Tourist Office: Vicolo Aquila Nera, 2
> Tel: 035 242226 Fax: 035 242994
> email: iat.bergamo@apt.bergamo.it
> www.apt.bergamo.it
> Markets: P.della Cittadella, Friday am

churches, adorning façades with the lion of St Mark. They also ringed the city with high 16th-century walls that held out further invaders until 1796, when French troops arrived and declared a Republic of Bergamo. By 1814, the city was under Austrian rule and remained so until 1859, when liberated by Garibaldi.

Bergamo has long enjoyed a lively artistic and cultural life. Lorenzo Lotto, a Venetian, painted here in the 1570s and influenced many local painters for the century that followed. Commedia dell' Arte, the popular theatre form starring masked characters such as Harlequin, originated here in the 16th century. Donizetti, the composer of light operas, was born and died here, a much-celebrated son of the city. The people of Bergamo, who speak a distinctive local dialect, are justly proud of their city and you'll find the tourist office awash with promotional material. Bergamo would make a good base to explore the foothills of the Alpi; ask at the tourist office for the map of *sentieri* in the province.

Bergamo Alta itself is pleasantly green, ringed by parks on the walls and with a traffic-free centre. Not surprisingly, Bergamo is a haven for the Milanese, who escape here on weekends seeking fresh air and good food, but it is not overrun by tourists. For those happy to amble, it is one of Italy's gifts.

A Bergamo bakery

The intricate Cappella Colleoni >

DON'T MISS:
① Piazza Vecchia
② Piazza Duomo
④ Castello di San Vigilio
⑧ S. Michele al Pozzo Bianco

# A WALK IN BERGAMO ALTA

*Every alleyway of the Città Alta yields up some treasure, perhaps a glorious Renaissance building or a shop crammed with delicacies.*

Bergamo's train station lies at the end of a broad boulevard in the lower town. From there you can catch a bus to the funicular station and then take the funicular (built in 1887) up to Città Alta. You disembark at Piazza Mercato delle Scarpe, where shoemakers once sold their wares under the covered market.

Walk on up Via Gombito passing, on the right, the church of San Pancrazio and below the **Torre del Gombito** on your left. The very helpful tourist office is tucked down the next street to the right. On your left, however, is

① **Piazza Vecchia**, the heart of the town, flanked by attractive buildings and decorated with a Venetian fountain of stone lions. The 16th-century Palladian **Palazzo Nuova** houses the library. You can climb the 12th-century **Torre Civica** for a wonderful roofscape view but, be warned, the 15th-century bell tolls very loudly!

A 14th-century covered stairway adds to the charming stage-set appearance of the piazza that is dominated by the Venetian-Gothic **Palazzo della Ragione**, stamped with the lion of St Mark. Court cases were heard here (*ragione* means 'reason') and condemned prisoners were paraded in the piazza below.

Wander through the arcade of the Palazzo della Ragione, noting a *meridiana* or sundial on the ground, to leave the civic centre and enter the religious one in

② **Piazza Duomo**. Here, your eyes are drawn immediately to the rich and colourful façade of the **Cappella Colleoni**. This gem of a chapel was designed in the 1470s by Amadeo (architect of the Carthusian monastery at Pavia) as a mausoleum for the *condottiere* Bartolomeo Colleoni. The interior is almost as elaborate, with Colleoni astride a gilded horse. His favourite

daughter, Medea, has a more modest tomb.

The chapel was added on to the **Basilica di Santa Maria Maggiore**, which was built in the 12th century. The delicate porch, left of the chapel, was added in the 14th century in Lombard-Romanesque style. Inside, the basilica is lavishly decorated in baroque fashion, with tapestries and giltwork in abundance. The choir screen features stunning intarsia panels designed by Lotto, and you can see part of a medieval fresco of the *Tree of Life* on the south wall.

The octagonal **Battistero** once stood in the basilica but was demolished in 1660, stored away, and then rebuilt in 1898 on its present site on the right of Cappella Colleoni. Between the two is the **Aula della Curia** or Bishop's Court, a frescoed passage-way open only on some mornings.

Opposite the baptistry is the entrance to the **Duomo**, somewhat less grand than the basilica. Built on the site of a 6th-century church, it was begun in 1459 and the statue-topped dome completed as late as 1853.

Take the alley between the duomo and the basilica, passing the large **Fontanone**,

Piazza Vecchia

The view from Castello di San Vigilio

a 1342 cistern built to supply the city with water in case of war. Take a look at the 10th-century **Tempietto di Santa Croce** and view the rear porch of the basilica, another wonderful piece of stonework.

From the *piazzetta* here, turn right along Via Arena, passing Palazzo della Misericordia, home of the **Museo Donizettiano**, on your left. At the junction, detour a short way straight ahead to look through the gates of the Seminario Vescovile Giovanni XXIII but, otherwise, turn right and then left along pretty Via San Salvatore, descending to Piazza Lorenzo Mascheroni. Cross this diagonally to enter

③ the **Cittadella** complex, a military stronghold that once occupied this end of town. It now houses two science museums.

Cross the Piazza della Cittadella and leave by the arch left of the road, to walk around the Torre di Adalberto. You are now on Colle Aperto (the 'open hill') offering a view northeast. Cross Viale delle Mura and walk through Porta Sant'Alessandro to reach the lower station of Bergamo's second funicular.

Take the short funicular ride up to San Vigilio, a charming hill of villas. From the upper station, turn right to walk a short distance up to the remains of

④ **Castello di San Vigilio**, once part of the city fortifications. It now forms a small park with fine city views southeast and towards Bergamo's other hills northwest.

Catch the funicular back downhill and retrace your steps through the gate and the Cittadella. From here, head along the main pedestrian thoroughfare, Via Bartolomeo Colleoni, lined with tempting shopfronts, such as the *pasticcerie* that display *ucelli*, cakes topped with little birds. On the left you pass the garden of **Luogo Pio Colleoni**, a charity established to raise dowries for poor women. Soon, on your right, is the

⑤ **Teatro Sociale**, an atmospheric old theatre that now houses exhibitions.

Pass Piazza Vecchia and turn left, staying on level ground, to walk through the old hay market, Piazza Mercato del Fieno, and continue on to the ex-convent of San Francesco that now houses the

⑥ **Museo Storico**, the civic museum. You can wander in for free, which you should do to see its two cloisters. Turn left as you leave the museum and then right down Via Solata. At the campanile (belonging to San Pancrazio), turn left into Via Rocca, leading, as you'd expect, to

⑦ the **Rocca**. This 14th-century fortress, modified by the Venetians, is only open on weekends and holidays. A nearby gate on Piazza Brigata Legnano leads up to a balcony and the Parco delle Rimembranze.

Return along Via Rocca but keep left where it broadens to walk down past charming medieval houses. Turn left to skirt the ex-church of San Rocco and walk down Via Porta Dipinta, passing various palazzi on the right and Palazzo Moroni on the left. After you pass a medieval fountain on the left, veer up to the right to the door of

⑧ **San Michele al Pozzo Bianco**, named for a well that was nearby. Its beautifully spare interior is decorated with frescoes, including several painted by Lotto in 1525.

Continue down Via Porta Dipinta, past

The Rocca >

a grassy slope, to the large Gothic façade of ⑨ **Sant'Agostino**. The church contains some lovely frescoes; the ex-monastery beyond the church now houses exhibitions.

A path to the left of Sant'Agostino leads you into parkland and around the bulwarks of the 16th-century **Venetian walls**. Cross the road at Porta Sant'Agostino and walk along the path on the walls, now offering grand views over lower Bergamo. An avenue of trees at the aptly named Spalto delle Cento Piante (or 'Terrace of a Hundred Plants') offers pleasant shade and from there you can admire the palazzi up to the right, including the Palazzo Suardi, which accommodates the funicular station.

Ahead on the left is the attractive viaduct bearing Via Sant'Alessandro, a pleasant pedestrian-only route down to the lower town, should you wish to head that way. Otherwise, return to the upper funicular station or Piazza Vecchia by turning right at the Porta San Giacomo and walking up Via San Giacomo.

## OTHER EXCURSIONS

While Bergamo's Città Bassa has less to offer the visitor than its historic upper town, a trip to the **Accademia Carrara** is definitely worthwhile. One of Italy's most important, the gallery contains Italian paintings of the 15th-18th centuries by such artists as Botticelli, Pisanello and Perugino, plus works from other European countries.

Leave upper Bergamo by Porta Sant' Agostino and turn left down the cobbled Via della Noca to Piazza dell'Accademia.

Further afield, the peaks of the **Alpi Orobie** have much to offer walkers. Ask the tourist office for the map titled *Carta dei Sentieri della Provincia* that includes estimated walking times for various trails.

| OPENING HOURS | |
|---|---|
| Duomo | daily 7.30-11.45, 3-6.30 |
| Cappella Colleoni | Tue-Sun 9-12.30, 2-4.30 (until 6.30 in summer) |
| Basilica di S.M.Maggiore | daily 9-12.30, 2.30-5 |
| Tempietto di Santa Croce | daily 9-12.30 |
| Museo Storico | Mon-Sat 9.30-1, 2-5.30; Sun 9-7 |
| S.Michele al Pozzo Bianco | daily 8-6 |
| Accademia Carrara | Tue-Sun 10-1, 3-6.45 (in winter 9.30-1, 2.30-5.45) |

# THE DOLOMITI

The north of Italy has a plethora of beautiful Alpine mountains, but none can compare with the Dolomiti, or the Dolomites as they are also known. These mountains have a distinctive verticality: tall, sharp towers and spires rise abruptly from gentle Alpine pasture or from rocky tundra plateaux. The mountains change colour in the light and glow pink and purple in brilliant sunsets, a sight known as the 'alpenglow'. The massifs and their valleys are in several clusters: this chapter visits the northeast Dolomiti around Cortina, known as the Dolomiti d'Ampezzo and the Dolomiti di Sesto. Other areas are mentioned in less detail at the back of the book. Each offers countless days of pure walking delight.

Named after French geologist Deodat de Dolomieu, who described their mineral composition in 1788, these peaks were once coral and marine sediment deposited during the Triassic period (some 250-200 million years ago) in what was then a tropical sea separating Europe from Africa. Later the Dolomiti (along with the Alpi) were uplifted by continental collision;

NOTES

Suggested base:  Cortina d'Ampezzo

Getting there:  rail to Calalzo or Dobbiaco, then bus to Cortina

Tourist Office:  P.tta San Francesco, 8

Tel: 0436 3231  Fax: 0436 3235

email: apt1@sunrise.it

www.dolomiti.it/apt

Map:  free APT hiking map 1:40000 or Tabacco #03 1:25000

Best timing:  June-September

glaciation and erosion did the rest.

Cortina d'Ampezzo is the 'capital' of the northeastern Dolomiti and it makes an ideal walking base. It hosted the 1956 Winter Olympics and is Italy's most fashionable winter resort, a fact attested to by the elegance of its shops and visitors, best observed during the evening *passeggiata*. Cortina is set in the sunny basin of the Valle d'Ampezzo on the river Boite, encircled by dramatic mountains. The three pyramidal peaks of the Tofane group rise up from the west. To the north is the red blockish bulk of the Croda Rossa. Cristallo dominates the northeast, massive Sorapiss the east and the shapely Anteleo

A chapel at Passo Falzarego >

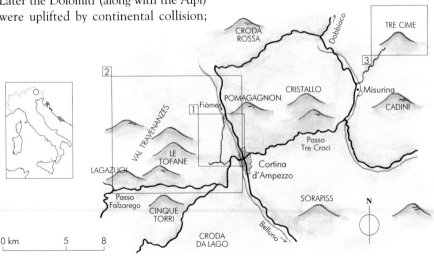

the southeast. To the south and southwest the mountains are lower but no less compelling, particularly the Cinque Torri whose stone towers resemble an archaeological ruin from a distance.

Apart from the fascinating geology of the region, there is also a wealth of alpine flora and fauna to enjoy. Meadows are tinted with wildflowers in spring and summer; gentians and alpenrose bloom at higher levels. In the nature parks, cute marmots are in abundance and you may see chamois as well as *cervo* and *capriolo*, two types of deer.

You may notice bilingual (Italian and German) and sometimes trilingual (Ladin) signage in this former frontier area. Ladin is an ancient Romansch or Raeto-Roman tongue, derived from the integration of the Latin of the Roman conquerors with the language of the earlier Celtic inhabitants known as Raetians. It is still spoken in some of the more isolated valleys.

Once part of the Venetian Republic, Cortina joined the Hapsburg Tyrol in 1511 and generally remained within the Austro-Hungarian Empire until WWI when battle was waged on the very mountains. Walks 2 and 3 provide grim reminders—barbed wire, trenches, tunnels, galleries and rusty cans—of the fierce war of attrition waged between Austria and Italy in the most bitter conditions. At the war's end the Austrian Dolomiti were ceded to Italy, however, the region's architecture, language and cuisine continue to bespeak its Tyrolean heritage.

With an exceptional infrastructure of paths, *rifugi*, public and mountain transport as well as many tourist facilities, the Dolomiti d'Ampezzo provide unlimited walking possibilities. Walking can be as easy or as demanding as you wish: Walk 1 takes you just a short distance from the town to a pretty forest lake. Other walks require no special expertise or equipment as long as the snow has melted. All walkers will enjoy the wealth of natural beauty that the Dolomiti have to offer.

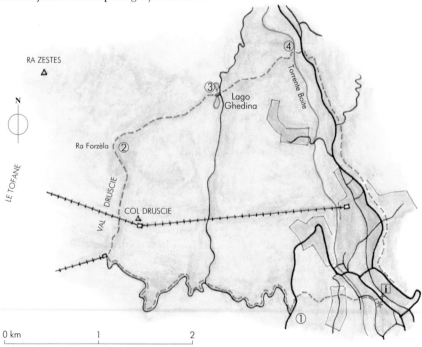

Lago Ghedina,
above Cortina >

## WALK 1: LAGO GHEDINA

*This easy walk leads you beneath the jagged flanks of the Tofane to pretty Lago Ghedina, nestled in its forest setting, before you descend to cross the green waters of the Torrente Boite.*

| | |
|---|---|
| Distance | 11.5 km (7 miles) |
| Time | 4 hours |
| Difficulty | easy |
| Start/Finish | Cortina |

From Cortina's 1775 parish church, descend to the river and cross at the nearby bridge. Cross the road and follow a lane up between houses, then cross another road and continue uphill. Turn left on a lane just past the first buildings and, at the bend, cross a meadow and turn left onto the road. Soon, in the district of
① **Gilardon**, turn right at a sign to Lago Ghedina (path #407); this road winds uphill with lovely views back to Cortina and beyond. An hour or so from the start, you pass a chairlift base. Path #406 joins in at the left and the Tofane range looms ahead.

Where the bitumen ends, pass a signpost and keep right on #410, now a gravel track into the Val Druscie. You soon pass a water spout and descend gently. Head straight through a path junction, with a close view of needle formations up to the left. At
② **Ra Forzèla** (1670 m), take the narrow path #410 right, descending through woodland filled with alpenrose, a type of small rhododendron. Continue downhill until a signpost directs you right to
③ **Lago Ghedina**, where you turn right onto the road. Left of the lakeside restaurant (open seasonally), steps lead down to a path around the lake, from where the view features the Tofane as a backdrop.

From the parking area, cross the paved road and pick up path #416/410 signed to La Vera. A short distance downhill, turn left onto the grassy path #416. Turn right onto a vehicular track and then left onto a footpath (still on #416). It descends to the
④ **Torrente Boite**, crossed by a wooden bridge, a delightful spot for a picnic.

Climb the opposite bank to soon meet the main Cortina road and turn right. At a nearby parking bay take the side road uphill, then immediately turn right onto path #208, a pleasant level footpath/cycleway which follows the old train route back to the centre of Cortina.

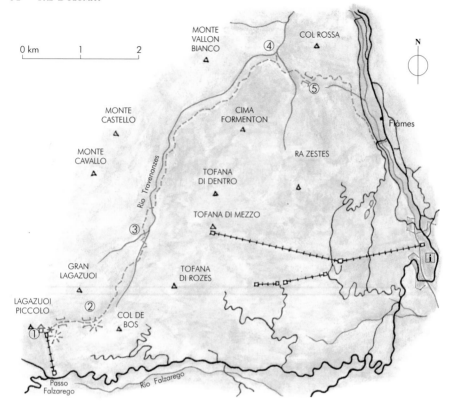

0 km    1    2

MONTE
VALLON
BIANCO
▲

④

COL ROSSA
▲

N

MONTE
CASTELLO
▲

CIMA
FORMENTON
▲

⑤

Fiàmes

MONTE
CAVALLO
▲

*Rio Travenanzes*

TOFANA
DI DENTRO
▲

RA ZESTES
▲

TOFANA DI MEZZO
△
▯

③

GRAN
LAGAZUOI
▲

TOFANA
DI ROZES
▲

▯

LAGAZUOI
PICCOLO

②

COL DE
▲ BOS

①
▯▯

Passo
Falzarego

*Rio Falzarego*

ⓘ

## WALK 2: VAL TRAVENANZES

*Make use of a cable car to gain height for spectacular views and a hike down the lovely Val Travenanzes. Take plenty of food, for you will be some distance from civilisation.*

| | |
|---|---|
| Distance | 16.5 km (10.25 miles) |
| Time | 7 hours |
| Difficulty | moderate |
| Start | Passo Falzarego |
| Finish | near Fiàmes |
| Transport | bus to start and from finish |

The route commences at the Passo Falzarego, 13 km (8 miles) from Cortina (a bus service operates from July) and finishes near Fiàmes where you can return to Cortina on a local bus. Passo Falzarego (2105 m) lies beneath the Lagazuoi Piccolo, one of the main theatres of WW1 combat in the Dolomiti. From the pass, looking north to the Lagazuoi Piccolo, you can see

two rock slides caused by Austrian and Italian mine explosions. Take the Lagazuoi cable car to the summit of

① **Lagazuoi Piccolo** (2752 m) to be met with one of the Dolomiti's most stunning panoramas: NE to the Tofane, E to Sorapiss and SE to the Croda da Lago, Cinque Torri, Nuvolau and Averau.

From the Rifugio Lagazuoi, take path #401 zigzagging down over scree and late snow below the *rifugio* and turn right at the path junction. You pass through a WW1 battle zone beside cutaway galleries and beneath tunnel openings in the mountain walls, with the Lagazuoi Grande ahead. Continue on #401 at a path junction at Forcella Lagazuoi (2573 m) to soon reach the pass of

② **Forcella Travenanzes** (2507 m). If you are lucky you may see chamois hereabouts. Continue ENE on #401/402. At a junction

The view back to Rifugio Lagazuoi >

you fork left on #401 with the awesome pyramid of the Tofana di Rozes ahead to begin a gradual descent of the U-shaped glacial Val Travenanzes. This landscape, seemingly barren, is home to tiny alpine rock flowers and, further on, the light woodland shelters alpenrose. You pass the ruins of an earlier *rifugio* and a junction for the Scala del Menighel where you keep left. Soon after path #17 joins left from Monte Cavallo, you reach the abandoned shepherd's hut (now an emergency shelter) at
③ **Malga Travenanzes**. Look and listen for the resident marmot colony hereabouts. Nearby rocks overlooking the river make a pleasant spot for a picnic lunch or just a rest break.

The route follows the course of the Rio Travenanzes and then crosses it; you may need to remove boots for this and the water will be cold! To your right is the flank of Tofana di Mezzo, to the west is Monte Cavallo with water cascading off the rock walls after rain or snow. The valley sides close and steepen as you descend and you cross sides of the torrent twice more before the path curves and steepens. Ahead is the Croda Rossa. Shortly after you enter woodland, an unsigned detour left down to a footbridge over the
④ **Rio Travenanzes** offers dramatic chasm views; alternatively, you might detour further along to the nearby Ponte de Cadoris for a similar view. At a junction, take path #408 right to Passo Posporcora, the Val Fiorenza and the Pian de Ra Spines. This path re-enters forest, crosses a stream and climbs steadily to
⑤ **Passo Posporcora** (1711 m); look up left to view a WW1 military ruin. From here, the path makes a long zigzagging descent to the Pian de Ra Spines. Eventually you turn right onto a broad track (#417) which follows above the right bank of the Boite and reaches a minor road at the Olympia camping ground at Fiàmes, from where you can catch a bus back to Cortina.

< Malga Travenanzes

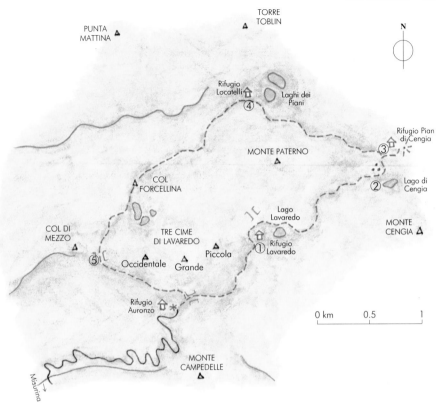

## WALK 3: TRE CIME DI LAVAREDO

*This high-level circular walk around the extraordinary Tre Cime di Lavaredo and Monte Paterno is considered to be one of the Dolomiti classics and is deservedly popular.*

| | |
|---|---|
| Distance | 14 km (8.75 miles) |
| Time | 6.5 hours |
| Difficulty | reasonably strenuous |
| Start/Finish | Rifugio Auronzo |
| Transport | bus to and from Rif. Auronzo |

The walk commences at Rifugio Auronzo, some 14 km of winding road northeast of Cortina. To get there, catch a seasonal bus (operating from July to mid-September) from Cortina and change at the picturesque Lago di Misurina for the bus to Rifugio Auronzo. Check return times at Cortina's

< Tre Cime di Lavaredo

tourist office before setting out or book a *rifugio* bed!

From the bland and busy Rifugio Auronzo (2320 m), walk along the level jeep track (path #101/104), passing beneath the towering spires of Tre Cime that dominate this furrowed limestone terrain. There are actually four peaks, rather than three, though the fourth seems to be unnamed. To the south are admirable views of the Cadini group of spires and needles. There will probably be plenty of company on this stretch of track which leads to

① **Rifugio Lavaredo** (2344 m), set beneath the Croda Passaporto. Ten minutes after this *rifugio*, veer right to head SE along the less walked #104 passing left of a tiny lake. This broad WW1 mule path descends into the pasture of the Pian di Lavaredo and, after meeting path #107, climbs to reach

② **Lago di Cengia** and a monument. Take path #104 north to cross a barren slope

The strange landscape of a WWI battlezone

and zigzag steeply up to numerous WW1 fortifications above a natural amphitheatre. Continue climbing to reach
③ **Forcella Pian di Cengia** (2522 m) at a path junction. Detour right here, traversing a rock ledge on wooden planks before contouring left to reach the small Rifugio Pian di Cengia, a charming *rifugio* where simple meals are available. Take time to enjoy the exceptional panorama; you may be able to pick out Monte Popera's tiny glacier visible due east.

Return to Forcella Pian di Cengia where there are wonderful views NW to the Tre Scarperi group. Now follow #101 NW, descending a steep gully (take care on the loose rocks) and then crossing the scree of Monte Paterno's northern flanks, with its spires looming high on your left. During WW1 the Italians held this mountain and a local Austrian guide, Sepp Innerkofler, was given the task of scaling it. He died near the summit and a later investigation suggests that his own troops, who held nearby peaks, mistakenly shot him.

Your path passes above a tiny glacial tarn

and, after a short climb, above two more such alpine tarns, the Laghi dei Piani. A gentle ascent then takes you to the popular
④ **Rifugio Locatelli** under the Torre Toblin. Occupying a strategic position near the battle front, the original building was burnt during WW1 hostilities. The views of the Croda Rossa (west), the Cristallo group (southwest) and, of course, the Tre Cime di Lavaredo are exceptional and you will want to linger for a while.

The return to Rifugio Auronzo on path #105 (Alta Via #4) around Tre Cime's western flanks takes longer than the more direct #101 but is less crowded. You descend into a flat rocky cirque, cross a stream and ascend again, crossing barren rock and traversing scree before reaching
⑤ **Forcella Col di Mezzo** (2315 m), where the views are panoramic. The path now tends SE and provides distant views of the Sorapiss, Antelao and Marmarole peaks en route back to Rifugio Auronzo. With luck, you'll have time for a well-earned drink before catching the bus back to Cortina.

## OTHER WALKS IN THE REGION

You can devise hundreds of itineraries of all lengths and degrees of difficulty! Here are a few possibilities.

### The Old Rail Track

If you wish to admire the mountain scenery but stay on level ground, you can stroll the length of Cortina's valley along path #208. This path, shared with cyclists, follows the track of the disused railway line and can be picked up from the bus station in Cortina's centre and then followed north or south to a point on the local bus route for a return journey. *Length is at your discretion.*

### Lago di Federa

This is a fairly easy circular walk beneath the Croda da Lago south of Cortina to reach the Lago di Federa. Take bus #3 from Cortina to Col. Backtrack to the Falzarego road, walk south uphill for 25 minutes and take path #451 left. Soon turn right onto a track (#428) and cross the Ponte Alto. Leave the track right for an unnumbered path which soon joins track #430. A short detour left at a crossroads leads to Lago d'Aial and the Bar Lago d'Aial.

Return to the crossroads and turn left onto #431, a road which becomes a footpath. Follow #431 south through woodland to Lago di Federa, reached in 2 hours or so. In summer the Rifugio Palmieri serves lunch. There is a path around the lake, fringed with larch and pine, offering superb views north to the peaks of Cristallo, Sorapiss and Antelao across the Valle d'Ampezzo.

The return path #432 is a car-free forestry track which descends the Val Federa to Campo on Cortina's outskirts, a walk of around 2 hours. You first emerge from forest at Malga Federa, a summer farm (fresh water from tap) with wonderful views over Cortina and behind to the Croda da Lago. Descend through more forest and cross the Torrente Federa near cascades. At a path junction you could follow #428

to return to Col. Otherwise continue on #432 down to Campo di Sotto. You may wish to detour right a short distance (signposted) to Lago di Pianoze where there is a chalet. Local bus #2 returns to Cortina from Campo or you could walk back along path #208 which parallels the Torrente Boite and the main road. *Allow 4 to 5 hours.*

### Cinque Torri

This popular moderate-grade walk rewards your efforts with dramatic mountain scenery, including views of the Tofane and Sorapiss massifs and Croda da Lago. Check the chairlift schedule before leaving Cortina. Catch the Passo Falzarego bus but get off early at Rifugio Bai de Dones and catch the Cinque Torri chairlift. From the top, take path #439 to the base of Averau. Continue on #439 to Rifugio Nuvolau which offers a complete panorama.

Return to the path junction and take path #452 which contours the slope of Nuvolau. Before you reach Passo Giau, pick up path #443 which heads north to Rifugio Cinque Torri. From here, pick up #439 back to the chairlift. *Allow 4 to 5 hours.*

Cortina d'Ampezzo

## Fanes-Sennes-Braies Nature Park

This spectacular 2-day walk takes you into the heart of nature reserve to overnight at a *rifugio*. Although not overly strenuous, the total distance is 41 km (26 miles) with some steady inclines.

Take the local bus to Fiàmes and at the *albergo* take the track up the valley (path #10) above the Torrente Boite with views of Col Rosa and Croda de R'Ancona. At Ponte Felizon you enter the Dolomiti d' Ampezzo Nature Park. Continue on #10 up through woodland, crossing several streams and the Rio di Fanes with views of Taburlo. Cross the dramatic Ponte Outo; a short detour leads to the Cascata di Fanes. Path #10 then continues up valley and passes Lago di Fanes.

Cross the river and enter the Fanes-Sennes-Braies Nature Park in alpine meadowland. The valley widens and forms an amphitheatre beneath Monte Vallon Bianco. Before a footbridge, a short cut diverts right uphill on a WW1 mule path. Watch for marmots! Regain the track (now path #10/11) and ascend to the Lago di Limo and the Passo di Limo (2174 m). Descend steeply to the Rifugio Fanes (meals, accommodation). Detour to the Lago Verde and cross a footbridge (path #7/12) to the farm buildings and the Rifugio La Varella (meals, accommodation).

Follow the Rio San Viglio on a jeep track (#7) down to the Rifugio Pederü. A very steep switchback ascent on a WW1 mule path (#7) and then on a forest path (#9) takes you to the delightful Rifugio Fodara Vedla. Alternatively, a jeep-taxi service operates between the four *rifugi*!

On day 2, ascend on a jeep track (#7) to Rifugio Sennes, where marmots abound. Take the jeep track (#6) signed to Cortina and soon turn left uphill (also on #6). At Ota del Barancio (2190 m), divert down right on an unnumbered path to Lago de Fosses, a remote lake beneath the scree of Remeda Rossa. At the *malga* farm building,

Rio di Fanes and Taburlo

take path #26, passing left of Lago Piccolo on a boggy path and ascend to Croce del Gris (2188 m) with panoramic views. Continue on #26 signed to Campo Croce/ Malga Ra Stua and descend to the valley floor. Take the road down the valley (or the parallel footpath across meadow and through woods) to Rifugio Malga Ra Stua where food is served (no accommodation).

From the *rifugio*, backtrack briefly up the valley and take an unmarked (#8 on the map) forest track right uphill. Take a right-forking path (#8) signed to Forcella Lerosa/ Val di Gotres. Zigzag up through woods; at the edge of meadowland, turn right uphill at a path junction. At the Forcella Lerosa the track becomes a jeep track and descends through the Val di Gotres. Cross the Torrente Gotres; a brief detour here leads to a cascade. Reach a gate and soon fork right on a minor footpath (#8c) that drops steadily through forest, skirts right around a fenced-off military area and eventually reaches the main road. Turn right and follow the road to the Rifugio Ospitale where you catch the bus to Cortina. *Allow 2 days, 7 to 8 hours each day.*

< High pasture near Fodara Vedla

# VENEZIA

In the city of Venezia or Venice, the walker gains his or her just rewards. Here, in the spiderweb of canals and narrow bridges, there are no mopeds to mow you down or tourist coaches to obscure your views. The only noises come from puttering boats and the bells of countless churches. The only cause for delay is not traffic lights but the endless perfect scenes that catch your eye as you weave through alleys and past piers. There is an air of unreality—Venezia is more of a floating museum than a working city—but there's no reason its charms should be resisted.

Built on a cluster of over a hundred flat islands, Venezia was established in the 8th and 9th centuries by inhabitants of other islands in the lagoon who were under attack by Charlemagne's Franks. In 828 two Venetian merchants stole the bones of San Marco from Alexandria and the young city, with its new patron saint, didn't look back for centuries. The Venetian Republic developed and flourished under the rule of successive doges and their councils, its great wealth drawn from trade with the East as well as conquest in the Crusades. Its power peaked in the 15th century when Venezia ruled a large portion of northern Italy as well as lands in the east.

Trouble from the Turks and the loss of

NOTES
Population: 275,000
Getting there: bus from Marco Polo
    airport (6 km N on the mainland);
    rail from Milano, Bologna or Trieste
Tourist Office: Palazzo Selva, P.S.Marco
    Tel: 041 5226356 Fax: 52998730
    www.provincia.venezia.it
Markets: west of Ponte Rialto

its trade monopoly with Asia undermined the strength of the Venetian empire and, when Napoleon's forces arrived in 1797, the city was more a playground than a centre of business. Today its reduced population is boosted by tourism, made viable by the construction of the mainland bridge in the 19th century.

Venezia is traditionally divided into six *sestieri* or districts. We have devised two walks, one on either bank of the Canal Grande, but you should do a bit of aimless wandering as well. A few tips: a street is a *calle* or *salizzada*, a quay is a *riva* or *fondamenta*, a canal is a *rio*, a filled-in canal is a *rio terrà*, a square is a *campo*. Three *ponti* or bridges cross the Canal Grande: the Scalzi, the Rialto and the Accademia. Ferries or *vaporetti* zigzag between its banks or you can catch a *traghetto* for a very cheap gondola ride across the canal at certain points. In winter and spring, the occasional high tide or *acqua alta* floods areas such as San Marco for a few hours. On these occasions, boardwalks are laid on main thoroughfares and La Serenissima continues on regardless.

A canal view >

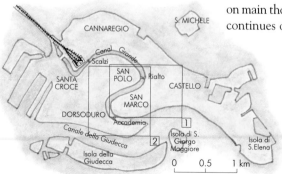

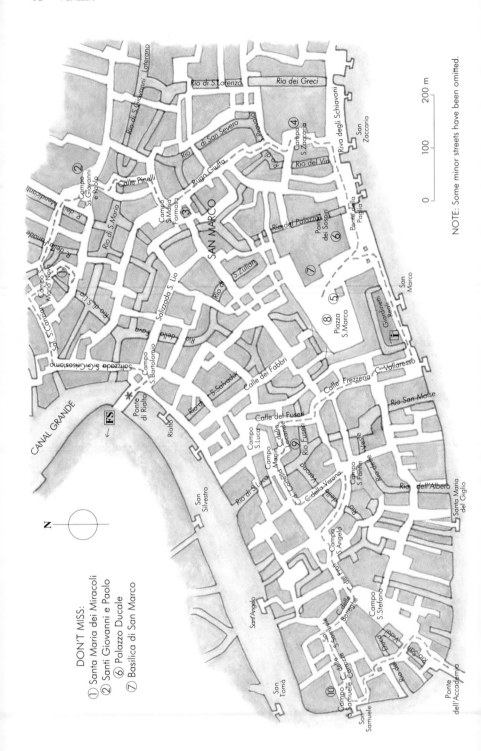

NOTE: Some minor streets have been omitted.

200 m

100

0

CANAL GRANDE

FS

N

SAN MARCO

Rio di S.Lorenzo

Rio dei Greci

Rio di S.Giovanni Laterano

Rio di San Severo

Campo S.Giovanni e Paolo

Calle Pinalli

Ruga Giuffa

Rio di San Severo

Campo S.Zaccaria

San Zaccaria

Riva degli Schiavoni

Rio del Vin

Campo S.Maria Formosa

Rio di S.Maria

Campo S.Maria Nova

S.Zulian

Rio del Palazzo

Ponte dei Sospiri

Ponte della Paglia

Salizzada S. Lio

Salizzada S.G.Grisostomo

Campo S.Bartolomio

Campo S.Bartolomio

Piazza S.Marco

San Marco

Giardinetti Reali

Ponte di Rialto

Rialto

San Silvestro

Rio di S.Salvador

Calle dei Fabbri

Calle Frezzeria

C. Vallaresso

Rio di

Rio d.

Calle dei Fuseri

Rio Fuseri

Rio San Moisè

Rio di S.Luca

Campo S.Luca

Campo Manin

Calle della Mandola

C. della Verona

C. della Chiesa

Campo S.Fantin

Rio delle

Rio dell'Albero

Santa Maria del Giglio

Sant'Angelo

Campo S.Angelo

Campo S.Stefano

Rio San

Vidal

San Tomà

Campo S.Samuele

Calle S.Samuele

Campo S.Samuele

Calle dale Botteghe

Campo S.Maurizio

Ponte dell'Accademia

Rio dale

Samuele

① ② ③ ④ ⑤ ⑥ ⑦ ⑧ ⑨ ⑩

DON'T MISS:
① Santa Maria dei Miracoli
② Santi Giovanni e Paolo
⑥ Palazzo Ducale
⑦ Basilica di San Marco

## WALK 1: CASTELLO & SAN MARCO

*A meander along the east side of the Canal Grande takes you to Venezia's most striking sights, plus a few of her hidden gems.*

Begin your walk at the Ponte di Rialto, a shop-lined 16th-century bridge designed so that an armed galley could pass below. Turn left off Salizzada Pio X and walk through Campo San Bartolomio. Walk north and look inside the Fondaco dei Tedeschi, a palazzo once owned by German merchants and now the main post office. Walk north on Salizzada San Crisostomo and right on Salizzada San Canzian to Campo Santa Maria Nova. Beside the canal is the small but charming Renaissance
① **Santa Maria dei Miracoli**, with its multicoloured marble façade. Built in the 1480s, this is the church of choice for Venetian weddings. To enter, you'll need to cross a bridge and encircle the church.

From the *campo*, cross the Rio di Ca', Rio della Panada and then Rio dei Mendicanti, a canal frequently painted by Canaletto and

Canal Grande near the Ponte di Rialto

Guardi, to reach Campo Santi Giovanni e Paolo. On your left is the richly sculpted façade of the Scuola di San Marco. Further on is a powerful statue depicting Colleoni the mercenary. Sculpted by Verrochio in 1488, it is thought by many to be the best equestrian statue ever created.

Dominating the *campo* is the huge ② **Santi Giovanni e Paolo**. This Gothic church was built by the Dominicans to compete with the Franciscans, who were building the Frari across the Canal Grande. Built in exposed brick in an unadorned style, it holds the tombs of many Venetian doges, as well as a beautiful altar polyptych by Bellini and ceiling paintings by Veronese. Leave south of the church by the *sottoportego* of Calle Bressana and turn left along Fondamenta Felzi to a lovely iron bridge facing diverging canals. Cross this and head down the narrow Calle Pinelli. Turn right into Calle Lunga S. Maria Formosa to reach ③ **Campo Santa Maria Formosa**. This is one of Venezia's most characteristic *campi* or squares; *formosa* means 'shapely'. Its church contains a polyptych of Santa Barbara by Palma il Vecchio.

*< Ponte dei Sospiri*

San Marco and San Teodoro, booty from conquest abroad. These stand in the Piazzetta San Marco, a space once reserved for the city's patricians and a foretaste of the larger piazza beyond. The solid brick ⑤ **Campanile** on your left was first built in the 16th century as a watchtower and lighthouse, then rebuilt following an earthquake in 1902. It offers amazing views if you are prepared to queue. On your right is the ⑥ **Palazzo Ducale**, which held the doge's apartments, the parliament and offices of government. It was built in the 12th century but modified over the next few centuries. Its exterior is a work of art: a geometric pattern in pale marble, a porticoed ground floor and a lovely upper gallery all add a light touch to the massive building. The main entrance, in the *piazzetta*, is a wonderful piece of Gothic design. Your entrance, somewhat less spectacular, is quayside.

Inside, the famous Scala d'Oro or Golden Staircase leads up to a long series of rooms, including a fascinating map room and the **Sala del Maggior Consiglio**, the great hall

Crossing Rio di S.M.Formosa, head along Ruga Giuffa, then dog-leg into Calle Corte Rotta, cross over Rio di S. Provolo, and turn right and walk through Campo San Provolo, then left to reach ④ **San Zaccaria**, an attractive 15th-century church with a façade designed by Codussi who marked a shift from Gothic style to the classical principles of the Renaissance. Inside, a work by Bellini adorns the second altar to the left.

From Campo San Zaccaria walk south to reach Riva degli Schiavoni, with a view across the lagoon to the **Isola di San Giorgio Maggiore** and its Palladian church (*vaporetti* #52 or 82 from the nearby wharf will take you across to the island). Turn right, cross the Ponte del Vin, pass the famous Hotel Danieli and compete with the crowds on Ponte della Paglia to view the **Ponte dei Sospiri**, the Bridge of Sighs, over which prisoners were led from the Palazzo Ducale to the dungeons.

The waterfront here is known as the Molo and was the traditional arrival point for important visitors to Venezia. They were greeted by the two columns representing

*The view from the Palazzo Ducale >*

built in 1340 and redecorated following a fire in 1577. Once the largest hall in Europe, this features Tintoretto's gigantic depiction of paradise and a ceiling work by Veronese. You can also troop over the canal to view the adjoining prisons, which most famously incarcerated Casanova.

Head back to the main piazza to enter ⑦ the **Basilica di San Marco**, though you should pause to admire its fantastic façade before doing so. The church, a mixture of Byzantine and Western styles, was built in the late 11th century to house the stolen relics of St Mark. In fact many decorative elements—columns, bas-reliefs, statues such as the four bronze horses—were booty from the Crusades, augmented with a fulsome use of gold to highlight the Republic's wealth and glory. Inside are beautiful 12th-century mosaics and the renowned Pala d'Oro, a 10th-century gold altarpiece heavily encrusted with jewels.

Back out in the daylight, take a stroll around the expanse of ⑧ the **Piazza San Marco**, designed by the architect Sansovino at the height of the Renaissance. The **Torre dell'Orologio** (the

Piazza San Marco

1496 clock tower is currently being restored) was designed by Codussi, as was the long **Procuratie Vecchie** next door. The **Procuratie Nuove** opposite was Sansovino's work; both buildings housed judicial offices—*procuratori* were magistrates—and now shelter famous cafés. The **Ala Napoleonica** at the end of the piazza was contributed by the Napoleonic occupiers and contains the Museo Correr, a collection of Venetian history and art.

Return to the quayside, passing the **Libreria Sansoviniana**, which contains rare illuminated manuscripts. Along the waterfront you pass the **Zecca**, the old city mint designed by Sansovino, and then the Giardinetti Reali. Turn right at Harry's Bar, once frequented by Ernest Hemingway, and walk up Calle Vallaresso and then up Calle Frezzeria. At the end, turn left and then right to cross Rio Fuseri. Head along Calle dei Fuseri but watch for a left turn into the narrow Calle delle Locandi. Turn left at a signed alley to reach the charming

< Palazzo Contarini del Bovolo

< Gondolas at San Marco

Stefano with its tilted campanile and remarkable wooden ceiling shaped like a boat's keel. You soon reach the large Campo Santo Stefano as it is known; locals have never caught on to the official name of Francesco Morosini. Leave the *campo* by Calle delle Botteghe at the northwest: the area you're entering is home to a number of local artisans. Turn left on Salizzada San Samuele which soon becomes Calle delle Carrozze to reach

⑩ **Palazzo Grassi** on the Canal Grande. This 18th-century palazzo was restored and opened as a cultural centre in 1985, at private expense. Its changing exhibitions are extremely popular with Venetians and Italian visitors.

Cross Campo San Samuele and zigzag to Calle Fruttarol to cross Rio del Duca and Rio San Vidal. Turn right through the grassy Campo San Vidal to the Ponte dell' Accademia. This simple wooden bridge was built as a temporary measure in 1932 to replace an ugly iron one. As yet, no one has dared commit to a new design.

⑨ **Palazzo Contarini del Bovolo**. A very elegant external staircase built in 1499 gives the building its name: *bovolo* is a local word for snail. The combination of graceful loggias and open arches is delightfully Venetian and a lovely view over rooftops can be had once you've climbed to the top.

Continue to Campo Manin, graced by a statue of Daniele Manin, a hero of the 1848 Venetian uprising against its Austrian rulers who succeeded the French. Cross Rio di San Luca on Calle di Cortesia which becomes Calle della Mandola. A detour left on Calle dei Assassini would take you to Campo San Fantin to view the scaffolded neoclassical exterior of **Teatro La Fenice**. Built in 1792, the opera house and its elegant interior is being restored following a disastrous 1996 fire. It suffered a similar fate in 1836 and is once again earning its name: *fenice* means 'phoenix'.

Otherwise, keep straight on to enter the graceful Campo Sant'Angelo, which contains the Oratorio dell'Annunciata. Leave by Calle dei Frati, passing Santo

Twilight over the lagoon >

The map shows a street map of Venice with the following labels:

Campo S.M. Mater Domini
C.d.Campanile
C.d. Bottari
C.d. Pescarie
Calle Saccaril
Ruga dei Oresi
Campo S.Cassiano
SAN POLO
Rio di San Cassiano
Rio della Due Torri
Rio di San Aponal
C. Bernardo
Rio della Madonnetta
Rio d.Meloni
Fondamenta del Vin
Rialto
Ponte di Rialto
Campo San Polo
C.Sec Saoneri
Sal.S.Polo
Rio di San Polo
Rio Terra S.Tomà
San Silvestro
Sal.di S.Rocco
④ Campo dei Frari
⑤
Rio della Frescada
C.dei Preti
⑥ Campo S.Pantalon
Rio di Cà Foscari
San Tomà
San Angelo
Sant' Angelo
Campo Santa Margherita
San Samuele
⑦ C.della Pazienza
Rio di San Barnaba
Campo S.Barnaba
Ca' Rezzonico
Fond. Gherardini
Fonta di Borgo
Rio Malpaga
DORSODURO
Rio Ognissanti
Fond. Bonlini
Campo S.Trovaso
Rio di San Trovaso
⑩
Ponte dell'Accademia
S.Maria del Giglio
S.Maria della Salute
Rio Terra Foscarini
Campo S.Vio
⑨
C. Bastion
Rio di San Vio
C. Rio Terra
Fond. di Cà Bala
⑧
Rio del Forner
Rio della Salute
Ponte Lungo
Fondamenta Zattere
Zattere
Rio Piccolo del Legname
Rio di San Vio

DON'T MISS:
① Rialto markets
④ Santa Maria Gloriosa dei Frari
⑤ Scuola Grande di San Rocco
⑩ Gallerie dell'Accademia

N

0    100    200 m

NOTE: Some minor streets have been omitted.

## WALK 2: SAN POLO & DORSODURO

*The west bank has fewer tourists and will reveal more about Venetian life. This route also offers a viewing of the many art treasures tucked away in Venezia's public buildings.*

Begin again at the Ponte di Rialto and head to the west bank of the Canal Grande. First, detour by strolling southwest along the Fondamenta del Vin. Towards the end,

you have a view across the canal of two handsome Byzantine palazzi: Ca' Loredan and Ca' Farsetti. *Ca'* is short for *casa* and is usually followed by the first owner's name.

Back at the bridge, head along Ruga dei Oresi and into
① **the Rialto**. This area was the first to be settled as it was the safe, high bank or *rivo alto*. Here is Venezia's oldest church: San Giacomo di Rialto with its 1410 clock face.

The Frari in San Polo

A squat column in front is supported by *il Gobbo*, the hunchback. Pass through a *sottoportego* at the corner of the Fabbriche Vecchie to emerge at Campo de la Cordaria where the Erberia or fruit market does business each morning except Sunday. Walk past the Fabbriche Nuove to reach Campo della Pescaria to visit the Pescheria, the fish markets (closed on Monday): Venetians eat a lot of fish, though little is now caught in the lagoon.

Leave Campo della Pescaria along Calle Beccarie. Turn right to cross Rio di Beccarie and then right down Calle dei Botteri to view the magnificent Gothic façade of the Ca' d'Oro across the Canal Grande. Walk along the waterfront and then down Calle del Campanile to reach Campo San Cassiano. Cross the canal and turn left then right to cross Rio di Due Torri and reach
② the tiny **Campo Santa Maria Mater Domini** in a district of lovely 13th- and 14th-century houses.

Leave on Calle della Chiesa and continue over Rio di San Boldo then turn left into

Shop windows are a Venetian art >

Calle Bernardo, which crosses a canal and zigzags to arrive at Campo San Polo, a spacious *campo* popular with children and mothers. Leave on Salizzada San Polo, where you'll find the entrance to
③ **San Polo**. This much rebuilt church contains the Via Crucis del Tiepolo, 14 images of the Stations of the Cross painted by Tiepolo in 1749, as well as paintings by Veronese and Tintoretto.

Continue on over Rio di San Polo then turn right into Calle Seconda Saoneri. Turn left on Rio Terrà, right into Fondamenta dei Frari and left over a bridge into Campo dei Frari. Dominating the *campo* is
④ **Santa Maria Gloriosa dei Frari** or, as Venetians known it, simply the Frari. The Franciscans built a church here in the 13th century but it was replaced with this vast Gothic building in the mid-15th century. Its 83-metre-high campanile dominates this side of the city. Its airy interior is furnished with an intricate 1475 rood screen, beautiful choir stalls and a dramatic tomb for the sculptor Canova. Its art treasures include works by Titian, Bellini and Donatello.

Circle the Frari's exterior to
⑤ the **Scuola Grande di San Rocco**, with its graceful Renaissance façade. *Scuole* were very Venetian institutions, something akin to clubs with a charitable role. The wealthy members of this *scuola* commissioned Tintoretto in 1564 to decorate the interior of their meeting house, and he did so with

56 paintings, the work of 18 years.

Head down the Calle Fianco della Scuola and cross the Rio della Frescada. Continue south to reach Campo San Pantalon and its late 17th-century church of

(6) **San Pantalon**. This church is worth a visit for its painted ceiling, a huge assemblage of some 40 scenes which, together, create an amazing sense of height. This was the life work of the artist Fumiani; he allegedly fell off the scaffolding on completion of the ceiling and died.

Cross the Rio di Ca' Foscari and soon reach the long and pleasant Campo Santa Margherita, lined with houses of many different ages. At the south of the *campo* is (7) the **Scuola Grande dei Carmini**. This 1663 building also features a splendid ceiling, this one painted by Tiepolo in 1744. Walk south alongside the church of Carmini on Calle della Pazienza and cross the charming Rio di San Barnaba. Turn left along Fondamenta Gherardini to reach Campo San Barnaba. Leave via a *sottoportego* and head south on Calle della Casin, cross Rio Malpaga and turn right to follow it, then head south on Fondamenta di Borgo and southeast on Fondamenta Bontini to reach Campo San Trovaso. A gondola workshop, Squero di San Trovaso, is sited here but is closed to the public. Note: if time is short and you wish to visit the Accademia, head direct from here.

Otherwise, cross over Rio Ognissanti and wend your way to the Ponte Lungo. Walk along Fondamenta Zattere past various churches and continue along the waterfront of the Canale della Giudecca. Eventually you turn left up the lovely Fondamenta di Ca' Bala. A quick detour right at Calle Rio Terrà and across Rio della Salute takes you to the great baroque church of

(8) **Santa Maria della Salute** at the mouth of the Canal Grande. It was built in thanks for deliverance from the plague of 1630— *salute* means health—a salvation which is still celebrated each 21 November. Its architect, Baldassare Longhena, understood the value of the setting and La Salute's

dome is a landmark visible across the city. Its interior, built to an octagonal plan, is relatively spare; the sacristy contains works by Tintoretto.

Recross the canal into Calle Abazia and the attractive district of San Gregorio. Continue down Calle Bastion to

(9) **Ca' Venier dei Leoni**, home of the Peggy Guggenheim Collection. This palazzo was begun in 1749 but never completed, so that only a ground floor exists. The collection of contemporary art is beautifully displayed, both inside and out in the garden.

Wend your way west past Campo San Vio, which offers a view across to Palazzo Babaro where Henry James worked—it is the second building down from the bridge— to reach Rio Terrà Foscarini and the

(10) **Gallerie dell'Accademia**, which houses a totally different collection of art, covering Venetian painting from the 14th to the 18th centuries. There are wonderful cityscapes, portraits and religious pieces by such masters as Bellini, Veronese, Canaletto, Tintoretto, Lotto and Tiepolo, to name a few. Once you have had your fill of art, you are back at the Ponte dell'Accademia.

A house in San Gregorio

< La Salute from the Ponte dell'Accademia

## OTHER EXCURSIONS

The Laguna Veneta contains a number of islands and a trip to one of these can refresh you for another intense day in Venezia. The one *vaporetto* (#12 from Fondamenta Nuove, north of Campo Santi Giovanni e Paulo) visits Murano, Burano and Torcello, so you could spend a day visiting all three.

**Burano** is a charming island famous for lace-making and for the brightly painted houses that line its waterways. From Venezia, it is a 30-minute boat trip to the island.

**Torcello** is almost deserted and now has an air of seclusion but it was a powerful stronghold before Venezia was a city. Around a grassy square stand its main buildings, including the oldest in the lagoon: the cathedral of Santa Maria dell'Assunta. This church dates back to 639 and houses wonderful mosaics. The adjoining church of Santa Fosca is a Byzantine addition.

**Murano**, closer to Venezia and reached on the same *vaporetto* line or from San Zaccaria, is famed for its glassworks. There

*Frutta e verdura* from a barge

is a museum of glass here and also the splendid 12th-century Basilica dei Santi Maria e Donato.

**Lido** is the long strip of land opposite the tip of the Dorsoduro and is renowned for its beach and casino. Cars have access to it, making it less of a walker's paradise.

| OPENING HOURS | |
| --- | --- |
| Santi Giovanni e Paulo | daily 7-12.30; 3-6 |
| San Zaccaria | daily 10-noon; 4-6 |
| Campanile | daily 9-7.30 |
| Palazzo Ducale | daily 9-7 |
| Basilica di San Marco | M-Sat 9.30-5; Sun 2-4.30; Galleria daily 9.30-5 |
| Contarini del Bovolo | daily 10-6 |
| Rialto markets | Erberia Mon-Sat till noon; Pescheria Tue-Sun |
| S. Maria dei Frari | Mon-Sat 9-noon; 2.30-6; Sun 3-6 |
| Scuola Grande di S. Rocco | daily 9-5.30 |
| San Pantalon | Mon-Sat 4-6 |
| Scuola dei Carmini | Mon-Sat 9-6; Sun 9-4 |
| La Salute | daily 9-noon; 3-5.30 |
| Peggy Guggenheim Collection | Mon, Wed-Fri 10-6; Sat-Sun 10-10 |
| Gallerie dell'Accademia | Mon 9-2; Tue-Sat 8.30-7.30; Sun 9-7 |

# VERONA

Though Verona has its fair share of historic sites and works of art, this attractive city doesn't seem distracted by the demands of tourism. You can wander its streets or relax with a drink in the popular Piazza Bra, and the fact that there are monumental Roman ruins beside you seems almost incidental.

Verona is located in the valley of the Fiume Adige, on the western side of the Veneto plains. It was a strategic centre of great importance to the Romans and it enjoyed immense cultural development. The old city, enclosed in a loop of the Adige, retains the traditional grid layout of Roman towns. The Forum, once the heart of the city's religious and civil life, is now the Piazza delle Erbe, a lively and attractive marketplace.

Christianity was supposedly brought to Verona by San Zeno during the 4th century and the Romanesque church dedicated to him, San Zeno Maggiore, is one of the city's main attractions.

After the fall of the western Roman empire, Verona's key position made it the subject of various invasions by Ostrogoths, Lombards and Franks. In the 12th century it became a free *comune* and began a programme of rebuilding after a major earthquake in 1117.

Following a 33-year period of tyranny under the ruthless Ezzelino da Romana, power was claimed by the Scaligeri family and the city enjoyed a period of growth. Within a century, Verona was the capital of a state that included most of the Veneto and reached as far as Toscana. Dante Alighieri was a welcome guest at the court of Cangrande I, who extended the city walls. The Castelvecchio was built to

NOTES
Population: 255,000
Getting there: bus from airport 14 km SW;
rail from Milano, Venezia or Bologna
Tourist Office: Via Leoncino 61, 37121
Tel:045 8068680  Fax:045 8003638
email: info@tourism.verona.it
www.tourism.verona.it
Markets: daily in Piazza delle Erbe
Note: many monuments close Monday

preserve power over the city but this tactic apparently failed and, in 1405, Verona came under the rule of Venezia. New fortifications were planned in the 16th century and the focus of city life shifted to Piazza Bra beside the Arena.

In 1796 the French invaded and ruled the city with ferocity until the Austrians won control in 1814, holding Verona until, in 1866, it joined the kingdom of Italy. Much damage was incurred during WWII—all bridges were bombed—but the city was painstakingly restored.

A walk around Verona's ancient centre is a pleasant one and en route you will pass many handsome palazzi built of the local pink-hued limestone. If you have time, extend your walk a little on the north bank of the river to visit the Renaissance Giardino Giusti.

< The view over Verona

The Roman Arena

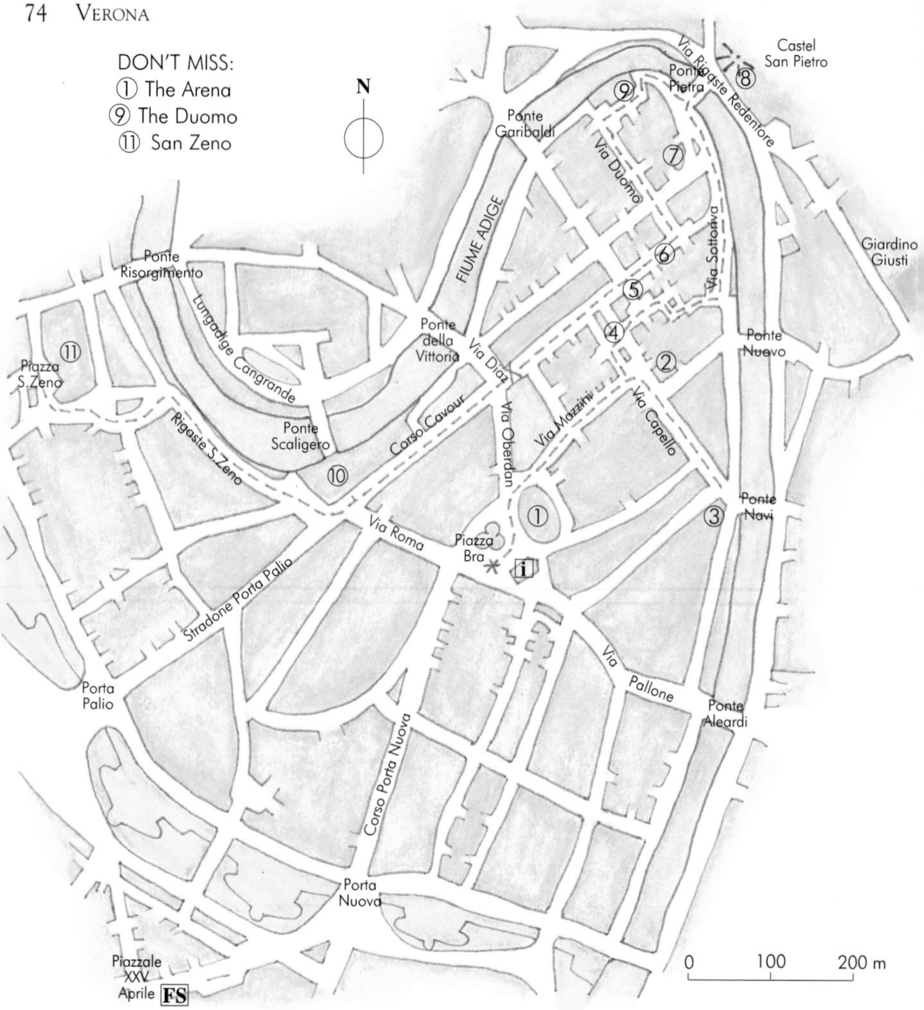

DON'T MISS:
① The Arena
⑨ The Duomo
⑪ San Zeno

N

## A WALK IN VERONA

*Discover the rich mixture of Roman and medieval elements in this charming city on the meandering Fiume Adige.*

Start in Piazza Bra, a large restaurant-lined open space hedged on the southeast by the neoclassical Palazzo Barbieri (now the town hall) and on the south by the Palazzo Gran Guardia, built in the 17th century. Despite these edifices, the piazza is dominated by the magnificent Roman Arena and softened by the clover-leaf park. ① The **Arena**, one of the most important and best preserved Roman amphitheatres,

was completed in AD 30. Its 44 tiers of steps can seat 22,000 people and while the audience was once entertained with gladiatorial combat and battle scenes, it's now filled each summer by opera lovers. Clamber up to the top row for an excellent city view.

Leave behind the Arena and head down the fashionable Via Mazzini, then turn right into Via Capello. At #23 on the left, you will find what is known as Juliet's house, ② **Casa di Giulietta**, supposedly the home of the Shakespearean heroine. There were Capulet and Montecchi families in medieval Verona; the rest appears to be enchanting fiction. Crowds throng to see the balcony to which Romeo might have climbed (and many to fondle the statue of Juliet). An even more unlikely 'tomb of Juliet' can be found near the Ponte Aleardi.

Continue along Via Capello and then on Via Leoni, past Roman ruins, to reach the Romanesque-Gothic façade of

③ **San Fermo Maggiore**. This church, begun in the 11th century but later remodelled, contains Pisanello's fresco of the *Annunciation*. Pisanello was probably born in Pisa, as the name suggests, but grew up in Verona and worked here at various times.

Retrace your steps along Via Capello and continue on to

④ **Piazza delle Erbe**. This marks the site of the old Roman Forum and today, as in the past, a colourful market enlivens the square. At the far end you can see Palazzo Maffei, a beautiful baroque building, and on its left, the Torre delle Gardello, erected by one of the Scaligeri in 1370. He also added the fountain in the square; the statue above it dates from Roman times. On one side stands a *capitello*, a 16th-century rostrum from where decrees and sentences were proclaimed and, on the other, a Venetian column.

To the right of the square is the medieval

Juliet's balcony

Palazzo del Comune dominated by its campanile, the 83-metre-high **Torre dei Lamberti**; a climb up its 368 steps can provide views of the Alpi.

Now turn right and walk through the **Arco della Costa** (the 'Arch of the Rib', as a whale rib once hung from it) and into

⑤ **Piazza dei Signori**. Once the centre of government, this piazza features a 19th-century statue of a grim-faced Dante, as well as the elegant 1493 **Loggia del Consiglio** topped by important Veronese figures. Another arch to the right leads you to the Cortile Mercato Vecchio (old market yard), where the Gothic staircase, the **Scala della Ragione**, is worth seeing. Walking back into the Piazza dei Signori and turning right, you come in sight of the impressive

⑥ **Arche Scaligere**, a compound designed to hold the tombs of the medieval ruling family and erected in the grounds of the Romanesque Santa Maria Antica. The most important of these tombs, high above the church's entrance, is that of Cangrande I, who died in 1329.

Walk down the Vicolo due Stelle and turn left at the end along Via Sottoriva,

< Piazza delle Erbe

one of the most picturesque streets of medieval Verona. Soon on your left is Verona's largest church,

⑦ **Sant'Anastasia**. Completed in 1481, this Dominican church has a remarkable campanile. Inside are various artworks, including a 1380 fresco by Altichiero in Cappella Cavalli and a Gothic masterpiece in the sacristy: a 1436 fresco by Pisanello of San Giorgio and the princess.

Across the river from the church you can see San Pietro's hill, used as a fortress since ancient times and fortified with barracks by the Austrians in 1853. From the small Piazzetta Bra Molinari, head over **Ponte Pietra**, or 'the stone bridge'. This was erected in the 1st century but it was rebuilt with original materials after being blown up by retreating Nazis in WWII.

On the steep bank across the Fiume Adige lie the

⑧ **Teatro Romano** and Museo Archeologico, one behind the other. The Roman theatre was built in the 1st century BC and was uncovered only in the 19th century. Although little now remains of the stage area, much of the seating is still visible and is it now used for concerts and theatre.

Steps to the left of the complex lead up to the Venetian **Castel San Pietro**, the terrace of which offers a wonderful panorama over Verona. Retrace your steps over Ponte Pietra and then head right along Via Sabbionaia to

⑨ **the Duomo**, built shortly after the 1117 earthquake destroyed its predecessor. It's something of an encyclopaedia of styles, with a Romanesque chancel, a Gothic nave and a Renaissance campanile. Note the doorway, sculpted by Maestro Nicolò. Inside, among pink marble pillars, is an altarpiece by Titian.

Turn left into the palazzi-lined Via Duomo and then right at Piazza S.Anastasia and walk down the Corso, lined with more palazzi and antique shops. This was the main street of Roman Verona and it passes through the **Porta dei Borsari**, a Roman arch in white stone. Look back, as the other side is far more richly ornamented.

As you near the *castello*, you pass the Roman **Arco dei Gavi**, a 1st-century arch destroyed by French troops and only reassembled last century: a good point from which to view Ponte Scaligero. Further along the Corso is the entrance to the huge ⑩ **Castelvecchio**, built in the 1350s by Cangrande I. The inside has been modified

< Ponte Pietra

to house a museum that focuses on Veronese art from the 12th to the 16th centuries. Between the two sections of the *castello* runs a passageway, guarded by a keep, leading onto the battlemented **Ponte Scaligero**, also reconstructed after WWII.

From the *castello*, follow the river, walking along Rigaste San Zeno and then veer away on Via Barbarani. Cross Piazza Corrubbio, Piazza Pozzo and then Piazza San Zeno to reach the splendid façade of ⑪ **San Zeno Maggiore**. San Zeno was appointed bishop of Verona in 362 and his church is one of northern Italy's finest examples of Romanesque architecture. Built in Lombard style in the 12th century, it features wonderful bronze doors from that period. The rose window, dated around 1200, was the first of its kind in Italy.

Inside, a tall bare nave continues the pure Romanesque style, only marred slightly by a 14th-century apse. The high altar bears a famous 1459 triptych by Mantegna and a chapel holds a painted statue of a smiling Zeno. A passage to the left of the church leads to lovely 12th-century cloisters, decorated with twinned columns.

Here our itinerary ends, but you could return to Piazza Bra along the following route: cross nearby Ponte Risorgimento, go left along Lungadige Cangrande (past the Arsenale), cross Ponte della Vittoria and head straight on Via Diaz and Via Oberdan.

## OTHER EXCURSIONS

**Giardino Giusti** lies on the northern bank of the Adige, hidden behind Palazzo

San Giorgio in Braido

Giusti, which was built in 1580. The terraced garden was landscaped in the 18th century and its current state preserves much of that Italianate design. The lower garden is formal; uphill is more of a woodland.

A pleasant walk north out of town takes you soon into **hilly countryside**. From Ponte Pietra, head directly north on Via Madonna Terraglio and turn left into Via Colli. The land here is cultivated with vines and groves of olives. At the top of a hill you'll enjoy a good view over Verona, and there's a pizzeria and bar for sustenance before you return. *Allow 2 to 3 hours.*

| OPENING HOURS | |
|---|---|
| Arena | Tue-Sun 8-7, on opera days 8.15-3.30 |
| Casa di Giulietta | Tue-Sun 8-7 |
| Torre dei Lamberti | Tue-Sun 9-6 |
| Teatro Romano | Tue-Sun 9-3; in summer till 7 |
| Castelvecchio | Tue-Sun 9-7 |
| San Zeno Maggiore | Mon-Sat 8-noon, 3-6 |
| Giardino Giusti | daily 9-sunset; in summer till 8 |

# PADOVA

University towns usually have a certain buzz about them, and they always have good cafés. Padova, or Padua, has the added attraction of the Cappella degli Scrovegni, Giotto's rich masterpiece of pigment and a seminal work of the Renaissance. What more can one ask for?

Padova began its existence as Roman Patavium, prospering as a centre for horse trading. It thrived until the barbarian scourges began and was all but destroyed by the Lombards in the 7th century. By the 12th century, the city had recovered sufficiently to become an independent city-state. Italy's second university was established here in 1222, attracting intellectuals from far afield. One of its lecturers was Galileo Galilei, who taught physics here from 1592 to 1610.

From 1337 to 1405, control over the city was exerted by the Da Carrara family, enlightened rulers who encouraged artistic and cultural activity, attracting the likes of the poet Petrarch. Following conquest by Venezia in 1405, Padova became a part of the Venetian Republic and remained so until 1797 when Napoleon took over. He then passed the territory on to the Austrians, who held it until Unification.

NOTES
Population: 215,000
Getting there: rail from Milano, Venezia or Bologna; bus from Venezia, Trieste or Genova
Tourist Office: Riviera Mugnai 8
 Tel: 049 8767911 Fax: 049 650794
 email: apt@padovanet.it
 www.apt.padova.it
Markets: daily, P. delle Erbe & Frutta

Padova was heavily bombed in WWII and much was lost as a result. Much, however, remains and here you can see the masterly works of artists such as Donatello and Mantegna, and of course the Florentine fresco painter Giotto di Bondone.

The city has also long been a magnet for pilgrims following the death and speedy canonisation of Sant'Antonio, a preacher who promoted much the same values as San Francesco, in the early 13th century. No doubt Padova prospered greatly from the constant arrival of devout pilgrims who still file past the saint's tomb in Il Santo: a variant form of tourism, as the many souvenir kiosks outside the basilica will attest.

Another excellent place for observing Italian life is the marketplace of Piazza delle Erbe. This is one of Italy's finest markets, with delicious produce arriving from all parts of Italy and beyond; though it isn't frenetic like many in the south, it's serious business, and an enjoyable place to linger and soak up the atmosphere.

Often overlooked by visitors is the lovely baptistry of the duomo, which is near the end of our itinerary. Padova's various highlights are linked by arcaded streets and pleasant piazzas, making Padova an attractive proposition to explore on foot.

Piazza dei Signori

A detail of Il Santo >

DON'T MISS:
① Cappella degli Scrovegni
② Chiesa degli Eremitani
⑤ Il Santo
⑧ Battistero

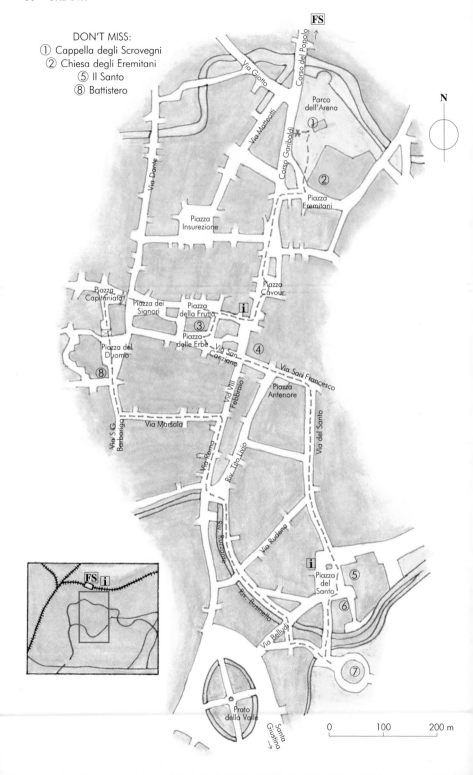

# A WALK IN PADOVA

*You don't have to tread much ground in Padova to glimpse the religious, aesthetic and intellectual strengths that underpin this ancient city.*

Our route starts in the **Giardini dell' Arena**, just 600 m south of the rail station along Corso del Popolo. This was the site of a Roman theatre and it lies by a fragment of the medieval city walls.

Here you'll find the artistic jewel of the city, the small but perfect

① **Cappella degli Scrovegni**. In 1303, Enrico Scrovegni commissioned this chapel to save the soul of his dead father, who had been a harsh usurer. The Florentine artist Giotto frescoed the walls with a cycle of the most wonderful paintings; the combination of fine perspective, naturalism and narrative power makes this one of the turning points in Western art. It's a difficult place to leave but you may have a time limit imposed on you by the guardians!

Just beside the chapel are the **Musei Civici**, housed in a former Augustinian monastery. They contain a varied collection of archaeological finds and some fine artworks, including a crucifix by Giotto.

Also nearby is the

② **Chiesa degli Eremitani**, built in 1276–1306. Bombing in 1944 caused immense damage to the structure of the church and, tragically, to the 15th-century frescoes by Andrea Mantegna that once filled the walls. The church retains a magnificent wooden ceiling and two of Mantegna's frescoes, one pieced together from fragments and the other removed before the war, are displayed in the Cappella Ovetari.

Walk down Corso Garibaldi, passing through the pleasant Piazza Cavour. Keep straight on, now on Via 8 Febbraio, turning right at Via Oberdan. The neoclassical **Caffè Pedrocchi**, on the corner, was designed in 1831 and gained notoriety as the café that never closed. Students, poets and intellectuals have been coming here

ever since; the upper floor hosts concerts and lectures in curiously decorated rooms.

Via Oberdan brings you to Piazza della Frutta, home to the daily market that also occupies nearby Piazza delle Erbe. Despite the names, most of the stalls in the first piazza sell clothing; food produce is sold with gusto in Piazza delle Erbe and on the ground floor of the building between them. This is the

③ **Palazzo della Ragione** or Palace of Reason, named because this was where citizens came to argue their cases and plead for justice. When it was built in 1218, the vast hall or *salone* on the upper floor was an architectural wonder. Sadly, the frescoes painted here by Giotto were destroyed by fire in 1420. The 15th-century frescoes by Miretta that replaced them depict astrological subjects. A 15th-century loggia along the palazzo's exterior offers a good view over the markets.

Leave Piazza delle Erbe on Via San Canziano. On a nearby corner is

④ **Palazzo del Bò**, the ancient seat of the university. Bò or 'ox' refers to the name of

Capella degli Scrovegni

< Cloisters of
Il Santo

an inn that once stood on the site. In its 16th-century courtyard there is a statue of Elena Piscopia, a student of 1678 and the first woman graduate. A tour takes you to see the lectern from which Galileo taught physics and the wonderful 1594 anatomy theatre. The medical school was renowned throughout Europe; its graduates include many of medicine's great names.

Walk east along Via San Francesco, passing the Tomba di Antenore on your right, and turn right into Via del Santo, which brings you to the busy Piazza del Santo. Among the souvenir stalls stands the bronze equestrian statue of a *condottiere* or mercenary leader known as **Gattamelata** or the 'Honeyed Cat'. Donatello sculpted this masterpiece in 1453 and its grand scale and quiet power mark it as one of the formative works of the Renaissance.

Now you can give your attention to ⑤ **Il Santo**, or the Basilica di Sant' Antonio. The church was begun shortly after the death of the saint in 1231 but wasn't completed until the beginning of the 14th century. Its attractive exterior is a mixture of Romanesque and Gothic, with domes and minaret spires that betray an eastern influence. Inside, modern-day pilgrims wait in line to visit

the tomb of Sant'Antonio, bedecked with votive offerings, but the basilica also contains works by Donatello, Altichiero and other artists of note.

Beside the basilica is the ⑥ **Oratorio di San Giorgio**, built as a funerary chapel. It contains 21 frescoes painted by Altichiero and his students in 1377. More frescoes are to be found in the adjacent **Scuola del Santo**, some attributed to a young Titian.

Leave the piazza south to cross the canal and reach Padova's fascinating ⑦ **Orto Botanico**, laid out in 1545 as a medicinal herb garden for the university. It is claimed to be the oldest botanical garden in Europe. Plants new to Italy, such as the sunflower and potato, were cultivated here. Much remains unchanged and there are

Piazza della Erbe >

trees here that are centuries old, such as a palm that Goethe came to inspect in 1786, when it was already 200 years old.

Cross the canal again and walk along Riviera Businello/Ruzzante. Cross a junction and walk up Via Roma past Santa Maria dei Servi. Turn left into Via Marsala and, with Palazzo Papafava on your left, turn right into Via Barbarigo. Keep on to reach Piazza Duomo and the city's **duomo**, begun in 1552 using modified sketches by Michelangelo, though to no great effect.

Of much greater interest is the domed ⑧ **Battistero**. Built by the De Carraras around 1200, this contains a vibrant 14th-century fresco cycle by Giusto de'Menabuoi.

Leave Piazza del Duomo by an archway and walk through porticoes behind the Palazzo Capitana (1599-1605) to Piazza Capitaniato, where the building of the university's arts faculty, the **Liviano**, stands.

Turn right to walk through the arch of the Torre dell'Orologio, which features an astronomical clock made in 1344. You are now in the Piazza dei Signori, edged by attractive arcades that shelter cafés and interesting shops.

OTHER EXCURSIONS

Padova's **Prato della Valle** lies on the site of a Roman amphitheatre just west of the botanic gardens. This huge green oval garden was reclaimed from marshy ground in 1775 and is now planted with plane trees, encircled by a canal and ringed with statues

The dome of the Battistero

of 78 famous figures. South, just across a busy road, is the classical **Santa Giustina**, a 16th-century domed church with an altarpiece by Veronese.

The **Colli Euganei** or Euganean Hills are the conical remnants of extinct volcanoes, southwest of Padova. The tourist office in Padova can advise you on good walking trails there. A car is a great advantage in this area, but a train takes you to the attractive medieval town of **Monsélice**, from where you could reach the lovely village of **Arquà Petrarca** (home of Petrarch's last years) by bus or on foot.

| OPENING HOURS | SUMMER | WINTER |
| --- | --- | --- |
| Cappella degli Scrovegni | daily 9-7 | daily 9-6 |
| Musei Civici | daily 9-7 | daily 9-6 |
| Chiesa degli Eremitani | Tue-Sun 9-7 | Tue-Sun 9-6 |
| Palazzo della Ragione | Tue-Sun 9-7 | Tue-Sun 9-6 |
| Palazzo del Bò (guided tours) | M,W,F at 3,4&5pm; T,T,Sat at 9,10,11am | |
| Il Santo | daily 6.30am-7.45pm | daily 6.30am-7pm |
| Oratorio di San Giorgio | daily 9-12.30, 2.30-7 | daily 9-12.30, 2.30-5 |
| Orto Botanico | daily 9-1, 3-6 | Mon-Sat 9-1 |
| Battistero | daily 9.30-1.30, 3-7 | daily 9.30-1, 3-6 |

# GENOVA

Italy's main port is not easy to classify. Unlike its great maritime rival Venezia, Genova (or Genoa) did not stop the clock when naval power sank in importance. Despite its great churches and rich palazzi, the city has never really chased the tourist market and continues to go about its business. This makes it hard to embrace at times, particularly when the business is being dealt in the narrow alleys of the *centro storico*. Don't overlook Genova though; it's a fascinating and vibrant city.

The city sits almost in the middle of the crescent coastal strip of Liguria, a piece of land settled for thousands of years, and its fortunes have always been tied up with the sea. By the 11th century, Genova ruled the Tyrrhenian Sea, having defeated the Saracens. The Genovese took part in the Crusades as a means of establishing trading posts in the east. Conflict with other great maritime powers arose, with Pisa over Corsica and with Venezia over various trading rights.

Great fortunes were made, particularly on the strength of trade with the Orient. Rival families—Doria, Spinola, Fieschi, Grimaldi—tussled for internal power and, to limit the havoc, the city opted to elect

> **NOTES**
> Population: 725,000
> Getting there: bus from Cristoforo Colombo airport 6 km (4 miles) west; rail from Milano, Torino and Roma
> Tourist Office: Via Roma, 11
>   Tel: 010 576791 Fax: 010 581408
>   email: aptgenova@apt.genova.it
>   www.apt.genova.it
> Markets: Loggia dei Mercati, P.Bunchi

a doge or ruler for life. The most famous of these was Andrea Doria, a successful admiral and legislator.

The Genovese have always had a reputation for thrift and shrewd dealing, but they missed the boat when they failed to fund the voyages of their native son, Cristoforo Columbo. The opening up of the Americas contributed to Genova's decline as a port. Other famous mariners passed through the city: the English explorer John Cabot was born here and Marco Polo imprisoned here. The ship that brought the Black Death to Europe was Genovese. Patriotic ideals were openly discussed here, encouraging the climate for the Risorgimento, and it was from Genova's harbour that Garibaldi pushed off for Sicilia.

Mercantile wealth is on full show in the renowned Via Garibaldi and other palazzi-lined avenues. Parts of Genova are less salubrious and can become unsafe when shops are closed, so avoid walking the route on a Sunday, or at night. That said, the old town, with its narrow alleyways or *caruggi* dotted with medieval churches, is perhaps the most fascinating part of Genova. It's here that you'll find the best cafés and pastry shops selling delicacies invented by the sweet-toothed Genovese.

Piazza de Ferrari

Detail of stonework, main portal of San Lorenzo >

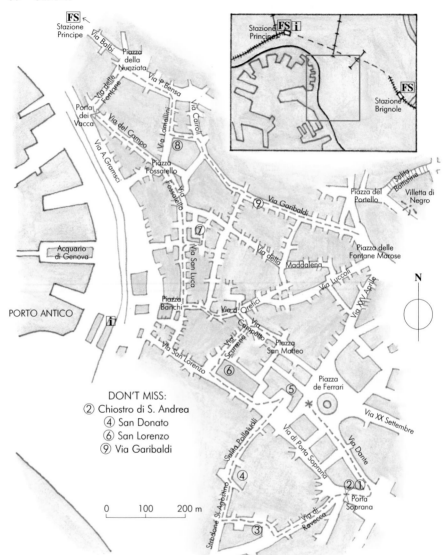

DON'T MISS:
② Chiostro di S. Andrea
④ San Donato
⑥ San Lorenzo
⑨ Via Garibaldi

0    100    200 m

## A WALK IN GENOVA

*Monumental reminders of Genova's glorious past stand close by alleys decorated with fluttering laundry: this walk takes in both aspects of the city-port.*

Our route starts in the centre of the city, in **Piazza de Ferrari**, which lies between Genova's two main rail stations, Principe and Brignole.

Piazza de Ferrari is a grandiose public space, a little out of keeping with much of the city. Behind the monument to Garibaldi is **Teatro Carlo Felice**, rebuilt some decades after WWII bombs destroyed the historic opera house. On the jutting corner is the **Palazzo della Borsa**, the old stock exchange. South is the baroque 16th-century **Chiesa del Gesù**, which houses two paintings by Rubens. Head down Via Dante between these last two and, at Piazza Dante, take a sharp turn right. On the corner stands the picturesque, 15th-century ① **Casa detta di Colombo**, an ivy-wrapped brick house reputed to have belonged to Christopher Columbus's father, who was, purportedly, the keeper of the nearby eastern gate.

Set in a small adjoining garden is a charming sight, the ② **Chiostro di Sant'Andrea**. These are the ruined cloisters of a 12th-century convent that was bombed in WWII. Though small, they offer a tranquil space that you won't find elsewhere in the city.

Now walk up through Porta Soprana, a robust medieval gate with twin towers, to enter Genova's *centro storico*. Turn left into Via Ravecca and then right into Vicolo Tre Re Magi to the 13th-century ③ **Sant'Agostino**. This church and convent were also bombed during the war but the bell tower and cloisters remain. The latter have been converted into a museum, containing fragments salvaged from Genova's various damaged churches.

Go right into Stradone S. Agostino to see the 12th-century octagonal bell tower of ④ **San Donato**. This lovely Romanesque church was built in the 11th century and

The official home of Columbus

enlarged in the centuries that followed. Inside are columns from Roman temples along with striped ones added in the 12th century. The left aisle contains a charming 1515 triptych by Joos Van Cleve.

Walk along Salita Pollaiuoli, which dips and rises to Piazza G. Matteotti and the entrance to ⑤ **Palazzo Ducale**, once the seat of the doges of Genova. The grand building, which

< The cloisters of Sant'Andrea

San Lorenzo

contains two 16th-century courtyards and arcades, is now a cultural centre.

Now head downhill on Via San Lorenzo to reach Genova's duomo, the

⑥ **Cattedrale di San Lorenzo**, an imposing Gothic design in black-and-white stripes. It dates back to the 9th century but most of the church is 12th-16th century; even then, the second of two bell towers was never completed. The side portals are older than the main one, an intricate design of twisted, fluted columns. The chapels inside are decorated in various styles. The museum in the sacristy houses some fabulous relics.

From the duomo, turn right into Via Scurreria and right again at the end to reach the charming **Piazza San Matteo**. The tall, narrow buildings here were home to the powerful Doria family. Look out for a bas-relief of San Giorgio—the protector of Genova—above a doorway on Palazzo Quartara. The elevated church of San Matteo, also built by the family and inscribed with their praises, houses the tomb and sword of Andrea Doria.

Return along Via San Matteo, continue

A shop in the *centro storico* >

on Via Campetto and detour briefly to the church of Santa Maria della Vigne, one of Genova's oldest churches, with a Romanesque bell tower. Backtrack a little and turn down Via degli Orefici or Goldsmiths' Street: watch for the *Nativity* bas-relief above the door of #47.

Continue down Via Banchi, passing on the right the 16th-century **Loggia dei Mercanti** where a market is held. On your right is the 16th-century San Pietro in Banchi. Turn right and walk up the medieval Via San Luca in the territory of the Spinola family; the shabby exteriors of many buildings conceal rich interiors. At Piazza San Luca, turn right past the Spinola church of San Luca and then left into Piazza Pellicceria to

⑦ **Galleria Nazionale di Palazzo Spinola**, a mansion with Renaissance Italian and Flemish paintings displayed in beautifully decorated apartments.

Return to Via San Luca, which becomes Via Fossatello. The church of **San Siro**, which has its origins in the 4th century, is a short detour off to the right. Continue through Piazza Fossatello. On the right, in the small Piazza Vacchero, is a ruined fountain and a *colonna d'infame*: the

column's Latin inscription curses the memory of Giulius Caesaris Vachery, beheaded for villainy.

Continue along Via del Campo to exit the *centro storico* by the 12th-century **Porta dei Vacca**.

Turn right uphill on Via delle Fontane to Piazza della Nunziata and right into Via P. Bensa. Turn right once again into Via Lomellini. Down on the right at #11 is ⑧ **Casa di Mazzini**, birthplace in 1805 of Guisseppe Mazzini whose writings inspired great political change; hence the building now houses the Museo del Risorgimento.

Turn left just before it and then right to walk along Via Cairoli. This brings you to ⑨ **Via Garibaldi**, Genova's renowned street of palazzi for the newly rich merchant bankers of the 16th century. Most were built to designs by Galeazzo Alessi, a student of Michelangelo. Peek into some of the grand courtyards, such as that of #7, **Palazzo Podesta**. Two mansions, **Palazzi Bianco** and **Rosso** (#11 and #18) are open as art galleries; the former has the more acclaimed collection, while the latter boasts particularly lavish decor. **Palazzo Doria Tursi** at #9 is now the town hall.

Via Garibaldi ends at Piazza delle Fontane Marose, leaving you well-placed for the first excursion below.

## OTHER EXCURSIONS

For a good view and some peace, climb to the park of **Villetta di Negro**. From Piazza delle Fontane Marose, walk up Via Interiano and cross busy Piazza del Portello

A courtyard on Via Garibaldi

by the pedestrian underpass. Turn right and, just before cars enter the tunnel, climb the steps of Salita Battistine. This brings you to a labyrinth of palms, cascades and artificial grottoes, and to the terrace viewpoint.

The old port area or **Porto Antico** was redeveloped for the 1992 Expo to designs by Renzo Piano. It offers various attractions, including the **Acquario**, and is best reached by Via San Lorenzo, down from the duomo.

To view the city from across the harbour, visit the **Lanterna**, Genova's medieval lighthouse and the city's emblem. Fires were once lit on top of the tower to guide ships.

---

OPENING HOURS

| | |
|---|---|
| Museo di S.Agostino | Tue-Sat 9-7; Sun 9-noon |
| Galleria di Pal. Spinola | Tue-Sat 9-7; Sun & Mon 9-1 |
| Museo del Risorgimento | Tue & Thur-Sat 9-1 |
| Palazzo Bianco | Tue, Thu-Fri 9-1; Wed & Sat 9-7; Sun 10-6 |
| Palazzo Rosso | Tue, Thu-Fri 9-1; Wed & Sat 9-7; Sun 10-6 |
| Acquario di Genova | M-W & F 9.30-7.30; Thu 9.30-11pm; Sat-Sun 9.30-10.30pm (last entry 2 hrs before) |

# THE CINQUE TERRE

The Cinque Terre or Five Lands is a short but beautiful strip of the Ligurian coastline backed by the foothills of the Appennini. It is named after five small neighbouring villages—Monterosso al Mare, Vernazza, Corniglia, Manarola and Riomaggiore—which cling to the terraced hills. These haven't suffered the excessive development that has affected many coastal towns and, while they attract plenty of visitors, they still retain the charm of fishing and farming communities.

Any arable land, terraced with dry-stone walls or *muretti*, is planted with olive trees for oil or with grapevines to make the white Cinque Terre wines, most famously *sciacchetrà*, a blended dessert wine. Fishing boats are dragged or winched up each day from harbours so small there is no space

NOTES
Suggested base: Riomaggiore
Getting there: rail from Genoa or Pisa;
  change at La Spezia
Tourist Office: Viale G.Mazzini, 47
  La Spezia  Tel: 0187 770900
  Fax: 0187 770908
  email:info@aptcinqueterre.sp.it
  www.aptcinqueterre.sp.it
Map: CAI Cinque Terre 1:40000
  or Kompass #644 1:50000
Best timing: avoid June-August

for moorings and then stacked in the narrow streets. The villages are also delightfully car-free, making an evening *passeggiata* extremely pleasant, obstructed only by brightly painted boats. There is some excellent seafood to be eaten in the local restaurants, often grilled in the Ligurian tradition.

Much history abides here. Corniglia, the oldest of the five villages, dates back to the Roman Age, while the others were founded between the 8th and the 11th centuries. They were fortified in the 13th century by the powerful Genovese and

The village of Manarola >

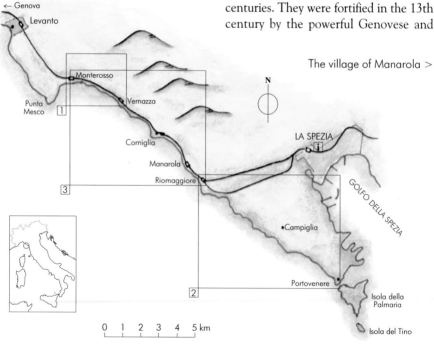

traces of this are still visible. A number of medieval sanctuaries, perched high inland, also served as a refuge when raiding forces threatened the villages.

The train line, which now tunnels through the coastal spurs, links each of the five villages and connects them with La Spezia and Levanto, giving the walker great flexibility. The only town not accessible by train is Portovenere, which is reached by a bus service from La Spezia. Riomaggiore, our suggested base, is an attractive fishing village with a good number of hotels and private rooms. More attractive still is the village of Vernazza, but accommodation is scarcer.

Many visitors to the region come merely to linger on its beaches, but many others come to walk the *Sentiero Azzurro* or Blue Path which traverses the coastline. This is deservedly famous but the area boasts a whole network of ancient paths, all clearly numbered by the CAI, linking the isolated sanctuaries and hamlets.

The first walk outlined in this chapter takes you to two such sanctuaries overlooking the Cinque Terre. Walk 2 follows the ridge path known as the *Sentiero Rosso* or Red Path above the wild, uncultivated coast of the Portovenere peninsula. We also describe the classic Sentiero Azzurro and each of its villages in full and outline a few other possible walks in the area. Liguria enjoys a mild Mediterranean climate and walking is possible around the year, though rainfall can be heavy in late autumn. All paths in this network are well waymarked and relatively straightforward but be prepared for plenty of steps, with compensating views to enjoy while you catch your breath.

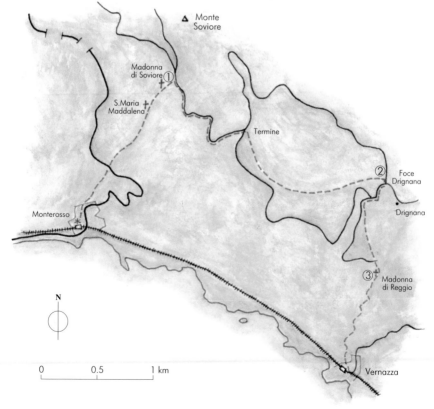

## WALK 1: HILL SANCTUARIES

*Head inland (and uphill) to visit two of the historic sanctuaries of this region and to stroll through the pleasant woodland on the ridge.*

| | |
|---|---|
| Distance | 7 km (4.5 miles) |
| Time | 3.5 hours |
| Difficulty | easy–moderate |
| Start | Monterosso |
| Finish | Vernazza |
| Transport | train at start and finish |

Madonna di Soviore

Catch a train to Monterosso; you will find a few notes on this Cinque Terre town at the end of Walk 3. You might wish to buy some picnic provisions before leaving the town, though in summer months refreshments are available at Soviore.

Our route is waymarked as #9 and starts from the road that crosses the old part of the town. The path climbs through olive groves and then crosses the Monterosso road. Continue heading northeast, climbing steeply. Pass the small chapel dedicated to Santa Maria Maddalena and, a short distance on, you reach the square of
① **Santuario della Madonna di Soviore**. This is Liguria's most ancient sanctuary, built in the 9th century and modified in the 13th century and beyond. Its magnificent

ogival portal and rose window make a contrast with its façade. The charming square, shaded by ancient holm oaks, provides an excellent viewpoint from its position some 464 m above Monterosso.

From here, turn right to pick up route #1 (the Sentiero Rosso) which follows the provincial road uphill through woodland. Where the road divides at a spot known as Termine, the #1 path leaves the road and heads through woods, frequented by locals in search of edible funghi. It emerges at
② **Foce Drignana** where there is a road junction. Turn right onto a minor road, following route #8 which heads downhill to Vernazza. Half way down you reach the
③ **Santuario della Madonna di Reggio** with its linear façade sheltering the black Madonna known locally as *l'Africana*. The church, originally built basilica-style at the beginning of the 11th century, was altered to a Latin cross in the 14th century.

Your scenic descent to Vernazza now follows a broad, stone-laid path which is still used for pilgrimages to the sanctuary.

The village of Vernazza makes a fitting end to the walk and you may well want to linger here for a meal in one of its excellent *trattorie*. From Vernazza you can catch the train back to Riomaggiore, or wherever you have chosen to stay.

< A local woman tends to the olive grove

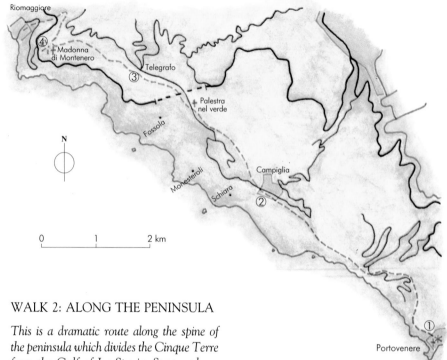

## WALK 2: ALONG THE PENINSULA

*This is a dramatic route along the spine of the peninsula which divides the Cinque Terre from the Gulf of La Spezia. Start early so you have time to explore the charms of Portovenere before you walk. You could buy lunch provisions here, or dine at the trattoria at Colle del Telegrafo.*

| | |
|---|---|
| Distance | 11.5 km (7 miles) |
| Time | 4 hours |
| Difficulty | moderate |
| Start | Portovenere |
| Finish | Riomaggiore |
| Transport | train and bus to Portovenere |

Catch a train to nearby La Spezia and, from there, catch an ATC bus to ① **Portovenere**, an ancient harbour town on the tip of the peninsula, facing the Isola della Palmaria. In Roman times Portus Veneris was a port for Roman galleys en route to Spain or Gaul. It was rebuilt as a fortified town in the 12th century by the Genovese who built the Castello Superiore (reconstructed in the 15th century) as a defence in the wars between Genova and Pisa. Old Portovenere is a narrow, single-street town, entered through an archway in the walls which descend from the castle. The tall houses squeezed between street and sea were originally built as defensive towers and face inwards. Spectacularly sited on high cliffs at the end of the promontory stands the church of San Pietro with its black-and-white façade. It was built in Genovese-Gothic style in the 13th century, supposedly on the site of a temple dedicated to Venus. The 12th-century Romanesque church of San Lorenzo in the upper town bears an unusual carving depicting the saint's martyrdom, roasted alive on a grill.

The walk begins in the Piazza Bastreri at a signboard just outside the village gate. The route, waymarked with red and white stripes, is the CAI path #1, the *Sentiero Rosso*, a ridge walk following the watershed between coast and hinterland.

Initially the path climbs steeply, skirting the castle walls. In fair weather you will have excellent views over the Golfo della Spezia to the Appennini and, looking southeast, a wonderful view of San Pietro and Isola della Palmaria. Continue along #1 to meet a minor road at a hairpin. Follow this past an old quarry, diverge right to short cut a bend and rejoin the road for 500 m. At a sign which warns of seasonal wild boar hunting, the path leaves the road to follow a spur high above the rocky coast, providing dramatic views. This part of the walk is the most exposed and care should be taken negotiating it. Further on, the path touches another road at a bend and continues through forest, rejoining the road briefly before reaching the medieval village of ② **Campiglia** at the church of Santa Caterina. Through Campiglia (ignore branch paths 4a, 4b and 11), path #1 leaves the road at a crossroads and climbs steps left between outlying dwellings. It ascends a steep ridge through chestnut woodland before levelling. Walk through the Palestra nel Verde, a forest gymnasium replete with exercise paraphernalia and pass a building that serves as both chapel (Sant'Antonio) and bar (La Bignetta) before briefly joining a road near the junction with #4. Leave the road, forking left to reach ③ **Colle del Telegrafo**, about an hour from Campiglia, where several paths and three roads all converge. There is a trattoria here, open seasonally.

In front of the trattoria, pick up route

Coastal view from Portovenere

#3 which descends in a westerly direction and passes through the hamlets of Lemmen and Casarino. After passing a right-forking path marked #3a, your path arrives at ④ the **Santuario della Madonna di Montenero**, a beautiful sanctuary built in the 14th century to shelter pilgrims and now housing a restaurant. The church square offers a wonderful panorama extending from Punta Mesco to the islands which lie south of Portovenere. On a clear day you might see Elba and Corsica.

From here path #3 veers sharply northeast and then west to cross the main coast road. It then continues downhill, alongside a stream in the Valle di Riomaggiore, crosses a lesser road and brings you to the carpark above Riomaggiore's traffic-free main street. Walk down into the village's vibrant centre; the rail station lies near the sea.

< Madonna di Montenero

## WALK 3: THE SENTIERO AZZURRO

*This extremely scenic coastal walk links up all five villages of the Cinque Terre. It is, quite understandably, very popular so you probably won't be alone!*

| | |
|---|---|
| Distance | 9.5 km (6 miles) |
| Time | 4.5 hours |
| Difficulty | easy–moderate |
| Start | Riomaggiore |
| Finish | Monterosso |
| Transport | train back to start |

The path, which hugs the coast but still includes some ascents and descents, can be walked in either direction. It is marked throughout as path #2. From time to time, a section of the path is closed due to rockfalls and must be bypassed by train. Before you leave from
① **Riomaggiore**, make sure you take time to explore the village, linked to its station by a long tunnel. The tiny harbour is reached by narrow lanes.

The Via dell'Amore, or Way of Love as this first section of the path is known, leaves via steps from the piazza beside the station. Despite its name, this is the dullest stretch, as the concrete gallery built to protect you from rockfalls detracts from the natural

< The view from the *Via dell'Amore*

beauty of the coastline. A short, level walk brings you to steps which descend to another tunnel and then to
② **Manarola**. Clustered like Vernazza on the side of a rock spur, Manarola's picturesque waterfront comprises a tiny harbour protected by a breakwater and a well-fenced promenade high above the crashing surf. Vine-terraced hills form the backdrop to the staggered lines of tall pastel buildings which crowd the harbour.

The Sentiero Azzurro continues northwest over a headland and past the local cemetery. It then follows the route of the old railway and passes above a desultory beach resort to arrive at the next station, from where a brick stairway leads ups to
③ **Corniglia**. This tiny village sits high atop a rocky pinnacle, terraced vines cascading down its slopes, and commands superb views of the other towns. Unlike the other four harbour villages, Corniglia is a true hilltown, its origin lying in farming not

Vernazza and its harbour

fishing. It is also the oldest, the most isolated and seems the least touched by modernity. It was once larger—in the 13th century it even boasted a castle—but the sea has claimed sections following landslides. The 1351 church of San Pietro remains.

From Corniglia, route #2 climbs to the few buildings of Prevo. From here the path meanders more gently through some of the Cinque Terre's most photogenic olive groves before descending, with stunning views of your next destination, reached eventually by narrow laneways.

④ **Vernazza** is possibly the most lovely and dramatic of the Cinque Terre villages. Tall houses in pastel shades tumble down the promontory to Vernazza's tiny harbour and breakwater, overlooked by the ruined tower of the Castello Belforte, a reminder of the port's importance to the 13th-century Genoan Republic. Bright boats adorn both the harbour and Vernazza's main pedestrian

A boat serves as market stall >

street where many are accommodated overnight. A maze of paths and stairways (*arpaie*) connect the houses with the street.

The Sentiero Azzurro leaves Vernazza's main street up stairs then on a steep path beside the church of Santa Margherita d'Antiochia. The path climbs high above the sea, providing wonderful vistas back over Vernazza to Corniglia and beyond, all framed by sea cliffs and the deep blue of the Ligurian. The narrow path levels and you pass through tiny terraced plots and negotiate narrow bridges over rushing streams as the path zigzags down on stone steps to the last of the Cinque Terre villages.

⑤ **Monterosso al Mare** is truly the last; it was added to what had been previously known as the Quattro Terre some time in the 15th century. Its two beaches are divided by a small headland which also serves to separate the old town from the new. On the headland, the 13th-century Torre Aurora (Dawn Tower), a remnant of fortifications, is now undercut by a road tunnel. Sited on fairly level land, Monterosso has grown in recent years to accommodate the needs of tourism. You should visit the 16th-century Capucchin convent to view a crucifixion painting attributed to the Flemish master Van Dyck. The elegant church of San Giovanni Battista, built in Genovese-Gothic style, is also worth seeking out.

## OTHER WALKS IN THE REGION

### Punta Mesco

This is another lovely coastal walk, taking you from Monterosso to the point and back, or further on to Levanto, from where you can return by train.

The walk (marked as #10) begins along the Monterosso waterfront and leads to the rock sculpture *il Gigante* depicting Neptune. Climb the steps behind the adjoining trattoria and briefly join a road which you leave at a bend to climb many more steps on a path to Punta Mesco, with good views back along the Cinque Terre. Where #10 joins #1, turn left to reach the ruins of **Eremo di Sant'Antonio** at Punta Mesco and the old *semaforo* (beacon) with memorable views in both directions: a great lunch spot. Head back to the junction from where you can retrace your steps to Monterosso. To walk to Levanto instead, keep left, taking path #1 which descends gradually through forest; eventually you join a minor road and then continue on a path between road and sea. Steps lead beneath a 13th-century *castello* and down to the sea.

To return from Levanto by train, head inland along the main street, Corso Roma, for about 1 km to reach the train station. *Allow 3 hours.*

### Above Corniglia

Here is another jaunt up to the ridge and back, passing through small hamlets and over terraced hillsides on the way; this one starts at Vernazza and ends at Manarola.

Leave Vernazza on route #2 heading towards Corniglia then soon veer left up onto path #7 which climbs to the church of **San Bernadino** and then to the pass of Cigoletta at 607 m. Turn right to follow the *Sentiero Rosso* #1 which rises for a short distance to another path junction where you turn right onto path #6. This descends to the **Santuario di Madonna della Salute** and down through the pleasant village of **Volastra**. Continue the descent on path #6

on a beautiful stone-laid path through picturesque olive groves. Cross the winding road and then rejoin it to descend through the outskirts of Manarola. *Allow 3.5 hours.*

Eremo di Sant'Antonio at Punta Mesco

### The hamlets

Between Riomaggiore and Portovenere lie a string of isolated hamlets perched above rocky cliffs and sandy beaches.

To reach them, leave Riomaggiore on route #3 which climbs to Telegrafo and take route #1 southwest (reversing the end of Walk 2). Shortly before Sant'Antonio, take the right-branching path marked #4c which descends to the hamlet of **Fossola**. Steep steps from here lead down to the sea. Path #4b links Fossola to **Monesteroli** and then **Schiara**, each with steps to the sea, and then climbs steeply to the village of Campiglia which lies on the main #1 path.

From here you can either go northwest back to Riomaggiore or southeast to Portovenere (see Walk 2). *Allow 4 to 5 hours.*

# FERRARA

NOTES

Population: 132,000

Getting there: rail from Bologna
or Venezia

Tourist Office: Castello Estense
Tel: 0532 209370
Fax: 0532 212266
email: infotur@provincia.fe.it
www.provincia.fe.it

Markets: Mon 8-2 Piazza Travaglio
Fri 8-2 Piazza della Cattedrale

Note: many monuments close Monday

To a visitor, Ferrara seems at first to have a dual personality. South of the broad road which bisects the walled city is a maze of narrow medieval lanes, criss-crossed with arcades. North is an airy expanse of broad streets, interspersed with parkland and large palaces. The contrast highlights just how modern the Renaissance rulers of this city were in their thinking.

Ferrara's origins are uncertain but it first came to prominence when the Este clan seized control in 1208. Their rule was characterised by sensational and bloody family dramas, but also by good government and by an enlightened patronage of the arts. Their Renaissance court rivalled the important European centres.

A university was founded here in 1391. Such artists as Pisanello, Veronese and Titian visited and worked for the Dukes of Este, as did the poets Ariosto and Tasso. Musicians and architects also found good employment, the latter put to service designing the city extensions and Castello Estense, among other things.

The main *dramatis personae* for the Este dynasty runs as follows: Niccolò III was a successful diplomat and libertine; his young wife Parisina was caught in the act of adultery with his illegitimate son Ugo and the two lovers were beheaded in the castle in 1425. Lionello and Borso, the next Este generation, were both excellent administrators. Ercole I was the great builder and both he and his daughters, Beatrice and Isabella, famously patronised the arts. Ercole's soldiering son Alfonso married the infamous Lucrezia Borgia and Ercole II married the intellectual Renée of France.

Powerful neighbours such as Venezia eventually managed to curb the Estes'

great influence and Ferrara became a province of the Papal States in 1598. Its low profile from then on ensured that it remained unspoilt, and today Ferrara is a wonderful provincial city in which to walk.

The city lies on the fertile plain of the River Po and the land hereabouts is flat. Possibly for this reason, bicycles are the preferred mode of transport for young and old alike. If you wish to travel into the flatlands of the Po Delta, you would do well to hire a bicycle from one of the many bicycle shops in town. However, Ferrara is also a lovely place for walking, with many of its cobbled streets closed off to car traffic, but remember to watch out for those bicycles!

< One of Ferrara's medieval alleys

The Romanesque-Gothic Cattedrale

DON'T MISS:
④ Via delle Volte
⑤ the city walls
⑦ Casa Romei
⑨ Castello Estense

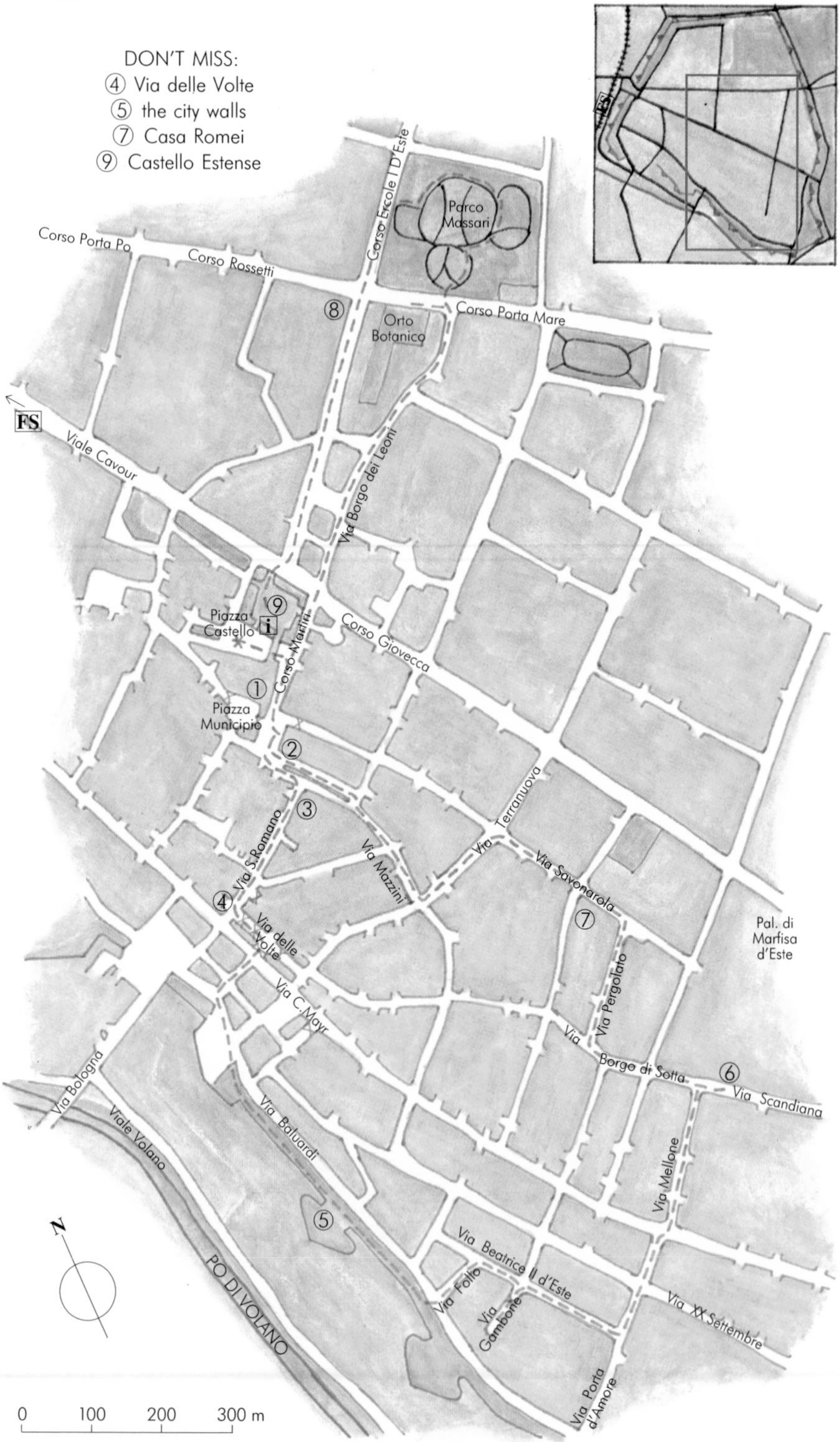

Parco Massari

Corso Porta Po

Corso Rossetti

Corso Ercole I D'Este

Corso Porta Mare

⑧ Orto Botanico

**FS**

Viale Cavour

Via Borgo dei Leoni

Piazza Castello ⑨ **i**

① Piazza Municipio

Corso Martiri

Corso Giovecca

② 

③ 

Via S. Romano

④ Via delle Volte

Via Mazzini

Via Terranuova

Via Savonarola

⑦ 

Pal. di Marfisa d'Este

Via delle Volte

Via C. Mayr

Via Pergolato

Via Bologna

Viale Volano

Via Boluardi

Borgo di Sotta

⑥ Via Scandiana

Via

Via Mellone

⑤ 

Via Beatrice II d'Este

Via Fatta

Via Gambone

Via XX Settembre

PO DI VOLANO

Via Porta d'Amore

N

0    100    200    300 m

# A WALK IN FERRARA

*This route takes you through time, from the lanes of medieval merchants to the Renaissance grandeur of the Este urban vision.*

The centre of town is 1.4 km (almost a mile) from the rail station and is dominated by the castle; we begin our walk in the adjoining Piazza Castello. A tour of the *castello* comes later, but the tourist office is situated in its courtyard should you wish to visit. Across the piazza is the crenellated ① **Palazzo del Municipio**. Built in the 13th century, this was the ducal palace before the castle was built. The courtyard features an elegant Renaissance stairway.

In the adjoining piazza is a wildly gesticulating statue of the monk Savonarola, who was born in Ferrara and burned to death in Firenze. Turn right into Corso Martiri della Libertà to arrive at the ② **Cattedrale**, a building dating back to the 12th century but 'improved' through the centuries. Its stunning triple façade is sculpted in white and rose marble: the lower section is Romanesque; the upper parts were added a few decades later in Gothic style. The interior is disappointingly baroque, remodelled in the 18th century.

Turn left out of the cathedral and gain a good view of the 15th-century campanile behind the cathedral, then head to Chiesa di San Romano, which houses the ③ **Museo della Cattedrale**, a collection of artworks including masterpieces by Cosmè Tura and Jacopo della Quercia.

Head down the car-free and porticoed Via S. Romano to enter the network of Ferrara's medieval streets. Turn left along one of the most evocative, ④ **Via delle Volte**, criss-crossed by multiple arches. This haunt of medieval merchants is still riddled with quaint workshops.

Take the next alley right, cross Via C. Mayr, continue down the narrow Vicolo Leoncorno and cross Via Baluardi. Head up the ramp of a small carpark and you will find yourself on

⑤ the **city walls**. This section is the oldest part of the ramparts, dating back to 1451. Walk south along the path, passing above a ramshackle farm overrun with chickens and then head down steps before you reach the second *baluardo* or bulwark. Again, cross the aptly named (and quite busy) Via Baluardi and head up Via Follo. Turn right into Via Beatrice II d'Este.

A short detour right down Via Gambone takes you to the convent and church of Sant'Antonio in Polesine, which boasts a tranquil garden and a fine painted portico.

Continue along Via Beatrice II d'Este, and then turn left into the prettily named Via Porta d'Amore. At the corner is the **Museo Archeologico Nazionale**, in the house of Ludovico the Moor. Take a peek inside the masterly but unfinished 15th-century courtyard by Biagio Rossetti.

Cross Via XX Settembre and Via C. Mayr and walk up Via Mellone. At the end, turn right a short distance to the entrance of ⑥ **Palazzo Schifanoia**, the 14-15th-century

Sant'Antonio in Polesine

The imposing bulk of Castello Estense

pleasure retreat of the Estes (its name translates as 'away with boredom'). The palace, housing a collection of medieval arts, is a little overrated save for the wonderful *salone dei mesi* or 'hall of the months' which depicts various aspects of courtly life in bright and lively frescoes.

From the palace, walk east along Via Borgo di Sotto and turn right into Via Pergolato, walking below the walls of a monastery on the left. At the end of the street, you could detour for a visit to the **Palazzina di Marfisa d'Este**, another elegant residence (see map). Otherwise, turn left into Via Savonarola, where a doorway on your left gives entry to ⑦ **Casa Romei**, the well-preserved house of a merchant who married into the Este family. The house boasts a fine courtyard enclosed by porticoes and loggias and its ground floor rooms are decorated with medieval frescoes. The upper floor was redecorated when Cardinal Ippolito II d'Este moved in during the 16th century. The *palazzo* opposite seats part of the university.

Continue along Via Savonarola, past the bulky Chiesa di San Francesco, then turn left into Via Terranuova and right into the car-free Via Mazzini. The Estes exercised religious tolerance and welcomed Jewish refugees from Spain and other parts of Europe, many of whom settled in this section of the city. Later, the Papal government was less liberal and closed off the area as a ghetto. You pass the plain exterior of the synagogue and its **Museo Ebraico** on your right.

Veer right and stroll under the 15th-century merchant's portico alongside the Cattedrale. Turn right to walk past your starting point and along Corso Martiri della Libertà. On the right you pass the **Teatro Comunale**, one of the first modern theatres.

Corso Giovecca and Viale Cavour once marked the northern boundary of the city limits; the castello lay along its walls. The area to the north, with its more spacious street-scape, was planned as an extension to the city by Ercole I in the 16th century.

Cross Corso Giovecca and continue along Via Borgo dei Leoni, passing the Chiesa del Gesù. A short detour left at Corso Porto Mare allows you to enter the Orto Botanico, a modest but well-labelled botanic garden. Otherwise, cross Corso Porto Mare and enter **Parco Massari**, landscaped in English style with large cedars, and an ideal spot for a picnic lunch.

Leave the park by Corso Ercole I D'Este. Head south, soon reaching the dramatic ⑧ **Palazzo dei Diamanti**, studded with thousands of marble diamond bosses and designed specifically for a corner view. This sumptuous palace, built during the 15-16th centuries, houses the Pinacoteca Nazionale, featuring excellent works of the Ferrarese school of painters.

Continue south along the broad, cobbled street, passing various palazzi which now serve as public buildings. Cross the main road and make your way over the moat to ⑨ **Castello Estense**, the solid stronghold of the Estes. A fortification to protect the rulers from their own people became desirable following riots in 1385. It was constructed around the existing Lions' Tower (which can be climbed for a view over Ferrara; access is from within the castello). Entry to the castello is well worthwhile for its excellent prison cells, one of which hosted Don Giulio d'Este, who plotted against his brother the Duke and was imprisoned for 50 years before being pardoned. The ducal apartments include the *salone dei giochi*, a hall frescoed with depictions of various games and sports.

## OTHER EXCURSIONS

Stretch your legs on a walk around the **city walls** on a path for pedestrians and cyclists. There are two tracks: one runs

Palazzo dei Diamanti

along the top of the ramparts, the other follows what was once the moat outside the walls. The wooded concourse along the eastern perimeter is particularly pleasant. The easy 9km (6.5 miles) walk should take approximately 2.5 hours.

Ferrara offers a good base for visiting the **Po Delta**, a flat landscape rich in birdlife. Hire a bicycle from Ferrara and cycle out through the huge Parco Urbano, north of the city walls. A few kilometres through parkland, you reach the broad River Po, with a path along the river embankment.

OPENING HOURS

| | |
|---|---|
| Cattedrale | Mon-Sat 7.30-noon, 3-6.30; Sun 7.30-noon, 4-6.30 |
| Museo della Cattedrale | Tue-Sun 9.30-2 |
| Palazzo Schifanoia | Tue-Sun 9-7 |
| Casa Romei | Tue-Sun 8.30-7.30 |
| Palazzo dei Diamanti | Tue-Wed 9-2, Thur-Fri 9-7, Sat 9-2, Sun 9-1 |
| Castello Estense | Tue-Sun 9.30-5 |

# BOLOGNA

The capital of Emilia-Romagna is rich—culturally, financially and gastronomically. One of its nicknames is 'la grassa' or 'the fat one', but a full day spent walking its arcaded streets will earn you the right to enjoy its culinary pleasures.

Bologna is sited on the lowest foothills of the Appennini, where the fertile plain of the Po begins. It was established as a commercial centre by the Etruscans, who called it Felsina. The Boi Gauls invaded during the 4th century BC and their prosperous cultivation of the land attracted the Romans in 191 BC. They colonised it as Bononia and opened the major road, Via Aemilia, which linked the city to Piacenza and coastal Rimini, and thus to Roma by the Via Flaminia. The area was overrun by various barbarian tribes after the fall of Roma and the Papal State owned it for a period, before it became an independent *comune*.

In 1088 a university, Europe's first, was founded here primarily to teach law. Among its graduates are such luminaries as Dante, Copernicus, Tasso and, more recently, Guglielmo Marconi.

NOTES
Population: 381,000
Getting there: bus from Marconi airport 9 km (5 miles) NW; rail from Roma, Milano, Firenze or Venezia
Tourist Office: Palazzo del Podestà in P. Maggiore Tel: 051 6487607 Fax: 051 6487608 www.cst.bo.it email: info@cst.bo.it
Markets: Mon-Sat 7-1 & Mon-Wed 5-7 Pescherie Vecchie & V. Ugo Bassi 27

Following struggles between rival nobles, the Bentivoglio family effectively ruled Bologna during the 15th century. After that it fell under the control of the Papacy once more and Napoleon arrived in 1797. The Austrians quelled several insurrections in the first half of the 19th century before the region was annexed to the Kingdom of Savoy in 1860. A strong peasants' movement was active at the turn of the 20th century and Bologna was the site of much resistance against fascist forces during WWII. Bolognese politics continued to lean to the left: the city's other nickname 'la rossa' was not earned for the colour of its brick buildings alone.

Today Bologna is a thriving city, filled with students and visitors to its trade fair centre (which can make accommodation difficult to find at times). The city centre is supposedly closed to private traffic most days, but it remains a melee of vespas, cars and buses. Fortunately for pedestrians, most of its streets are lined with beautiful porticoes, built from the 12th century and onwards in varying styles but all high enough to accommodate a horse and rider.

Bologna is justly renowned for its local produce and cuisine; a meal in a *trattoria* and a stroll through the city's food shops are essential to any Bolognese itinerary.

A taste of Bolognese cuisine

Porticoes in Piazza San Stefano >

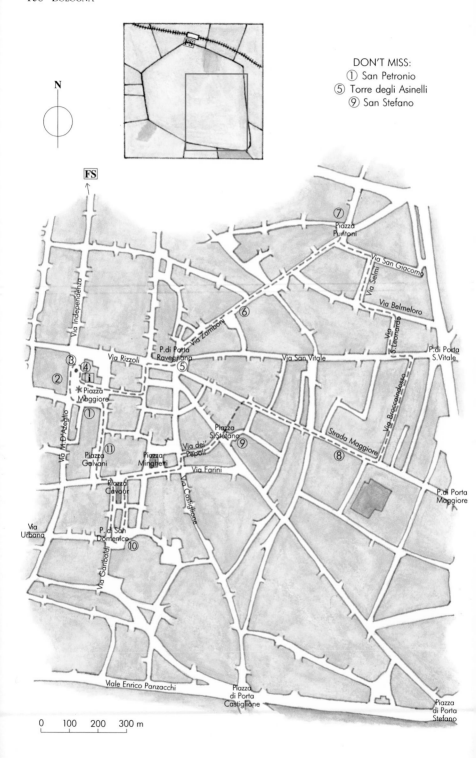

N

FS

DON'T MISS:
① San Petronio
⑤ Torre degli Asinelli
⑨ San Stefano

0   100   200   300 m

# A WALK IN BOLOGNA

*This route starts in the civic heart and leads you along porticoed streets lined with ochre-tinted palazzi and tranquil churches.*

Begin at the Piazza Maggiore, the heart of historic Bologna, some 1.3 km (0.8 miles) south of the rail station. This public space is edged by several imposing buildings. The tourist office is located in the 13th-century Palazzo del Podestà, which stands opposite ① the **Basilica di San Petronio**. This fine Gothic church was designed in 1390 by Antonio di Vincenzo. The upper section of the façade is exposed brick; the lower marble section features sculptures by Jacopo della Quercia on the central doorway. The three-aisled interior is airy and light and contains 22 chapels, including the lovely **Cappella di Re Magi** in the north aisle. On the floor, starting at the central doorway, is a 1655 meridian line which indicates the hour, day and month when the sun beams through a tiny hole in the ceiling above. The Council of Trent reconvened here in 1547 to avoid the plague and in 1529 the basilica hosted the crowning of the German Charles V as Holy Roman Emperor.

On the left as you exit San Petronio is ② the **Palazzo Comunale** or town hall, made up of two buildings: 13th-century to the left and 15th-century at right, plus a statue of one of the Popes Gregory in between. Inside the doorway designed by Alessi, an arcaded courtyard leads to the Museo Morandi, the council's art collection.

In the adjacent Piazza del Nettuno is the ③ **Fontana del Nettuno**, created in 1566 and decorated with the muscular bronze figure of Neptune and his water-spouting attendants. Flemish sculptor Giambologna designed the grouping in such a way that the viewer is engaged to circle the fountain.

On a wall beside the fountain are the chilling photographs of people who died at the hands of fascists, either in WWII under Nazi rule or in later right-wing attacks such as the 1980 bombing at Bologna's railway

Torre Garisenda from Torre degli Asinelli

station. On the other side of the fountain stands the 13th-century ④ **Casa di Re Enzo**, which housed the captive King Enzo for two decades from 1249. Enter to view the inner courtyard and magnificent covered staircase.

Walk past the Palazzo del Podestà and leave the piazza along narrow Via Pescherie Vecchie which hosts the city's outdoor market (an indoor one is located in Via Ugo Bassi), turn left into Via Drapperie and on along Via Calzolerie, then right into busy Via Rizzoli, lined with shops.

At the Piazza di Porta Ravegnana no less than seven streets converge. In the piazza are two leaning towers or ⑤ **Torri Pendenti**, which were built in the 12th century on shifting ground: the shorter Torre Garisenda (47 m high) has a tilt of over three metres. The 488 steps of the Torre degli Asinelli (97 m high) can be climbed for a panoramic view of the city and surrounding hills and is a fascinating, if exhausting, experience.

Leave the piazza on Via Zamboni, passing some palazzi. On the right is the church of ⑥ **San Giacomo Maggiore**, featuring the 15th-century Cappella Bentivoglio. Walk along the church's Renaissance portico and along Via Zamboni to Palazzo Poggi, home to Bologna's university. Turn left at Piazza Puntoni to reach

⑦ the **Pinacoteca Nazionale**, a superior collection of mostly Bolognese paintings from 1300 to 1700, including works by Perugino, Reni and Raphael.

Cross Piazza Puntoni once more and turn left down Via San Giacomo. Head right into Via Selmi, skirting university buldings, left into Via Belmeloro, right down Via San Leonardo, left briefly into Via San Vitale, then right into Via Broccaindosso, a narrow street lined with dilapidated houses in lovely ochre hues (and several good *trattorie*).

At this point there is a possible detour to view the **Portico degli Alemanni**, some of Bologna's most attractive arcades. Turn left down Strada Maggiore, pass Porta Maggiore and continue down Via Mazzini (an old Roman road) to see the arcades leading to Santa Maria Lacrimosa degli Alemanni: this was a 'sacred way' in the 17th century. Walk back up Strada Maggiore and along the beautiful quadriportico which belongs to the ⑧ **Santa Maria dei Servi**. Inside this Gothic

church, Cimabue's *Maestà* hangs in a chapel on the left.

As you near the towers, turn left off Strada Maggiore at the signed Corte Isolani, a string of small courtyards with shops. If you miss this, turn left instead down Via dal Luzo, a lane of antique shops, then left again down Via San Stefano to reach the lovely triangular Piazza San Stefano, enclosed with porticoes on two sides and, on the third, by the

⑨ **Basilica di San Stefano**, which now comprises no less than four Romanesque churches, two chapels, two cloisters and the 8th-century basin in which Pilate reputedly washed his hands, the Fontana di Pilato. Originally there were seven churches in this charmingly tangled complex.

Leave the piazza by Via de' Pepoli. Turn left into Via Castiglione and then right into Via Farini, pass Piazza Minghetti and then left into Via Garofalo to enter Piazza di San Domenico near a raised sarcophagus. Here is the 13th-century church of

⑩ **San Domenico**, remodelled in the 18th century. The famous tomb of St Dominic

San Stefano's Romanesque churches

was crafted by Nicola Pisano in 1267 with later additions by Niccolò dell'Arca and Michelangelo. A small work by Filippo Lippi hangs at the end of the right aisle.

Leave the piazza on Via Garibaldi along the other side of Piazza Cavour and under the painted ceilings of the Banca d'Italia portico. Turn left into Via Farini and soon right into Piazza Galvani. The Portico del Pavaglione leads to the entrance of ⑪ the **Palazzo dell' Archigennasio**, which housed the university from its Renaissance construction until 1803; the crests of former teachers and students still decorate the courtyard. It now hosts the Biblioteca Comunale and, upstairs, the intriguing **Teatro Anatomico**. This small chamber was bombed in 1944 but was reconstructed from the fragments. Note the flayed figures carved to support the professor's chair.

Continue along the portico past the **Museo Civico Archeologico**, a collection of prehistoric, Etruscan and Greco-Roman artefacts, to regain the Piazza Maggiore.

OTHER EXCURSIONS

For the full portico experience, head to **Santuario della Madonna di S.Luca** situated on a hill known as the Colle della Guardia 5km (3m) southwest of the city. From Piazza Maggiore, walk south down Via M. D'Azeglio. Turn right onto Via Urbana and continue along Via Saragozza to leave by the 19th-century Porto Saragozza. Walk ahead to the Arco del Meloncello (the #20 bus runs between here and Piazza Maggiore) and then head uphill, along the 666 arches

Fontana del Nettuno and San Petronio

of Portico di San Luca, to the mainly 18th-century sanctuary. Its piazzale offers a fine panorama of Bologna.

For a green respite, visit the **Parco de Villa Ghigi**, set on the Apennine foothills and offering more excellent views of the city. Walk directly south from Piazza Maggiore on Via M.D'Azeglio, through Piazza di Porta San Mamolo and continue south. A detour left along Via A. Codivilla leads to the gardens of **San Michele in Bosco**. Walk south along Via San Mamolo to climb to the large Parco de Villa Ghigi, the gift of a university rector to the city of Bologna.

OPENING HOURS

| | |
|---|---|
| Palazzo Comunale | Tue-Sun 10-6 |
| Torre degli Asinelli | daily 9-6 (winter 9-5) |
| Pinacoteca Nazionale | Tue-Sat 9-2; Sun 9-1 |
| Santa Maria dei Servi | daily 8-12.45, 3-7.30 |
| Basilica di San Stefano | daily 9-noon, 3.30-6 |
| San Domenico | Mon-Sat 9-noon, 3-5.30; Sun 3-5.30 |
| Palazzo dell'Archigennasio | Mon-Sat 9-1 |

# RAVENNA

NOTES
Population: 138,000
Getting there: rail from Bologna,
  Ferrara or Rimini
Tourist Office: Via Salara 8-12
  Tel: 0544 35404  Fax: 0544 35094
  email: turismo@comune.ravenna.it
  www.turismo.ravenna.it
Markets: Wed & Sat at P. Andrea Costa

While the rest of Europe fumbled through the Dark Ages, Ravenna blazed with glory. The glittering mosaics which evoke that period still draw travellers to this otherwise quiet provincial city and it should not be omitted from any itinerary.

The town was built on a series of islands in a lagoon in the 1st century BC and it prospered due to its proximity to Classis, the largest Roman naval base on the Adriatic. Its population converted to Christianity in the 2nd century AD. After the decline of Roma in the late 4th century, Honorius made Ravenna capital of the Western Roman Empire: the earliest mosaics you'll see date from this period.

In 476 the Ostrogoths invaded. Their kings, notably Theodoric, were also Christian and they continued to enrich Ravenna with mosaic-encrusted churches and baptistries. The city traded with Byzantium, the capital of the Eastern Roman Empire and, in 540, Ravenna came under Byzantine rule. It was administered by *exarchs* under the Emperor Justinian and flourished as the Empire's stronghold in Italy throughout the 6th century.

In 752 the Lombards gained control of Ravenna and its period of brilliance was over. Its port silted up, denying it much of its strategic importance. It fell under Venetian rule in the 15th century and was later held by the Papacy before Italy's unification. The nearby development of gas and chemical works has brought some prosperity back to Ravenna but it remains a pleasant town which happens to hold some of the world's finest mosaics.

These artworks are pieced together with *tesserae*, stone fragments glazed and positioned to catch the light. The mosaics of Ravenna are worked in vivid blues and greens, heightened by gold backdrops. Symbolic figures such as the Good Shepherd and the River Jordan are accompanied by historic identities. The images are laden with meaning: doves at a fountain denote the souls sipping eternal life; specific flowers lend symbolic value while their detailed depiction adds to the beauty of the whole. Ravenna's mosaics are a wonderful meld of classical theory with Christian iconography, the crowning achievement of Byzantine art, and a pleasure to behold.

Fortunately, walking between each of the monuments is a delight, as Ravenna is a compact town, with little car traffic and many fine buildings to admire. The town hosts a major arts festival in July and August, when it gets a little more crowded than usual.

< Mosaic detail, Sant'Apollinare in Classe

Piazza del Popolo

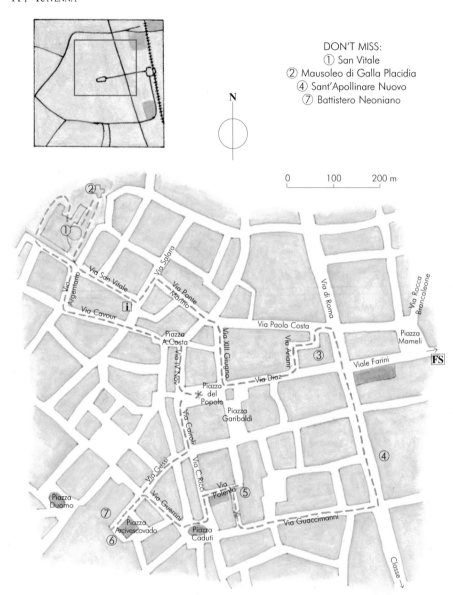

DON'T MISS:
① San Vitale
② Mausoleo di Galla Placidia
④ Sant'Apollinare Nuovo
⑦ Battistero Neoniano

## A WALK IN RAVENNA

*Our short itinerary takes in the major World Heritage sites, linked by a stroll through streets with character and charm.*

Piazza del Popolo is the heart of the town, some 600 m west of the rail station. This very attractive public space is edged by Renaissance palazzi built under Venetian rule and is a popular meeting place.

Leave the piazza at its northwest corner and head down Via IV Novembre to Piazza A.Costa and the main entrance to the indoor Mercato Coperto, a good place to buy provisions if you are planning a picnic lunch. Turn left down Via Cavour, passing near the tourist office (in Via Salara) which is stocked with excellent brochures. At Via

Argentario turn right, then left into Via San Vitale to enter the San Vitale complex. The former cloisters now house the Museo Nazionale. Adjacent is the ① **Chiesa di San Vitale**. Buy a comprehensive ticket giving access to all major sites. This wonderful octagonal basilica was built in the mid-6th century by the Byzantine conquerors and it marks the birth of the Romanesque style. The interior is filled with carved capitals and geometric floor mosaics but it is the mosaic-crammed apse which catches the breath. On one side of the chancel are Justinian and his court; facing it are his Empress Theodora and her retinue. Above, Christ is enthroned between San Vitale and Bishop Ecclesius, who founded the church and holds a model of it.

Emperor Justinian and his court

In the grounds behind the church is a small building in the shape of a Latin cross, ② the **Mausoleo di Galla Placidia**. This was built around AD 428 for Honorius' half-sister who ruled as regent for her young son, though it seems she was buried in Roma. Its mosaics, which include a cobalt sky pierced with stars, are Ravenna's oldest.

Leave the grounds, keeping the church on your right and exiting at a small gate, then turn left up Via S.Vitale to the tourist office. Turn left briefly into Via Salara and then right into Via Ponte Marino to pass another entrance to the markets. Turn right around the base of the leaning 12th-century Torre Comunale and walk along Via XIII Giugno to gain another view of the Piazza del Popolo. Turn left up modern Via Diaz but then turn left into Via Ariani where, as you round the corner, you are back in ancient Ravenna. Tucked away is the tiny ③ **Battistero degli Ariani**, built by the Gothic Arian sect during the 6th century. The dome is embellished with the baptism of Christ, surrounded by the Apostles.

Pass the fairly nondescript Chiesa dello Santo Spirito, turn right onto Via Paolo Costa and then immediately right again on Via di Roma. Pass Viale Farini on the left, which leads to the FS rail station. This is a good point at which to detour to **La Classe** (see the end of this chapter).

San Vitale >

< The procession
of female martyrs

Continue down Via di Roma to reach
④ the **Basilica di Sant'Apollinare Nuovo**
with its round campanile. This lovely
structure was built as Theodoric's palatine
church at the end of the 5th century. Inside,
one wall depicts a procession of female
martyrs leaving the town and its port to
follow the Magi who bear gifts for the
Virgin. Opposite, a line of male martyrs
leave Theodoric's palace to honour Christ.

Back outside, turn left and pass the
evocative remnants of the 7-8th-century so-
called Palazzo di Teodorico, built too late
to have hosted Theodoric. Turn right down
Via Guaccimanni, lined with attractive
pastel buildings. Turn right into Via Santi
and walk under the arch and past the
church of San Francesco, facing onto its
pleasant piazza, to reach the
⑤ **Tomba di Dante**, constructed in 1780.
The great poet Dante Alighieri, exiled from
Firenze, ended his wanderings in Ravenna
where he completed *The Divine Comedy* and
died in 1321. The Florentines, who have
an empty tomb for their estranged son,
supply the oil for this sepulchre's lamp.

From the tomb, turn left and stroll down
Via da Polenta then left onto Via C. Ricci.
Skirt around Piazza Caduti and take the

second exit on the right, Via Guerrini. Turn
left into Via Gessi then reach the shady
Piazza Arcivescovado, which would make
a pleasant picnic spot, and straight ahead
to the steps leading up to the Episcopal
Palace museum:
⑥ **Museo Arcivescovile**. Inside, the Sant'
Andrea chapel bears a remarkable mosaic
of Christ in centurion's garb. Also on display
is the intricately carved ivory throne of the
6th-century Bishop Maximian.

Battistero Neoniano and campanile >

The dome in Battistero degli Ariani >

Head back down the steps and out. On your left is a door leading into the back of the 18th-century **Duomo** with its 10th-century crypt and campanile. Near the back entrance is a gate (opposite the park) which leads to the wonderful ⑦ **Battistero Neoniano**, the orthodox baptistry named after Bishop Neoni who likely commisioned its mosaic decoration in 458. Its baptism scene has fascinating similarities and differences to that seen in the Ariani baptistry. This building was converted from a Roman bathhouse, signs of which are still visible.

Exit through the same gate and turn left. Walk down Via Gessi and turn left onto Via Cairoli, a traffic-free alley lined with shops, to return to Piazza del Popolo.

## OTHER EXCURSIONS

The last of the mosaic treasures is found in **Sant'Apollinare in Classe**, some 5km (3miles) south but well worth the trip. Classe is one stop by train, or you can catch #4 bus from opposite the rail station (or from the newstand on Viale Farini near Via di Roma) and get off when you see the imposing basilica set among fields. The apse of the 6th-century church is adorned with a mosaic scene of immense harmony, showing Bishop Apollinare praying in a meadow while Christ is transfigured above.

In Ravenna, just across the rail line lies the final World Heritage site, **Mausoleo di Teodorico**. From Piazza Mameli, walk along Via Rocca Brancaleone which skirts the Venetian fortress of Rocca Brancaleone. At the end of this street, turn right into Circonvallazione alla Rotonda dei Goti, which crosses the railway line and becomes Via delle Industrie. The mausoleum is set in parkland on your left. Theodoric the Ostrogoth built this austere monument around 520. It is made with huge blocks of Istrian stone, assembled without mortar.

| OPENING HOURS | Apr-Sep | Oct-Mar |
|---|---|---|
| San Vitale & Mausoleo | daily 9-7 | daily 9-4.30 |
| Battistero degli Ariani | daily 8.30-7.30 | daily 8.30-4.30 |
| Sant'Apollinare Nuovo | daily 9-7 | daily 9-4.30 |
| Tomba di Dante | daily 9-7 | daily 9-noon, 2-5 |
| Museo Arcivescovile | daily 9-7 | daily 9-7 |
| Duomo | daily 7.30-noon, 2.30-5 | |
| Battistero Neoniano | daily 9-7 | daily 9-4.30 |
| S.Apollinare in Classe | M-Sat 8.30-7.30; Sun 1-7 | |
| Mausoleo di Teodorico | daily 8.30-7 | daily 8.30-4.30 |

Fridays in Jul-Aug: S.Vitale, the Mausoleo & S.Apollinare Nuovo open to midnight

# HEART OF TOSCANA

The images of Toscan landscapes splashed across today's calendars and book jackets are remarkably similar to those adorning the paintings and frescoes of Florentine Renaissance masters. Not a great deal has changed over 600 or so years, despite such modern blights as electricity pylons and concrete grapevine supports. Even so, there is little that's pristine about a landscape shaped by at least 3,000 years of human toil. Rather it's the happy blend of forested hills with human interventions—terraced vineyards, olive groves, golden sunflower fields, cypress rows and stone farmsteads—that makes for the quintessential Toscan landscape.

The ancient hilltowns that tourists find so enticing in this part of Italy seem to emerge organically from their rocky platforms. Equally attractive are the tiny *borghi*, fortified *castelli* and solitary medieval churches, many of which have been restored as private residences or for the growing *agriturismo* business. Northwest of Siena, the rolling hills surrounding San Gimignano *delle Belle Torre*, that famous hilltown of medieval skyscrapers, are particularly pleasing. Colours change depending on the season and time of day,

NOTES
Suggested base: San Gimignano
Getting there: bus from Poggibonsi, Siena or Firenze
Tourist Office: Piazza Duomo 1, 53037 San Gimignano Tel: 0577 940008 Fax: 0577 940903
email: prolocsg@tin.it
www.sangimignano.com
Map: Kompass #660 1:50000
Best timing: avoid July-August

and everywhere you go you have views of the town's extraordinary silhouetted skyline. The countryside is peaceful and remarkably unspoilt; no industrial sprawl here, just the occasional farm or *fattoria* and the odd tiny hamlet.

San Gimignano, now a UNESCO world heritage site, is Italy's most touristed hilltown, a very good reason to roam its lovely countryside by day and enjoy its charms in the early morning or late evening. *Affittacamere* or private rooms offer a less expensive alternative to San Gimignano's hotels; enquire at the tourist office.

The town's remarkable preservation, as if in 14th-century amber, results from its rapid increase in prosperity and expansion followed by an almost instant decline. From the 11th century, prosperity came with its position on the Via Francigena pilgrimage route from Lombardia to Roma and from its trade in wine and saffron. Decline came in 1348 with the Black Death, which killed two-thirds of the populace and kept pilgrims away. Tourism

A Toscan landscape >

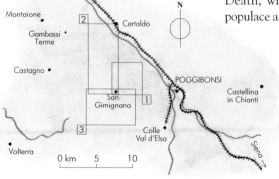

and delicious *Vernaccia* white wines have now revived its fortunes. Its trademark medieval towers—15 survive of an original 72—served as status symbols, granaries and fortresses from where the town's warring nobility could skirmish.

A walk through San Gimignano itself is described at the chapter's end. The three country walks are undemanding, allowing time for some practical oenology en route. Walk 1 takes you north via Ulignano, a sleepy ridgetop village and *castello* overlooking the Val d'Elsa. The second walk initially follows the ridgeline route of medieval pilgrims and then heads for Certaldo, one of Toscana's better-kept secrets and a gem of a hilltown. The third walk, to the hillier south, takes you into the forest of the Riserva Castelvecchio and through several delightful hamlets.

San Gimignano's southern gate

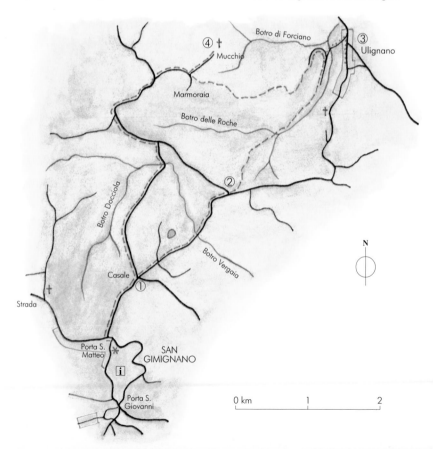

## WALK 1: VINES AND VIEWS

*This loop walk takes you along farm lanes, through woods and by vineyards for a taste of the countryside and wonderful views back to the San Gimignano skyline.*

Distance     14 km (8.7 miles)
Time         4 to 5 hours
Difficulty   easy
Start/Finish San Gimignano

Ulignano has a bar and several basic shops, but you might take a picnic with you. Leave San Gimignano by Porta San Matteo and cross Viale Garibaldi. Take the right-forking Via Cepparelli downhill and keep on this road, signed to Ulignano.

Almost 1 km out of town, you reach the ① **buildings** and church at Casale. Here, the road branches three ways; take the middle road, a gravel lane signed to Ulignano. This will be very quiet unless it's autumn and the *vendemmia* or grape-harvest is under way, in which case you'll need to watch out for laden trucks.

A kilometre further on, cross the Vergaia stream and pass the premises of winemakers Terruzzi & Puthod at Ponte a Rondolino. After a gentle climb, join a more major road by veering right and, after 50 m, turn left on a track marked with a red arrow and a trail sign for mountain bikers. Stay right on a track that passes below ② **Agriturismo Montegonfoli**. The track descends steeply into woods and can be muddy and slippery after rain. At a clearing, keep right on a level track (red-and-white waymarks) between an avenue of tall trees.

Vines are laid out on your left and Ulignano comes into sight on the ridge above to your right. The track becomes a paved road and loops sharply to the left. To visit the unassuming village of ③ **Ulignano** and its castle, you will need to detour right and then turn sharp right to climb the ridge.

Back on the route, the road now climbs above the vines, with a truffle reserve on your right. On your left you gain a view of the Castello Ulignano and then beyond to San Gimignano. Climb up past several villas and walk on through light woods on what has become a dirt track. Reach a gravel track just before a gate at the Marmoraia buildings. Here there are beautiful views, over vines, of villas set among cypresses. Turn right and, in 100 m or so, make a 500-metre detour right to reach the buildings of Mucchio and the ④ **Abbazia Camaldolese**, which you'll have to be content to admire from the outside. Retrace your steps, turn right back on the gravel lane and soon turn left onto a paved road descending gently.

At a junction some 1.5 km further on, turn right on the road to San Gimignano. This crosses the Botro Vergaia once again and rises to the junction at Casale to complete a loop. From here you retrace your steps south, back into San Gimignano, admiring its silhouette as you approach.

A country lane
at twilight >

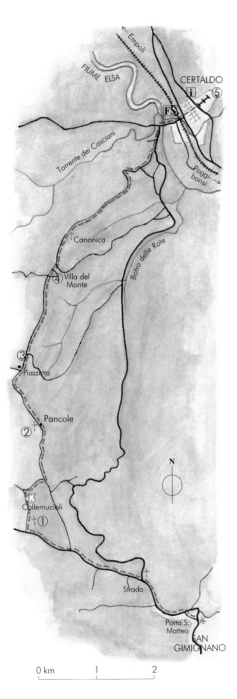

< Certaldo Alto's main street

## WALK 2: CERTALDO

*This wonderful ridge walk picks up the ancient Via Francigena pilgrim road and then wends past a picturesque villa to end at Certaldo, a historic and lovely hilltown.*

| | |
|---|---|
| Distance | 13.5 km (8.4 miles) |
| Time | 4 hours of walking |
| Difficulty | easy |
| Start | San Gimignano |
| Finish | Certaldo |
| Transport | bus back to San Gimignano |

Take some food and water as there's nothing available until near Certaldo. Also, check the time of the return bus from Certaldo before you head off.

Leave San Gimignano by the Porta San Matteo and cross Viale Garibaldi. Take the left-forking Via Niccolo Cannuci downhill and, at the bottom, turn left to walk down to Sant'Angelo a Strada, the church at the road junction. Here you keep left, watching out for traffic as you climb the next hill and gain a good view back over the town.

Pass the turn-off right for Pancole and continue a further 800 m to another junction. Turn right onto the lane signed to Cellole. This soon brings you up to the ① **Pieve di Santa Maria a Cellole**, tucked in to one side of a large clearing. This tiny church, with its lovely 13th-century façade, was once the centre of much ecclesiastic power, owing to its position on the Via Francigena, a principal pilgrimage thoroughfare to Roma from northern Europe. Unfortunately, the church will most likely be locked.

Cross the clearing and, a short distance on, you get a sight of the restored **Torre di Collemucioli**, first mentioned in 1059 and now a private residence. The lane now winds down by houses and you fork right to reach the Pancole road. Turn left onto this quiet road to soon gain a lovely view of the hamlet of Pancole on the next hill. The road passes under an archway to the ② **Santuario di Pancole**, built originally in

< Torre di Collemucioli

1670 to mark the miraculous cure of a deaf-mute girl and reconstructed after WWII.

Keep on through woods to the *borgo* of ③ **La Piazzetta**, where the Via Francigena veers off to the left (detour a short way for a view over the rolling hills) and you keep right. The road now drops a little and then heads along a ridge to pass Podere Ranucci and then to the left of ④ **Villa del Monte**, a grand residence with a stunning position high above the Val d'Elsa. Signs by the road inform you that this area is a private game reserve, unfortunately for the pheasants that are to be seen hereabouts.

Cypresses line the road straight ahead to the church of Canonica. From here you descend along the ridge, overlooking vines; the descent becomes steeper as you reach houses and a petrol station. Turn left and, at a T-junction, turn right to cross first the Fiume Elsa and then the rail line to reach Viale G. Matteotti in Certaldo's lower town.

Turn left through a small park then, with the rail station on the left, turn right to walk up through modern Certaldo and past Piazza Boccaccio. Cross the road to catch the funicular up to the walled, red-brick ⑤ **Certaldo Alto**. This small but perfectly formed medieval town clusters around Via Boccaccio, so named because the poet, son of a Certaldo banker, lived and died here. Make sure you visit the frescoed church of **S.S. Jacopo e Filippo**, with its lovely della Robbia tabernacles and altarpiece, and the **Palazzo Pretorio** (the Governor's Palace), which dates back to the late 12th century. Certaldo also affords delightful views over the Val d'Elsa.

Once you have explored Certaldo and caught the funicular back down, you can catch a bus directly to San Gimignano from Viale G. Matteotti. A less direct route, but with more frequent departures, would be to catch a train from Certaldo to Poggibonsi and then a bus to San Gimignano.

A Renaissance ceramic, Certaldo

## WALK 3: SAN DONATO LOOP

*South of San Gimignano, the countryside is hillier, with ever-changing landscapes and views. From San Donato, you could make a detour to the dramatic ruins of Castelvecchio.*

| | |
|---|---|
| Distance | 13.5 km (8.4 miles) |
| Time | 5 hours |
| Difficulty | moderate |
| Start/Finish | San Gimignano |

The only restaurant is at Racciano, so you'll probably need to carry lunch supplies as well as water. Leave San Gimignano by the 13th-century Porta San Giovanni and turn right to cross Viale del Fossi and take the lane downhill between a carpark and the Carabinieri. This is signed as La Strada della Vernaccia. About 600 m downhill, by two cypresses with a bench between them, turn left onto a farm track.

Shortly, fork left on the higher of two tracks then fork right up a stony track through woods. You emerge onto a paved road that heads uphill and then curves left. You approach a hamlet; the main road skirts it, but you can walk straight through this tiny settlement of

① **Racciano**, sited on a panoramic ridge, to view its little chapel and pick up the road again at the other side. Head downhill and then turn right on a broader road and follow this south through woodland, taking care about traffic. The road passes a turn-off to the picturesque hamlet of Pescille and keeps on gently uphill for a further 1 km to

② **San Donato**, set slightly off the road to the left. This lovely hamlet features a few medieval houses and a Romanesque church.

Detour: For walkers who have started early and will happily walk all day, an interesting detour to Castelvecchio is an option here. The return trip is 4.25 km or 2.6 miles but you should allow 2.5 hours.

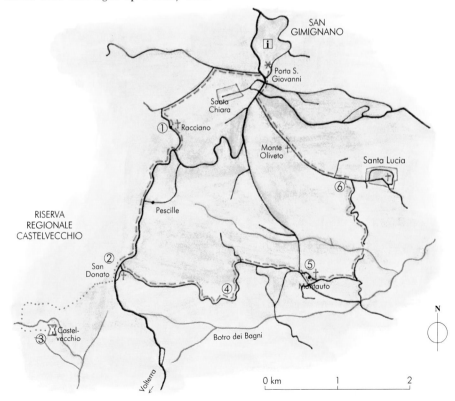

Castelvecchio

path to the evocative ruins of

③ **Castelvecchio**. This site, which probably has its beginnings as an Etruscan temple, was fortified in the Middle Ages but abandoned centuries ago following an outbreak of plague. Beyond the high entrance tower are the ruins of a church and other buildings, home to the small community who once lived here. Return by the same route to San Donato.

From San Donato, pick up the track with red-and-white waymarks from the back of the hamlet. This heads east downhill and passes Fattoria Voltrona, then crosses through the lovely grounds of Podere Voltrona. The track then curves and, before you reach another house, pick up

④ **a grassy track** forking left, signed to Montauto and San Gimignano.

Cross a creek bed (which can be muddy) and skirt left along the bottom of a vineyard. The path then heads up to the right between vines and, at olive trees, you turn right to reach a gravel track, by Podere Casavecchia. This descends to a road junction; keep straight on to climb steeply and skirt right of the small *borgo* of

⑤ **Montauto**, where you should make a quick uphill detour. Beyond Montauto, keep straight ahead on a gravel track that descends to a sharp switchback left; don't

Instead of turning off to San Donato, pick up a track heading off to the right; there is a trail sign for mountain bikers at the turn-off. Follow this track into a wood of dense Mediterranean maquis. The path continues to the farm of Caggio. Here you veer left and descend steeply to cross a stream, the Botro di Castelvecchio. A steep climb brings you to a junction; turn left to walk the easy

< The famous skyline of San Gimignano

go straight on at the Via Francigena sign. Your track descends by some cypresses and then skirts around a house and keeps heading downhill, now a grassy path between vines, to enter woods. Ford the Botro Imbotroni and veer left along the other bank to then pass right of a beautifully restored mill.

From here a gravel track winds slowly uphill on a long climb with lovely scenery. It eventually skirts left to avoid a property and then reaches
⑥ **a broad road**, 300 m west of Santa Lucia. Turn left and walk on its sidepath for almost 2 km, passing the convent of Monte Oliveto on the left, to reach a roundabout and enter San Gimignano by Porta San Giovanni.

## A SAN GIMIGNANO WALK

There is, of course, much to see and enjoy in the small town of San Gimignano itself. It's worthwhile buying a combined museum ticket if you have time to spend here. Start at **Porta San Giovanni**, the southern gate, and walk up Via San Giovanni. On your right is the former church of **San Francesco**, built in 12th-century Pisan-Romanesque style and now a wine shop.

Heading through the **Arco dei Becci**, part of the town's original fortifications, you reach the triangular **Piazza Cisterna**, named for the 1273 cistern that features in its centre. Lining the piazza is a jumble of medieval houses and towers.

The adjoining Piazza Duomo is the town's civic and religious centre. Above its **Palazzo del Podestà** (1239) is a 51-metre-high clock tower known as the Torre della Rognosa; it set the maximum legal height for any private towers. Up a broad flight of steps stands the plain façade of the 12th-century **Collegiata**. Inside, the walls are almost totally filled with brilliant frescoes by various artists of the 14th and 15th centuries. The Cappella di Santa Fina, dedicated to a girl who performed miracles in San Gimignano, contains beautiful lunette frescoes by Ghirlandaio.

View to Sant'Agostino

Left of the Collegiata is the 13th-century **Palazzo del Popolo**, which still serves as the town hall. In its courtyard, decorated with coats of arms and a fresco, are stairs leading to the **Museo Civico**, which displays paintings from the Florentine and Sienese schools of the 12th-15th centuries. You can climb to the top of the 54-metre Torre Grossa for a spectacular panorama.

Behind the Collegiata, on the top of the hill, is the **Rocca**, built in 1353 to preserve Florentine control over the town. Climb steps up the ramparts for excellent views. From the Rocca, had back down to Piazza Duomo and take Via San Matteo, lined with shops and filled with people. Before the northern gate, Porta San Matteo, turn right along Via Cellolese and then left to the Romanesque-Gothic church of **Sant' Agostino**. Built in 1280–98, the airy church contains various fine paintings as well as a remarkable fresco cycle by Benozzo Gozzoli, which depicts the life of Sant'Agostino.

Allow time to meander around San Gimignano's alleys, away from the madding throng, where you'll get a wonderful sense of the medieval town.

# FIRENZE

For the visitor to Firenze, or Florence, distance is not the problem. The compact city centre holds so many monuments containing, in turn, so many artistic gems, that the senses give up long before the feet.

The city lies on the banks of the tawny Arno amid the beautiful hills of Toscana, a setting that has inspired many great artists. Julius Caesar founded the colony of Florentia for veterans in the 1st century BC, but it wasn't until the 11th century that it became an important centre of trade, primarily in silk and wool.

A class of powerful merchants and bankers—Firenze was a European centre of banking—arose, including the Medici family who ruled unofficially. Cosimo the Elder and grandson Lorenzo the Magnificent liberally promoted the fine arts, architecture and literature, making Firenze the undisputed capital of the early Renaissance movement.

Civil unrest followed Lorenzo's death in 1492 but the Medicis were restored to power with help from Emperor Charles V. Cosimo I (confusingly numbered) defeated Siena and extended Firenze's territory, meanwhile further patronising the arts. By the beginning of the 18th century, however, the fortunes of Firenze had slumped and it was ceded first to Austria and then to Napoleon, joining a united

Italy at an early stage. Firenze avoided heavy bombing during WWII but in 1966 a swollen Arno flooded the city, killing 35 people and causing great damage to its art treasures.

Firenze had always been fiercely competitive with other cities and its artists were encouraged to innovate and excel. Many were lured to the city with great commissions and even, in the case of architecture, competitions for commissions. Collections of fine art were valued as a sign of wealth and power among the families of Firenze.

Today, the city is congested with cars and tourists, and those few travellers with absolutely no interest in art will wonder what all the fuss is about. For the rest, it is a magnet. We've suggested two walks but, if you can spare three or four days, break them up to allow more time in museums, galleries and chapels. The two routes can be linked by strolling along the lively Via dei Calzaiuoli.

NOTES
Population: 460,000
Getting there: bus or train from Pisa's Galileo Galilei airport (a 1-hour trip); rail from Roma or Bologna
Tourist Office: Via Cavour, 1r
Tel: 055 290832 Fax: 055 2760383
email: infoturismo@provincia.fi.it
www.firenze.turismo.toscana.it
Markets: Mercato Centrale, M-Sat am
Note: some museums close Monday

Michelangelo's *David* >

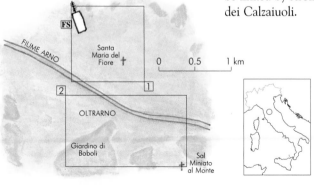

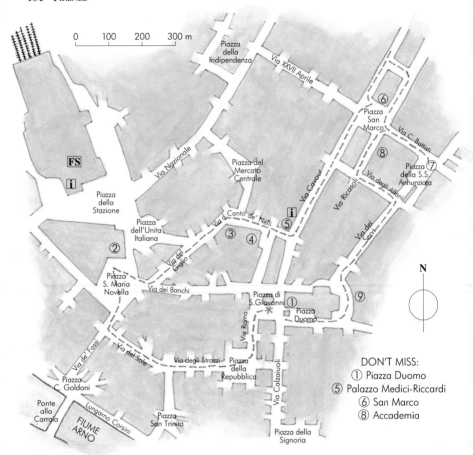

DON'T MISS:
① Piazza Duomo
⑤ Palazzo Medici-Riccardi
⑥ San Marco
⑧ Accademia

## WALK 1: NORTH of the DUOMO

*A walk from the city's religious centre north-wards takes in some of Firenze's medieval, Renaissance and baroque splendours.*

Begin your walk in the central squares of Piazza di San Giovanni and the adjacent ① **Piazza Duomo**, filled with a magnificent ensemble of buildings in white, pink and green marble. The oldest of these, and perhaps of any buildings in Firenze, is the huge octagonal **Battistero**. Generally thought to date from the 6th or 7th century, and possibly built on the site of a Roman temple, it was here that all Florentine children were baptised, cementing their loyalty to the city. Walk around to view its three sets of gilded bronze doors, notably those named the *Gates of Paradise*, designed by Lorenzo Ghiberti and made in 1452. The majestic interior is covered with magnificent 13th-century mosaics by Venetian masters of the art. Note: on weekdays, the baptistry only opens in the afternoon; you return here at the end of the walk.

The **Campanile di Giotto** was begun according to the artist Giotto's plans, but he died long before its completion in 1359. The bell tower, at 82 m, exceeded the maximum height permitted by Florentine law at that time. You can climb its 414 steps for wonderful views, but choose between this and an ascent of the cathedral dome; both would be excessive!

The **Duomo** or Santa Maria del Fiore is among the largest cathedrals in Europe and is a symbol of the city's position at the end of the Middle Ages. It was begun in 1296 to a design by Arnolfo di Cambio and consecrated in 1436, no doubt delayed by the terrible outbreak of plague in 1348.

The huge dome was, and is still, an architectural marvel. Filippo Brunelleschi won a competition to design it and he built it without any frame or support, an amazing feat. Climbing the 463 steps between the two shells of the dome can be claustrophobic but gives you unmatched views.

The façade of the duomo is neo-Gothic; 'neo' because it was added in the late 19th century, in the elaborate style of Giotto's campanile. In contrast, the duomo is quite sparsely decorated inside, accentuating its great space.

Just by the campanile but in danger of being overlooked, is the **Loggia del Bigallo**, a 14th-century structure where lost or abandoned children were set out so they might be claimed before a charity cared for them. Leave the piazza to walk down Via Roma. Cross the spacious Piazza della Repubblica, which is lined with renowned cafés. Now walk down Via degli Strozzi, passing along the solid Palazzo Strozzi, built in the 15th-16th centuries. Filippo Strozzi, a rich banker, had some 15 buildings demolished to make way for his mansion.

Veer into Via della Spada, noting the protected fresco on a sharp corner ahead on the right. Pass the ancient but deconsecrated church of **San Pancrazio** on your left; it now houses a museum dedicated to the 20th-century artist, Marino Marini. At Piazza Ottaviani, turn right to reach the grassy piazza in front of

② **Santa Maria Novella**, constructed for the Dominicans mostly between 1279 and 1357. The green and white façade is in two sections, the upper one completed in 1470. The church's masterpiece is a 1428 fresco, a *Trinity* by Masaccio, which was groundbreaking for its use of perspective. The Chiostro Verde or Green Cloister is so named for the pigment that predominates in its frescoes by Paolo Uccello.

Leave the piazza on Via dei Banchi but soon turn left into Via del Giglio to reach Piazza di Madonna degli Aldobrandini. Here you'll find the entrance to

③ **Cappelle Medicee**, the chapels of the

Firenze's magnificent duomo

*< Santa Maria Novella*

Medici family at the rear of San Lorenzo. The Cappella dei Principi or Princes' Chapel is an opulent family mausoleum, commissioned by Cosimo I in 1604. The simpler Sagrestia Nuova was Michelangelo's first architectural work and he also sculpted the figures on the tombs.

Around the corner, past the stalls of leather goods and woollen clothing, is the entrance to
④ **San Lorenzo**, the parish church of the Medicis. This was the work of Brunelleschi; he designed the old sacristy inside, but the façade was never completed. Through the cloister, you can enter the Biblioteca Laurenziana, which features a staircase by Michelangelo.

Leave Piazza San Lorenzo to visit
⑤ **Palazzo Medici-Riccardi**, home to the Medicis from 1459 to 1540. Cosimo the Elder cunningly avoided an ostentatious display of wealth when he had this palazzo built to plans by Michelozzo. However, the tiny chapel on the first floor contains a wonderful *Procession of the Magi*, frescoed by Benozzo Gozzoli in 1459; it's a true gem.

Walk up Via Cavour, passing the main tourist office, to reach the very pleasant Piazza San Marco. Seats in the shade make it a good spot for a rest, before you visit
⑥ **San Marco**. This former Dominican monastery is now a museum, dedicated to

the works of Fra Angelico who decorated the walls—including those of the monks' cells—with delicate frescoes. Savonarola, the fire-and-damnation preacher who held great sway in the 1490s (before he was hanged and burnt) was a prior here.

Continue along Via Cavour for a short distance to the modest portal of **Chiostro dello Scalzo** on the left. This cloister opens only a few morning each week, but you may be in luck. Its name derives from the shoeless nature of the cross-bearer in the order's processions; *scalzo* means barefoot.

Cross the road and walk along Via della Dogana then turn right along the Orto Botanico or Giardino dei Semplici (the entrance is around the corner on Via Micheli). Back at Piazza San Marco, turn left along Via C.Battisti to the charming
⑦ **Piazza della S.S. Annunziata**. This gracious piazza is flanked by two sets of porticoes and a church. On your right is the **Loggia dei Servi**. Opposite is the **Spedale degli Innocenti**, designed by Brunelleschi in 1445 and Europe's very first orphanage, as advertised by Andrea della Robbia's roundels above the columns. Its

*Piazza della S.S. Annunziata >*

A della Robbia
lunette >

upper floor now houses a modest museum; duck inside to view its two lovely cloisters.

Also on the piazza is the church of **Santissima Annunziata**, established in 1250 but rebuilt in the 15th century by Michelozzo. A pleasant atrium, decorated with frescoes, leads into the church, which houses a painting of the Virgin reputedly begun by a 14th-century friar but completed by an angel. Sadly, it's no longer on display.

Return along Via C.Battisti and then turn first left into Via Ricasoli, to walk along the side of the former Ospedale di San Matteo, passing three lunettes by della Robbia. This building now houses the ⑧ **Galleria dell'Accademia**. The 1563 academy was Europe's first school dedicated to teaching the techniques of art, and the pieces here were collected as models for students to draw and paint. The most famous work is Michelangelo's 1504 *David*, which made his name as the pre-eminent sculptor and which was moved here from the Piazza della Signoria in the 19th century. There are other works by the master, as well as important paintings by Florentine artists of the 15th and 16th centuries.

Continue down Via Ricasoli, then turn left into Via degli Alfani to pass, on the left, the Museo dell'Opificio delle Pietre Dure, founded in 1588 by the Medicis as a centre of inlay and mosaic work. Turn right into Via dei Servi, which leads you past a palazzo with a fine high loggia, to the north-east end of the duomo, where you will find the recently reopened ⑨ **Museo dell'Opera del Duomo**. This museum features original artworks from the duomo, campanile and baptistry, including the panels from the *Gates of Paradise*. The sculpture collection contains works by Donatello and Michelangelo, including the latter's unfinished *Pieta*.

Finally, if the baptistry was closed when you were here earlier, now is your chance to view its stunning interior.

Loggia dei Servi

N

FIUME ARNO

Piazzale Michelangelo

S. Miniato al Monte

Viale Galileo

Piazza d. Cavalleggeri

Via Magliabechi

Corso dei Tintori

Via dei Benci

Piazza S. Croce

④

Via Ghibellina

V. d. Vigna Vecchia

③

Ponte alle Grazie

Via dei Leoni

Piazza della Signoria

②

①

Via dei Calzaiuoli

Via dei Belvedere

300 m

200

100

0

Lungarno Torrigiani

Ponte Vecchio

Costa di San Giorgio

Forte di Belvedere

Piazza S. Trinita

Ponte S. Trinita

⑨

Borgo San Jacopo

Via Guicciardini

GIARDINO DI BOBOLI

⑤

Sdruc. de' Pitti

Piazza dei Pitti

⑥

FS

Piazza C. Goldoni

Ponte alle Carraia

Lungarno Guicciardini

⑦

Piazza Santo Spirito

Via Sant' Agostino

Via S. Monaca

Borgo San Frediano

Piazza del Carmine

⑧

DON'T MISS:
① Galleria degli Uffizi
④ Santa Croce
⑧ Cappella Brancacci
⑨ Ponte Vecchio

WALK 2: SOUTH & OLTRARNO

*From the city's seat of civic power and artistic heart, we cross the Arno to visit formal gardens and seek out an art masterpiece.*

Start this walk in **Piazza della Signoria**, the city's political hub for centuries and an outdoor sculpture gallery. A bronze plaque in the centre of the square marks the site of Savonarola's execution. The late 14th-century **Loggia della Signoria** shelters more statues, such as Cellini's bronze of Perseus with Medusa's head. Left of the loggia is a narrow *piazzale* leading to the entrance of ① the **Galleria degli Uffizi**, Italy's greatest gallery, so named because the 16th-century building held offices or *uffici* of Cosimo I. This collection, bequeathed by the Medicis, allows you to trace the evolution of Italian art from its Byzantine origins, through the heady Renaissance, to the Mannerist period, via many remarkable paintings. Giotto, Uccello, Leonardo da Vinci, Michelangelo, Raphael, Titian, Veronese and Caravaggio are just a few of the

Palazzo Vecchio >

< Neptune, Piazza della Signoria

'headline acts', but perhaps the most amazing works are the lyrical and enigmatic paintings by Botticelli. There are 44 rooms of masterpieces; Florentine Renaissance works are concentrated in the first 15.

Back on Piazza della Signoria stands the crenellated, medieval ② **Palazzo Vecchio** or Old Palace. This was designed in 1299 by Arnolfo di Cambio as the seat of government. Cambio, who also designed the duomo, gave his name to the 94-metre-high Torre d'Arnolfo. Cosimo I moved his residence here in 1540 and had the building renovated, including the courtyard. Upstairs, you can view the magnificent Salone dei Cinquecento, the Quartiere di Eleanora (Cosimo's Spanish wife) and other lavish chambers.

Even if you don't wish to view the apartments, you can stroll freely through the courtyard of the palazzo, re-emerging in Via di Leoni, named for the lions once kept at the back of Palazzo Vecchio. Turn left and walk through Piazza San Firenze. Beyond this, on the left, is the **Badia Fiorentina**, an abbey founded in 978 and rebuilt several times. If it's open, take stairs to the right of the altar to view the frescoed Chiostro degli Aranci; *aranci* or orange trees once grew

Santa Croce

here. Across the road is the
③ **Palazzo del Bargello**, begun in 1254 for
commanders of the local militia. Many
people were tortured and executed in its
courtyard, entered from Via Ghibellina. The
palazzo now houses a museum dedicated
to sculpture, particularly of the Florentine
Renaissance, and to decorative arts. There
are master works by Donatello and
Michelangelo, and glazed terracottas from
the workshops of the della Robbia family.

Walk back around the Bargello and turn
onto Via della Vigna Vecchia. Continue on
Via Lavatoi, then turn right into Via G.
Verdi to reach the large piazza, the scene
of past gladiator fights, executions and
jousting tournaments. Here stands
④ **Santa Croce**, a Franciscan church begun
in 1294, though the façade and campanile
are actually 19th century. The church's
massive interior contains the tombs of
Michelangelo, Machiavelli and Galileo and
a monument to Dante. There are also
chapels frescoed by Gaddi and Giotto, plus
many other artworks.

The 15th-century cloisters and Cappella

Giardino di Boboli >

de' Pazzi were designed by Brunelleschi
shortly before he died, and the chapel is a
masterpiece of line and proportion.

From the church and cloisters, turn left
and walk down Via Magliabechi, then left
again into Corso dei Tintori. Make a sharp
turn right and walk along the Fiume Arno,
to cross over on Ponte alle Grazie. The
Roman settlement of Florentia was confined
to the river's north bank. When the south
bank was settled, it was known simply as
Oltrarno, 'beyond the Arno'.

Head right along the Lungarno Torrigiani
towards the Ponte Vecchio and take Via
Guicciardini uphill to the imposing
⑤ **Palazzo Pitti**. The Pitti family of bankers
weren't averse to demonstrating their
wealth and commissioned grand plans from
Brunelleschi in 1448. Their fortunes
declined, however, (in part due to the cost
of the building) and in 1549 they sold the
palazzo to Cosimo I who extended it. Today
it houses several museums, the most
important being the Galleria Palatina,
which displays paintings from the 16th-18th
centuries in lavish apartments.

From the courtyard of the palazzo, you
can buy a ticket and enter the extensive
⑥ **Giardino di Boboli**, or Boboli Gardens.
Designed in 1549 and opened to the public
in 1766, the gardens are dotted with antique

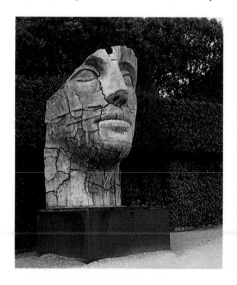

Ponte
Vecchio >

statuary, grottoes and fountains. A café or Kaffeehaus offers some refreshments, but it would be better to bring your own.

Outside once again, cross the Piazza dei Pitti and walk down the narrow Sdrucciolo di Pitti, then straight on. Much of this character-laden quarter is populated with workshops of artisans and restorers. You soon reach the basilica of
⑦ **Santo Spirito**, with its flaking baroque façade. Inside, the church is another of Brunelleschi's late designs, begun in 1444 and a beautiful example of Renaissance architecture. Its 38 side altars are decorated with artworks, including a *Madonna and Saints* by Lippi in the right transept. The high ceiling is painted with a coffered effect; a cost-saving technique.

Walk through the Piazza Santo Spirito, admiring Palazzo Guadagni's high loggia on the left, and turn right along Via Sant' Agostino and then along Via Santa Monaca to arrive at the unfinished façade of **Santa Maria del Carmine**. This 13th-century church was rebuilt in heavy baroque style after a fire, but through a side door you can visit a rare jewel,
⑧ **the Cappella Brancacci**. A merchant named Felice Brancacci commissioned frescoes for the chapel in about 1424. Most of the work was carried out by the young Masaccio, whose breakthroughs in dramatic realism and perspective inspired many Renaissance artists. The frescoes had to be completed by Lippi; Masaccio had left for Roma and died there at age 28.

Cross the piazza, used as a carpark, and turn right along Borgo San Frediano. Take the first street left to reach the Arno at the Ponte alla Carraia (by an excellent *gelateria*) and walk along the bank to the Ponte San Trinita. Here you must detour inland along Borgo San Jacopo, passing, on the left, the church of San Jacopo and, on the right, two medieval towers. The second of these is opposite a short lane to Hotel Lungarno, where there is a good river viewpoint.

You soon reach and cross over the
⑨ **Ponte Vecchio**, lined with ancient shops. There has been a bridge on this spot since Roman times; this one was built in 1345. Originally the shops held tanneries and other trades that dumped refuse into the river, but in 1593 they were replaced by goldsmiths. The enclosed passageway above is the Corridoio Vasariano, built in 1565 to allow the Medicis to walk from Palazzo Pitti to their offices. The Germans spared only this bridge when they retreated in 1944.

Walk straight on and then turn right along Via Vacche Reccia to regain Piazza della Signoria.

## OTHER EXCURSIONS

A visit to Firenze is incomplete without a walk up to **Piazza Michelangelo**, high above the Arno. Cross the river to the Oltrarno and walk up Costa di San Giorgio to the **Forte Belvedere**, built in 1590. Follow Via di Belvedere along to Piazza Michelangelo, adorned with a statue of David and offering a wonderful panorama. Now walk up Viale Galileo Galilei and climb steps off to the left to the church of **San Miniato al Monte**, an excellent example of Toscan-Romanesque style.

The ancient town of **Fiesole** is set on hills some 8 km (5 miles) north of Firenze. As well as offering stunning views over the city and the coutryside, it has several sites of interest, including its duomo, an archaeological museum and a well-preserved Roman theatre. Nearby lanes offer the option of a pleasant country walk. Catch one of the frequent #7 buses from the railway station in Firenze, up the winding road to Fiesole's Piazza Mino.

A view of the Florentine hills

< Mosaics in the baptistry dome

### OPENING HOURS

| | |
|---|---|
| Duomo (S.M. del Fiore) | Mon-Sat 10-5; Sun 1-5 |
| Battistero | Mon-Sat noon-6.30; Sun 8.30-1.30 |
| Campanile di Giotto | daily 9-5.30 (till 7.30 in summer) |
| Santa Maria Novella | Mon-Sat 7-noon, 3.30-6; Sun 3.30-5 |
| Cappelle Medicee | Tue-Sat 8.15-5; selected Sundays 8.15-2 |
| Pal. Medici-Riccardi | daily 9-7 in summer (check at other times) |
| Museo di San Marco | Tue-Sat 8.15-1.30; selected Mons & Suns |
| Chiostro dello Scalzo | Mon, Thur & Sat 8.15-2 |
| S.S. Annunziata | daily 7.30-12.30, 4-6.30 |
| Galleria d.Accademia | Tue-Sun 8.15-6.50 |
| Opifico Pietre Dure | Mon & Wed-Sat 8.15-2; Tue 8.15-7 |
| Museo dell'Opera | Mon-Sat 9-7.30; Sun 8.30-1.40 |
| Galleria degli Uffizi | Tue-Sun 8.30-6.35 |
| Palazzo Vecchio | Mon & Wed-Sat 9-7; Tue 9-2 |
| Badia Fiorentina | Mon-Sat 3-5 |
| Museo del Bargello | Tue-Sun 8.15-2; selected Sundays |
| Santa Croce | Mon-Sat 9.30-12.30, 3-5.30; Sun 3-5.30 |
| Giardino di Boboli | daily 8.15-5; closed selected Mondays |
| Santo Spirito | Mon-Tue & Thu-Sun 8-12, 4-6; Wed 8-12 |
| Cappella Brancacci | Mon & Wed-Sat 10-5; Sun 1-5 |

# LUCCA

NOTES
Population: 85,000
Getting there: bus from Firenze, Torino,
    or Pisa; rail from Firenze or Pisa
Tourist Office: Piazzale Verdi
    Tel:0583 442811 Fax:0583 442502
    email: uffturismo@comune.lucca.it
    www.comune.lucca.it
Markets: Via dei Baccettoni
Note: many monuments close Monday

When you cross the band of grass to enter the gates of Lucca, or climb up, as we did, through one of the narrow passageways in a bastion of the walls, you enter a whole new world. Or, rather, an old world. Lucca is a charming medieval city, small and intimate, where you can walk unhindered by cars and overwhelmed by splendid churches. It's no museum; this is simply a town prosperous enough to eschew the uglier aspects of urban life.

Settled early by local tribes who prized its location on a very fertile plain, Lucca became a Roman town around 180 BC. It has retained the two perpendicular streets of a Roman military camp, but the Roman amphitheatre evolved in the medieval era to become the wonderful Piazza Anfiteatro. Lucca's alleyways and oblique piazzas also developed in the Middle Ages, a time when the city flourished from its silk industry and from agriculture.

Prosperity also came from pilgrims who came to see the *Volto Santo*, a wooden crucifix said to have been carved by Nicodemus, eyewitness to the crucifixion. It supposedly came to Lucca from the Holy Land of its own volition, by crewless boat and then by unmanned ox-cart. Its fame was spread by Lucca's merchants and it brought money and influence. The town's architectural wealth belies its size and provincial status; it boasts not one but three of Italy's most exquisite Romanesque churches, reason alone to visit.

The city fell briefly under the control of Pisa but an adventurer, Castruccio Castracani, led the Lucchesi to regain their independence and expand their territory. After his death, Lucca slipped from its powerful status to being a quiet, wealth-amassing republic until the French arrived in 1805. Napoleon's sister, Elisa Baciocchi, was given rule of Lucca and managed it with great ability while patronising the arts. A strong musical tradition existed in Lucca, even before the composer Giacomo Puccini was born here in 1858.

Not much has changed in Lucca over the centuries. Silk is still manufactured here and the region remains a producer of excellent olive oil. Devoted Lucchesi still bear the *Volto Santo* through the streets in a twilight procession on 13 September. Residents ride through the walled town on bicycle and the city walls remain intact for you to stroll along.

Puccini enjoys the view

San Michele in Foro >

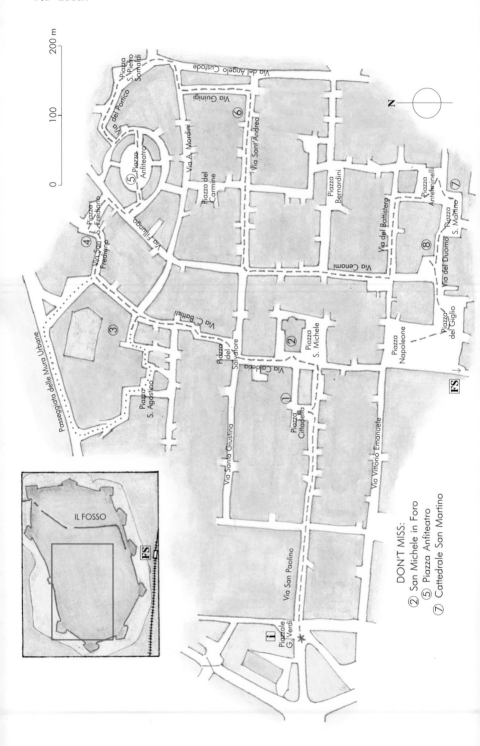

DON'T MISS:

② San Michele in Foro
⑤ Piazza Anfiteatro
⑦ Cattedrale San Martino

## A WALK IN LUCCA

*This route leads you around the web of medieval lanes west of Lucca's Fosso or ditch; according to the Lucchesi, this is the fashionable side of town.*

Our route starts in Piazzale G.Verdi, just inside the city walls, where out-of-town buses arrive and where you'll find a helpful tourist office.

Walk down Via San Paolino, a charming street leading to the centre of the walled town. On the right is the baroque church of **San Paolino**, dedicated to the first bishop of Lucca. You soon detour left into Piazza Cittadella, where there is a naturalistic bronze tribute to Puccini, who sits near ① **Museo Casa Puccini**. The composer was born here in 1858 and was later organist at San Paolino. The small museum contains his Steinway and other memorabilia.

Further along is Piazza San Michele and the stunning façade of ② **San Michele in Foro**, the most ornate of Lucca's trio of magnificent churches. As the name indicates, this piazza was once the Roman forum and is still the hub of town life. The church was built between the 11th and 14th centuries, but lack of funding prevented the raising of the nave, giving the fanciful façade an airy, floating appearance. The decoration mainly features pagan designs, save for the winged San Michele on high. The simple interior features a painting by Filippino Lippi and a chapel known as the Rifugio dei Peccatori, or the Refuge of Sinners.

Turn right out of the church and walk up Via Calderia to Piazza del Salvatore where there's a fountain. The 12th-century church of **San Salvatore** has a simple façade with a Moorish influence.

Walk up the twisting Via Cesare Battisti, then detour left to visit the privately owned ③ **Palazzo Pfanner**, built at the turn of the 18th century. It's possible to visit the apartments, but of more appeal is the small but beautiful garden, featuring statuary and a fountain. For a view of the garden, without the expense of the ticket, you can skirt Sant'Agostino to climb the city walls for a short distance.

Continue along Via Cesare Battisti and turn left into Via San Frediano to arrive at the front of ④ **San Frediano**. This 12th-century basilica was built before the Pisan influence was established in Lucca and it features a Byzantine-style mosaic on its façade (being restored at time of writing) in place of the usual loggias. The interior is beautifully Romanesque and features the remarkable Fonte Lustrale, a huge 12th-century baptismal font carved by three sculptors from quite different schools.

A nearby chapel holds the remains of St Zita, a local maidservant who, when caught red-handed giving the household's bread to the poor, found that the contents of her apron had been miraculously transformed into flowers. Her feast day is celebrated on 27 April when flowers fill the piazza outside. Across the nave, another chapel features

Giardini Pfanner

< Piazza Anfiteatro

16th-century frescoes by Aspertini, one of which depicts the arrival of the *Volto Santo*. Another shows San Frediano, an Irish monk who reputedly brought Christianity here in the 6th century, saving Lucca from flood.

Cross Piazza Frediano and turn right briefly into Via Fillungo, then left through an arcade and into the surprising ⑤ **Piazza Anfiteatro**; its aerial view graces many a tourist brochure, but it is still impressive from the ground. Much of the stone from the Roman amphitheatre that stood here was pillaged for other buildings, including San Frediano. Medieval houses were then built on the foundations, and slums grew up in the centre. These were cleared in 1830 at the order of the Bourbons (who held Lucca for a while after the French) to reveal the oval shape once more.

Leave the piazza by the passageway opposite, where you'll see remains of original columns embedded in the exterior. Turn left and then right into Via del Portico, which curves past the church of San Pietro Somaldi. Soon, turn right into Via Mordini then left into Via Guinigi. Turn right under the walls of the **Palazzo Guinigi**, built by Paolo Guinigi, who held political power in the beginning of the 15th century, and arrive at the entrance of ⑥ **Torre Guinigi**, distinctive on Lucca's

skyline because of the ilex trees growing on its roof! There were once a vast number of such towers in Lucca, which goes to prove that some things do change here. A climb to the top, up some 230 steps, provides a panorama over lovely rust-red rooftops.

Keep on along Via Sant'Andrea and then left into Via Fillungo, the 'long thread' and Lucca's main street, on which many old shops and cafés stand. You soon pass the town's clock tower, **Torre del Ore**, perhaps best viewed from outside the lovely façade of the deconsecrated San Cristoforo.

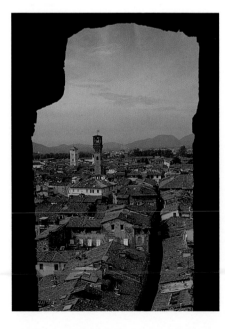

View from Torre Guinigi >

Keep on along Via Cenami, passing San Giusto on your right, and turn left into Via del Battistero then right at Via Donnino to reach Piazza Antelminelli, which features a fountain. You are now at the corner of ⑦ **Cattedrale San Martino**, the duomo of Lucca. Its campanile was begun in 1060 as a defensive tower and proved an inconvenience when the cathedral was rebuilt in the 11th century, hence the asymmetry of the Pisan-Romanesque façade. Nicola Pisano probably carved the relief above the left portal; the others are by the building's architect, Guidetto da Como. The interior is Gothic and features a 15th-century *tempietto* designed by local Matteo Civitali to house the *Volto Santo*. This venerated 'Holy Face' is now thought to be a 13th-century copy of a Byzantine work, rather than a contemporary image of Christ.

The famous tomb of Ilaria del Carretto has been removed from the duomo and is now displayed in the nearby **Museo della Cattedrale**. Ilaria, who died in 1405, was the young second wife of the powerful Paolo Guinigi. Sienese sculptor Jacopo della Quercia created the beautiful marble portrait of the young woman, who appears merely asleep, with her dog at her feet. The museum contains other treasures removed from San Martino.

Cross the piazza to gain entrance to ⑧ **San Giovanni**, Lucca's original duomo, rebuilt over the ages, but still with a Romanesque portal. Excavations have revealed various archaeological remnants inside the large basilica.

Walk along Via del Duomo to pass, on your left beyond a piazza, the 1817 **Teatro del Giglio**. Your walk ends in the spacious

Detail of San Martino's façade

**Piazza Napoleone**, cleared by the Bourbons and edged by the Palazzo del Governo.

## OTHER EXCURSIONS

The **city walls** are the most recent defensive ramparts to ring Lucca and were completed in 1645. The open space around them was cleared to prevent any would-be attackers taking cover. Fortunately for Lucca, they were never tested and have been turned into parkland. The ramparts extend 4.2 km (2.6 miles) and are wide enough to walk or cycle on, a particularly enjoyable activity in the late afternoon.

If you have time, wander **over the Fosso**, the canal that marks the edge of the medieval town. The unadorned church of **San Francesco** sits in the middle of this quarter. Just south is **Villa Guinigi**, built for Paolo Guinigi as his out-of-town house, and now home to an excellent museum. In the southeast corner, you'll find the Orto Botanico, Lucca's pleasant botanic garden.

OPENING HOURS

| | |
|---|---|
| Museo Casa Puccini | mid-Mar-Oct Tue-Sun 10-1, 3-6; Nov-Dec Tue-Sun 10-1 |
| Palazzo Pfanner | daily 10-6 |
| Torre Guinigi | Mar-Sep daily 9-7.30; Oct 10-6; Nov-Feb daily 10-4.30 |
| Museo della Cattedrale | Tue-Sun 10-6 (Oct-Mar 10-1) |
| Villa Guinigi | Tue-Sun 9-2 |

# PISA

To almost everyone, Pisa is synonymous with just one thing: the Leaning Tower. Pisans, and those who have stayed in Pisa, know better. For a start, the famous *Torre Pendente*, as they know it, is only one in a quartet of amazing buildings clustered in the Campo dei Miracoli or Field of Miracles. Secondly, the small city is an extremely pleasant place to wander around, and a good base from which to visit Firenze and Lucca.

Before its nearby harbour silted up, Pisa was a great maritime power. It had been a Roman naval base and became an independent republic at the end of the 9th century. In the 11th century, the Pisans won control of much of the Mediterranean after several victories over the Saracens. Much of its consequent wealth went into great public works.

A unique style of architecture—Pisan-Romanesque, displaying a strong Islamic

NOTES

Population: 93,000

Getting there: train from Galileo Galilei airport 5 km (3 miles) south; rail from Genova, Firenze and Roma

Tourist Office: Via Pietro Nenni, 24
Tel: 050 929777 Fax: 050 929764
email: aptpisa@pisa.turismo.toscana.it
www.pisa.turismo.toscana.it

Markets: am M-Sat, Piazza Vettovaglie

influence—developed and informed the later buildings of neighbouring cities. As a complement to architecture, the art of sculpture flourished in Pisa. The greatest masters tended to be simply referred to as Pisano—fortunately they had different first names—and while some were related, others weren't.

Pisa took the side of the Ghibellines in the struggle between Empire and Papacy, making it an enemy of Genova, which defeated Pisa in a 1284 naval battle. Internal political wranglings undermined the republic further and in 1406 the city came under Florentine control. The Medicis were good patrons, re-establishing Pisa's university and giving support to Galileo, who was born here. The great scientist taught here and carried out his famous experiments on gravity, employing the tower's convenient lean.

Today Pisa is a quiet town—apart from the throngs in its northwest corner—and the university is still an important part of the community's life. There aren't so many sights that you'll have to rush, so take it in a leisurely manner. Amble along the looping banks of the Arno with a gelato in hand, or parade up and down the arcaded Borgo Stretto. If you can, wander back to the Campo dei Miracoli after a good dinner; the sight on a fine evening is more affecting than any *digestivo*.

Piazza dei Cavalieri

The Torre Pendente >

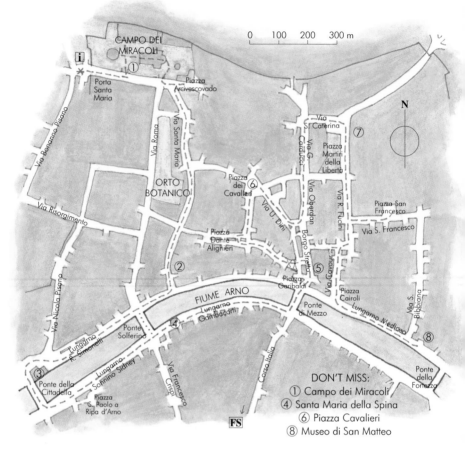

DON'T MISS:
① Campo dei Miracoli
④ Santa Maria della Spina
⑥ Piazza Cavalieri
⑧ Museo di San Matteo

## A WALK IN PISA

*The walk begins with the Leaning Tower (early to beat the inevitable crowds) and becomes a pleasant afternoon stroll around medieval streets with few tourists in sight.*

Pisa's main rail station lies in the city's south, from where it's a 20-minute walk or a #1 bus ride to Porta Santa Maria. Walk through this to the breathtaking ① **Campo dei Miracoli**. This lush green square contains a quartet of wonders, one of the most amazing architectural ensembles the world has known. No postcards or guidebook can prepare you for a first encounter with the exquisite **Torre Pendente**, the campanile begun in 1173 on sandy subsoil. By the time its third storey was completed, a lean—in the opposite

direction to the present one—was evident and corrections were made; the tower, completed in 1350, has a clear curve to it. The sheer weight of the building and its bells made it tilt further over eight centuries and, throughout the 1990s, elaborate work was undertaken to save the tower from eventual collapse. Its recent fetters have been removed and the tower, with its open galleries, once more appears to be spiralling off into the sky.

The immense **Duomo**, begun in 1064, is a solid counterpoint to its bell tower. Its four-tiered façade is the benchmark of Pisan-Romanesque style. Note the original bronze doors, near the Leaning Tower; the artist, Bonanno Pisano, was also the tower's first architect. Due to a fire in 1595, much of the interior is late Renaissance.

Highlights are the monumental pulpit carved by Giovanni Pisano in 1302–11 and Cimabue's 1302 mosaic in the apse.

Nearby stands the **Battistero**, Italy's largest, begun in 1152 on Romanesque principles, but finished a century later in Gothic style by Nicola and Giovanni Pisano. The 1260 pulpit is an early Nicola Pisano masterpiece! The vast interior is plain and the excellent acoustics are demonstrated on occasion by a custodian. You can climb to the top gallery on a narrow staircase.

Behind the baptistry is the **Camposanto**, the 'holy field' filled with soil from Golgotha, brought back by Crusaders. The cloister-like building constructed to house it is a lovely shelter to an array of tombs. Frescoes once covered these walls, but WWII bombs dropped by the Allies set fire to roofing and destroyed the renowned works of Benozzo Gozzoli. A room displays the 14th-century fresco cycle by a master known only for this work, *The Triumph of Death*.

Two museums stand beside the square, and the first is worth a visit, particularly if you've bought a comprehensive ticket. By the tower is the **Museo dell'Opera**, which displays artworks, notably sculptures by Giovanni Pisano, and treasures from Saracen raids and the Crusades. Its garden —this was the cathedral's chapterhouse— is also a lovely quiet spot to rest and enjoy the view. The less interesting **Museo delle Sinopie**, between the souvenir sellers,

The Battistero

contains the monochrome sketches for the Camposanto frescoes.

Tear yourself away from the *campo* and walk down the broad Via Santa Maria. On your left, as you near the Fiume Arno, is ② **San Nicola**, a mid-12th-century church, later enlarged. Its octagonal campanile was designed on mathematical principles set out by 13th-century Pisan, Leonardo Fibonacci. Inside the church is a delightful painting of San Nicola protecting Pisa from the plague.

Now pass under the arcaded walkway connected to the **Palazzo Reale**, which stands on the left-hand corner. Turn right to walk west along the river, past various palazzi, to the Ponte Solferino. If your time is limited cross the bridge; otherwise continue as follows. Walk along the north bank, past the **Arsenale Mediceo**, to the

< Campo dei Miracoli

< Santa Maria
della Spina

③ **Torre Guelfa**, a 15th-century watch-tower built by the Florentines and named the 'Guelph Tower' to distinguish it from a Ghibelline tower built in Pisa earlier. You can climb to the top for a fine view over the city and of the neighbouring Cittadella Vecchia, site of the old shipyards.

From the *torre*, cross the Ponte della Cittadella and walk east, pausing to view the church of San Paolo a Ripa d'Arno before you regain the Ponte Solferino. From this bridge, continue along the south bank to the exuberantly Gothic

④ **Santa Maria della Spina**, built in the early 14th century to house a thorn or *spina* of Christ's crown, and strongly resembling a reliquary itself. The church was originally even closer to the Arno, but was rebuilt here to protect it from flooding. The interior, simpler than expected, has copies of statues from the Pisano workshop.

Keep on along the Lungarno Gambacorti and cross the river once more on the Ponte di Mezzo to reach Piazza Garibaldi. This leads into the arcaded Borgo Stretto, a pedestrian street lined with tempting shops and cafés. On the right is the lovely Roman-esque-Gothic façade of

⑤ **San Michele in Borgo**, built on the site of a Roman temple. Inside the church, you'll find a beautiful crucifix by Nino Pisano.

Turn left into Via della Colonne and weave through these narrow streets past market stalls and small squares to Piazza Dante. This pleasant piazza contains shaded benches, a drinking fountain and several trattorie, making it an ideal spot for lunch or a break. Leave the piazza by the northeast corner where you'll find the church of **San Frediano**, begun in the 11th century, with some original capitals and a 12th-century wooden crucifix.

Walk up Via S. Frediano to the spacious

⑥ **Piazza dei Cavalieri**, possibly the site of the Roman forum, certainly the centre of political power in medieval Pisa. In the 16th century, Cosimo I de' Medici, whose statue stands here, created the crusading Cavalieri di Santa Stefano (Knights of St Stephen). The order made its base here and Vasari designed its buildings. Elaborate *sgraffito*, designs scratched in wet plaster, decorate the **Palazzo dei Cavalieri**, which is now a prestigious college. Opposite stands the archway and tower of the **Palazzo dell' Orologio**, adapted from a medieval tower in which Ugolino della Gherardesca was starved to death, along with his sons and nephews, as punishment for the military defeat by the Genovese in the 13th century. **Santo Stefano**, with its fine wooden ceiling, houses a display of Turkish spoils.

With the church to your left, walk down Via Ulisse Dini, named after a mathematician/politician whose statue you soon pass. Further along, on the right, you pass a 12th-century deconsecrated church (now a bank) featuring two Roman capitals.

Turn right into Via Oberdan, which then becomes Via Carducci, and left into Via S. Caterina to the Dominican church of ⑦ **Santa Caterina**. The lower Romanesque section of the façade dates from 1251; the upper section is Pisan-Gothic. Inside are works by Nino Pisano.

Walk along the parkland of Piazza dei Martiri della Libertà, which replaced the medieval layout in the 19th century, and then straight ahead down Via Renato Fucini. At the first junction, you could detour left to visit the nearby church of **San Francesco**. Otherwise, keep heading south and veer right to look into the narrow alley of Via Mercanti before walking down Via Cavour to Piazza Cairoli. This little piazza was once known as the Square of Derision, as prisoners were exhibited here for public scorn. The 1550 statue that adorns the piazza represents Abundance.

Turn left along the Arno to pass, at #30, the palazzo that was home to Byron from 1821–2 while he wrote *Don Juan*. Continue along Lungarno Mediceo to Piazza Mazzini, where you'll find the ⑧ **Museo di San Matteo**, housed in a medieval convent. Its strong collection comprises artworks from Pisa's churches, including sculptures from the Pisano school and paintings from the 12th-17th centuries.

Torre Guelfa

## OTHER EXCURSIONS

For a good view, climb the **Torre di Santa Maria** in the northwest corner of the Campo dei Miracoli, and walk atop a section of the city walls.

The magnificent **Certosa di Calci** stands 12 km (7.5 miles) to the east of Pisa. This 14th-century Carthusian monastery and church is replete with frescoed chapels and a refectory. To get there, catch an APT bus from Piazza S.Antonio, near Pisa's main rail station, to the village of Calci.

| OPENING HOURS | |
|---|---|
| Duomo | Mon-Sat 10-7.40; Sun 1-7.40 (shorter hours in winter) |
| Battistero & Camposanto | daily 8-7.40 in summer; daily 9-5.40 other seasons |
| Museo dell'Opera | daily 8-7.20 in summer; daily 9-5.20 other seasons |
| Museo delle Sinopie | daily 8-7.40 in summer; daily 9-5.40 other seasons |
| Torre Guelfa | Tue-Sun 11-1.30, 2.30- 6 (summer hours) |
| S. Maria della Spina | Tue-Sun 11-1.30, 2.30- 6 (summer hours) |
| Museo di San Matteo | Tue-Sat 9-7; Sun 9-2 |
| Torre di Santa Maria | June to October, daily 10.30-6.30 |
| Certosa di Calci | Tue-Sat 9-5; Sun 9-1 |

# CHIANTI

**NOTES**
Suggested base: Radda in Chianti
Getting there: bus from Siena or
    Firenze (avoid travelling on Sunday)
Tourist Office: P. Ferrucci 1, 53017
    Radda, Tel/Fax: 0577 738494
    email: proradda@chiantinet.it
    www.chiantinet.it
Map: Kompass #660 1:50000
Best timing: avoid July-August

Il Chianti is, for many, the embodiment of the Toscan idyll: balmy climate, gentle patchwork landscapes framed with stands of cypress, an abundance of olive oil and excellent wines. It lies between the two great cities of Firenze and Siena, edged to the east by the Monti del Chianti and to the west by Val di Pesa and Val d'Elsa. This is the 'Chianti Classico', from 1716 the oldest official wine-producing area. Though not far from the rolling San Gimignano hills, Chianti's terrain is less tamed; the soil is not as fertile, the hills higher and more craggy and thick woodland covers steeper slopes.

Inevitably, Chianti's charm has attracted wealthy expatriates. This gentrification has helped restore farmhouses abandoned after the 1960s when laws turned crop-sharing peasants into lowly paid farm workers. Tourists are easily absorbed by numerous *agriturismo* and winery accommodations throughout the countryside. The few scattered towns remain small and relatively unaffected. The quiet and mostly unpaved roads, farm lanes and cart tracks are ideal for those who enjoy Toscan cuisine and fine wine after a day's walk.

In your travels you'll come across the Gallo Nero or 'black cockerel', the trademark for Chianti Classico wineries. It was once the heraldic symbol of the 1384 Lega di Chianti or Chianti League, a defensive alliance of the three towns: Radda, Gaiole and Castellina. Prior to this, Chianti had been victim of the territorial claims of Firenze and Siena, as evidenced by the hilltop *castelli* that pepper the landscape.

Radda in Chianti, the most convenient base for these walks, is Chianti's most attractive town, spread along a high ridge and visible from afar. Its tiny medieval heart contains several choices of accommodation; book ahead in summer.

Our first two walks leave from Radda, the first heading north to the photogenic hill village of Volpaia, and the second south via a succession of remote Romanesque churches and exquisite *borghi* to the market town of Gaiole in Chianti. Walk 3 involves a return bus trip to Greve in Chianti and visits one of Toscana's most beautiful abbeys, Badia a Passignano.

A word of warning: in late autumn the *vendemmia* or grape harvest adds interest to a Chianti walk; however, this is the start of hunting season so expect loud noises in the forests, particularly on weekends.

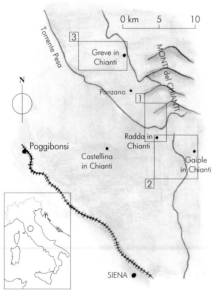

Grapes ripe for the *vendemmia* >

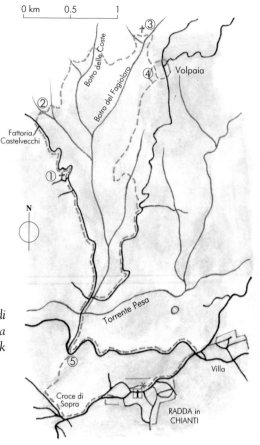

# WALK 1: VOLPAIA LOOP

*North of Radda, watching over the Val di Pesa, sits the fortified village of Volpaia, a charming destination for a half-day walk along lanes and woodland paths.*

| | |
|---|---|
| Distance | 14.5 km (9 miles) |
| Time | 4 hours |
| Difficulty | easy–moderate |
| Start/Finish | Radda in Chianti |

Leave Radda by its northeast gate and walk past the little cinema towards the district of Villa. Cross the overpass and fork right, then turn sharp right to walk under the bridge and west along the minor road for almost 2 km (the path is #52). After a sharp curve the road forks; take the right fork signed to Volpaia and cross Torrente Pesa. Soon fork left on the road signed to S. Maria Novella that ascends past a small fishing lake and up through ivy-wrapped woods to the 12th-century

① **Pieve di Santa Maria Novella.** The Romanesque church has a pretty setting with views of Radda from its terraced lawns; to see inside, ask next door for the key.

Continue on the road uphill as it winds past an old *borgo*, now the grand Fattoria Castelvecchi, an *agriturismo*. Just before a shrine, take a gravel track right down the hill. Where the track curves south to enter the gates of a residence, look for

② **an overgrown track** sharp left uphill. This soon narrows and climbs through woodland, traversing the head of the gully. Cross a small stream and emerge onto a gravel drive (belonging to an *agriturismo*) where you turn right down a dirt track. Pause at a clearing to admire the ridgetop view of Volpaia, framed by olive groves. Swing left down between olive trees and left again on a grassy track to traverse another gully and cross a stream.

At a large flat rock marked with directions, a detour left takes you in a few minutes to the small forest chapel of

③ **Madonna del Fossato.** Return to the signed rock and continue on, reaching a row of cypresses to enter

④ **Volpaia** near an ancient well. This medieval village probably marked the territorial border of Siena and Firenze. As well as a maze of covered passageways, it still has the castle keep at the centre of a small square. Also of interest is the deconsecrated Commenda di Sant'Eufrosino, built in the 15th century and now host to exhibitions. A bar, which serves food, stands in a *piazzetta* by the 13th-century dungeon.

Leave by steps to the right of the bar and then keep right to descend on a gravel track (#52) with red-and-white waymarks. Descend an avenue of cypresses, the Viale del Nonno, with Radda in view ahead. At a fork, keep left to Cassetto and then right at the next junction. Keep on the main path that veers left to cross a stream and rises to reach a gravel road. Turn right downhill and then right onto the paved road.

Follow this downhill and turn left at the junction (where you were earlier) to cross Torrente Pesa once again. Climb to the main road junction but then try the following short cut (it's a bit rough but cuts out much road walking). Cross the road at the switchback and pick up a faint ⑤ **footpath** signed #52. Climb through overgrown scrub and then keep left below

Santa Maria Novella

vines. Head through more scrub and over a ditch, then left along more vines and follow the creek uphill to exit at the drive of Podere Compassole. Turn left onto the road that climbs uphill with a lovely view of Radda. It brings you to the district of La Croce, where signs of Etruscan settlement have been unearthed. Turn left for the last leg into Radda, being wary of traffic.

Volpaia >

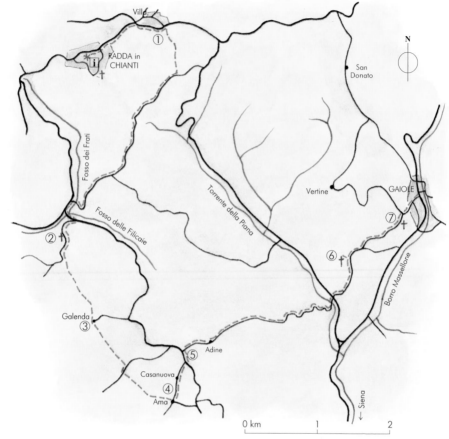

## WALK 2: RADDA TO GAIOLE

*A string of isolated churches and lovely hamlets leads you across country to the market town of Gaiole in Chianti.*

| | |
|---|---|
| Distance | 15 km (9.3 miles) |
| Time | 6 to 6.5 hours |
| Difficulty | moderate, some rough ground |
| Start | Radda in Chianti |
| Finish | Gaiole in Chianti |
| Transport | taxi from Gaiole, or walk |

Leave Radda east as for Walk 1, cross the overpass and fork right along the Gaiole road. You soon pass Albergo Villa Miranda on your right; now turn right down a lane signed to Agriturismo Canvalle. You are now on path #68, which you follow all the way to Ama, with sporadic red-and-white waymarks to guide you.

Cross a stream and keep right as you climb uphill past the medieval

① **Torre di Canvalle**, now someone's house. Keep left on path #68 and, once on the ridge, head right on a level track that soon passes a wooden cross. Shortly after, you gain a good view across the valley to Radda, though this is not its best side. The track continues southwest along the ridge and, at a junction, you turn right. The track now descends to cross the Fosso dei Frati and meet a road.

Turn left and continue on the paved road to cross Fosso delle Filicaie. After a further 150 m, take the lane up to the right that leads to the

② **Pieve di San Giusto in Salcio**, an 11th-century parish church by a shady wall. Built on the site of an Etruscan temple, the church has a beautiful outlook.

Walk uphill past the church and through the ancient *borgo* to where the road loops right and you turn left on a trail with red-and-white waymarks. Now keep right along an old stone wall, ignoring left forks. The track descends to cross a minor stream and rises to the photogenic farm buildings of ③ **Galenda**. Here you'll find a water tap once you've walked through a pretty passageway. Barking dogs will herald your coming and going. Continue on along a grassy path by an ancient drystone wall. The path then descends to an electricity substation and rises again. Go through an iron gate, closing it behind you, to pass left along olives and vines and then exit by another gate to reach a road.

Turn right and, at a nearby shrine, turn left on a stony track. Pass through a gate and head down along vines. Head right, past a dam, skirt a clump of bushes and then head uphill on a grassy track between vines to exit by another gate and reach the delightful *borgo* of ④ **Ama**. There is a bench in the *piazzetta*,

by the church of San Lorenzo ad Ama, and you'll find a tap to the right of the church door, making it a good spot to have some lunch and enjoy the neat buildings.

Pass the church and turn left on a road waymarked #68, which descends by vines and climbs to a winery at Casanuova di Ama. Continue ahead uphill and reach a chapel by a paved road. Keep left and walk on for 250 m, then turn right onto ⑤ **a dirt road** waymarked #66 to Adine. Keep the farm buildings of Adine on your right as the road dips and rises. As you round a hill, you gain a view of the fortified village of Vertine across the valley. Pass the buildings of San Bastiano and then fork right (red-and-white waymarks) on a track through light woods.

You now have a long descent on a rough stony track, with compensating views. From left to right in the foreground are Vertine, the hamlet of San Piero, and the *castello* of Meleto. At the bottom of the hill, you pass a power station and cross a paved road diagonally left to pick up a gravel track (#66, signed to S.Piero). Head uphill to a

The hamlet of Galenda

< Santa Maria a Spaltenna

tower and veer left to detour briefly to the abandoned church of

⑥ **San Piero in Avenano.** Note the ruins of an oven nearby. Backtrack a little and pick up the track heading off left downhill

midway between the church and the tower. This passes vines and then some scrub, before veering left uphill to pass a ruin and then swings right, above more vines. Now head to the splendid Romanesque

⑦ **La Pieve di Santa Maria a Spaltenna.** Built before 1060, this was a monastery and then a castle. The adjacent buildings are now upmarket accommodation.

From the church, head down the paved road to the market town of Gaiole. The heart of the town, its large triangular piazza, lies across the main road and over a stream. Here you can enjoy a well-earned gelato, before you head back to Radda. As there's no bus service, you'll need to arrange a taxi (try Tel: 0577 749258).

If you have to walk back, return to the junction just below Pieve di Spaltenna and take the road signed for Vertine. From this lovely village, continue on the road, north through San Donato and then turn left along the paved road to Radda, a distance of 9.5 km or 6 miles.

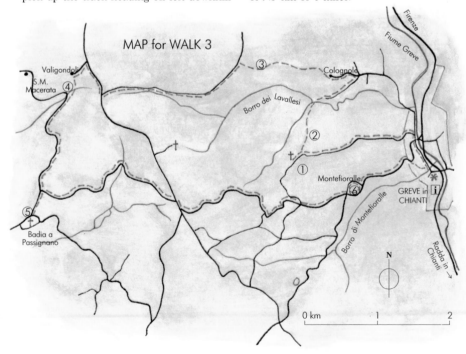

MAP for WALK 3

# WALK 3: BADIA A PASSIGNANO

*Greve in Chianti is the starting point for this longer walk above the Lavallesi valley to the majestic abbey of Passignano and back via the hilltown of Montefioralle.*

| | |
|---|---|
| Distance | 18.5 km (11.5 miles) |
| Time | 7 to 7.5 hours |
| Difficulty | moderate |
| Start/Finish | Greve in Chianti |
| Transport | bus from Radda and return |

If staying in Radda, this walk requires an early start. For lunch, there is a trattoria in Valigondoli and another by the Badia; otherwise take lunch supplies. From Radda, catch an early SITA bus to Greve in Chianti. From the triangular Piazza Matteotti, take Via Roma north. Pass a turn-off left signed to Montefioralle and cross a stream, then turn left onto Via di Zano, waymarked with a yellow triangle.

Walk up past the stately Fattoria Zano. At a cross, make a short detour left to ① **Chiesa di San Cresci**, a mainly 12th-century church with a façade of limestone and terracotta. Back at the cross, take the dirt track passing right of a telegraph pole; there's a yellow triangle on a vine support.

*Funghi in Chianti woodland*

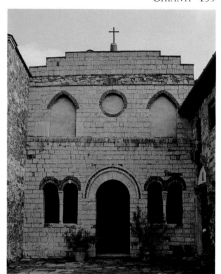

San Cresci

With Colognole in sight and a row of trees about 100 m ahead, watch carefully for ② **a pile of stones** on the left, indicating a footpath forking left into the trees. Take this path to descend through woods and come out at a paved road, where you turn right uphill, following yellow waymarks. The track becomes gravel and you turn left at a junction to climb to the gated villa of Colognole, which has a lovely outlook.

At gates, the track veers right. Just 50 m on, turn left on an unwaymarked track that passes below a stone wall and contours through lovely mixed woods. Almost 1 km on, just before the track rises and curves left, look carefully for ③ **a right-forking footpath**, heading uphill into the woods. Emerge at vines and head towards ruined farm buildings; beyond these you soon reach a track junction. Take a sharp left, once more following yellow waymarks. Soon keep right at a small ruin and then pass a dwelling to reach the paved road. Turn right uphill and, in a few minutes, turn left on a road signed to ④ **Valigondoli**. The handful of houses in this charming hamlet boast street numbers, and there is even a trattoria here where you can eat a hearty lunch.

Badia a Passignano

Follow the road left downhill before the trattoria and you soon reach a broader gravel track. Turn left onto this to contour around a hill and get a glimpse of the approaching abbey. The road then descends gently to a paved road. A short detour right leads to a cypress-lined ramp up to the ⑤ **Badia a Passignano**, with its crenellated towers. Probably founded in the 9th century, the abbey is privately owned, but its church is normally open (though restoration is underway). Inside are frescoes and the tomb of San Giovanni Gualberto who founded the Vallombrosan order in the 11th century.

Return to the junction and take Strada di Greve, a quiet country road. After half an hour, you gain a view back to the abbey. Pass an abandoned house where a plaque states that Domenico Cresti (the painter known as Il Passignano for his work in the abbey) was born here in 1558. You join a busier road and, after 100 m, turn left downhill on the road signed to Greve. This is narrow and winding so be wary of traffic.

You soon gain superb views across the valley. The road then dips and you pass a traffic light (a strange sight) and take steps

Montefioralle >

up into the charmingly restored hamlet of ⑥ **Montefioralle**. Make a circuit, anti-clockwise, around its single street and then pick up the road again at the other traffic light. Continue down the looping road. At a switchback, take the lane right to the convent of San Francesco to descend onto Via Roma near Piazza Matteotti in Greve.

## OTHER WALKS IN THE REGION

### Vertine loop

This walk through woods and vineyards leads to the delightful *borgo* of Vertine. Leave Radda east as for Walk 1 but stay on the Gaiole road and, just after the Monte-varchi turn-off, take the unpaved road left, signed to Vistarenni, descnding into woods.

At a sharp loop right, a detour 800 m up the road leads to **Vistarenni**, a 16th-century baroque villa and now a winery. Otherwise, ignore the DO2 waymark and keep straight on a grassy track. This heads through scrub, along vines, veers right briefly over a tiny stream, then along more vines. At a track junction, step over low electrified wire and head straight up to a ruin. Continue to **San Donato in Perano** and keep on the road south (path #50), forking left after 800 m to reach 10th-century, fortified **Vertine** after another 1.2 km.

Enter the *porta* and veer right of the bar to the 11th-century Romanesque church of San Bartolomeo. Leave the village at the far end and descend by a stone wall. Keep right at a junction to rise through woods and emerge at vines with a view back to Vertine. Head right to descend steeply by vines and cross a stream. Keep right, joining another track downhill. Turn right at a paved road, walking on a parallel footpath. Turn left on a gravel track that winds up past various villas. At a junction, turn right and head north for 1 km. Take a rough track forking left, heading northwest and bringing you to the convent of Santa Maria, on the edge of Radda. *Allow 4 hours.*

A busy street scene in Vertine

Piazza Ferrucci, Radda

## Albola ring walk

This pleasant route in the Monti del Chianti northeast of Radda takes you through forests of wild boar to the perched hamlet of Albola and then back on a scenic road by beautiful vineyards. Take lunch supplies and water with you. If you have a car, you would do well to drive to the Selvole turn-off and so avoid the road walk near Radda.

Leave Radda on the easterly road and, after the overpass, veer left down through woods. About 1.6 km further on, turn right on the quiet road signed to Selvole (paths #50/52). In just over 2 km you reach the lovely hamlet of **Selvole**, where there is a public telephone and church, but little else.

Return 500 m or so along the road, then turn right on a track uphill, signed to Pescinale. Before buildings, turn sharp right uphill. Just before the next dwelling, take a track left uphill (#52), winding up through chestnut wood. Eventually you pass an abandoned farm, Podere San Marco. Keep right at a sign warning of chemical hazard to ascend between berry thickets. At a path junction, keep right (left leads up to Monte Maione ruins). Continue uphill, ignoring left forks. At a broad junction with a red-and-white waymark, another track joins in from the right; keep straight on, now descending on path #00. Track #31 soon joins in from the right. At a clearing where four tracks converge, take the unmarked track left. Ignore a cross-path and keep right to skirt past new vines and a villa.

The track improves and sweeps around to **Castello di Albola**, privately owned, but detour down for a close view of the 12th-century *castello*. Return to the junction and take the road left. At the next road junction, turn left for a winding, pano-ramic descent over vine-clad hills, passing the Fattoria d'Albola and the hamlet of Bugialla before you reach your earlier turn-off for Selvole. Keep straight on and climb the hill back up to Radda. *Allow 5.5 hours.*

# SIENA

The medieval jewel of Siena is immediately enchanting. From the moment you enter its gates, you can't help but love this intimate city, with its beautiful piazza of Il Campo, its narrow lanes and its medley of attractive Gothic buildings. Even the setting contributes: it sits atop three ridges of red clay—giving us the hue 'burnt sienna'—with rural Toscana lapping at its very edges.

Legend would have it that the city was founded by Senius and Acius, the sons of Remus; hence the many she-wolves on view. More likely, it was an Etruscan settlement that evolved into a Roman one, named Saena Julia.

Siena's trade in textiles and skill at banking made it a major European city, a prosperous, independent republic that rivalled and fought Firenze. During the 13th century, Siena was governed by the Council of Nine, men of the middle or merchant class, responsible for many of Siena's fine buildings. Art also flowered in this period, with such painters as Duccio di Boninsegna, Simone Martini

NOTES

Population: 55,000

Getting there: SITA bus from Firenze; rail from Firenze (via Empoli) or Roma (via Grosseto or Chiusi), then local bus

Tourist Office: Piazza del Campo, 56

Tel: 0577 28055 Fax: 0577 281041

email:aptsiena@siena.turismo.toscana.it

www.siena.turismo.toscana.it

Markets: La Lizza, Wednesday 8-1

and the Lorenzettis developing a style full of decorative detail and brilliant colouring.

The glory days came to an abrupt halt with an outbreak of plague in 1348. Within five months, two-thirds of the city's population had died, dropping from 100,000 to 30,000. The city went into decline, putting an end to such plans as an extension of the duomo. Siena's native-born saints, Caterina and Bernardino, held sway over the people's hearts during two more episodes of plague. Internal conflicts left the way open for outside control, first by the Milanese Viscontis and then by the tyrant Pandolfo Petrucci.

Finally, in 1555, Charles V took the city following a two-year siege that decimated the population once more. Siena was soon handed on to Firenze's Cosimo de'Medici, who clamped down hard, forbidding any Sienese to operate banks.

The city's swift decline goes a long way to explaining the extraordinary state of its preservation. Little was built or demolished after the plague tragedy. Later, Siena avoided the damage that many other Italian cities suffered in WWII. It has prospered once more since then.

Factional rivalries are still the basis for life in Siena. It is divided into 17 *contrade* or districts, each with its own heraldic emblem, typically an animal. These feature on the fountain and church of each

Tethering ring, Palazzo Piccolomini

Palio flags adorn an alleyway >

*contrada*, as well as on its banner. A banner or *pallium* is the prize in the famous Palio, a wild, twice-yearly horse race around the Campo, contested by the *contrade* since the 13th century. No matter whether you're there for the Palio (on 2 July and 16 August) or not, it's on everyone's minds for much of the year.

Siena is brimming with fascinating sights and we've tried to encompass most of them; as a result, the itinerary is fairly full! If you can manage two or more days in Siena—highly recommended—you could break up the walk for greater enjoyment.

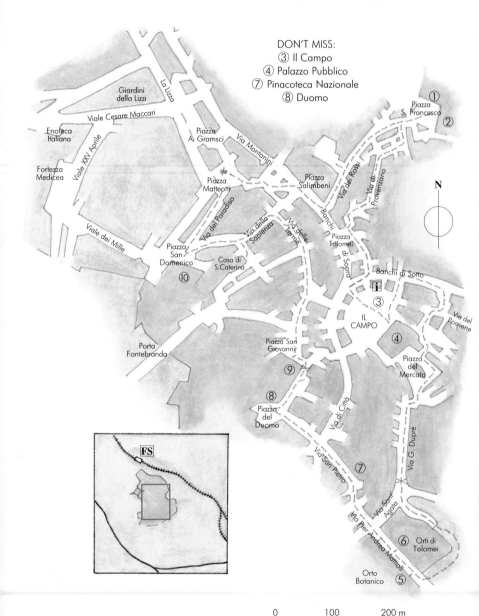

DON'T MISS:
③ Il Campo
④ Palazzo Pubblico
⑦ Pinacoteca Nazionale
⑧ Duomo

0    100    200 m

Il Campo

## A WALK IN SIENA

*This walk in Siena encompasses art-crammed buildings, winding medieval lanes and many panoramas, plus quite a lot of footwork!*

This walk starts in Piazza Matteotti, a destination for buses from the rail station below the city and near to the stop for intercity buses. Leave the piazza by its southeast corner, on the broad Via Pianigiani. You soon reach **the Piazza Salimbeni**, hemmed in by palazzi, all of which form the headquarters of the Monte dei Paschi di Siena, the 1472 charity-turned-bank that has largely underpinned Siena's recovery.

Continue down Banchi di Sopra then turn first left down Via dei Rossi. Detour briefly into Via dell'Abbadia to view the façade of San Donato (now housing the bank's art collection) and the rear of the late-Gothic Palazzo Salimbeni. Keep on down Via dei Rossi, veering right to reach the brick façade of the

① **Basilica di San Francesco**. A fire damaged this large church in 1655 and it was later used as a barracks, so it is now quite spartan. At the end of the right aisle is the 14th-century tomb of the Tolomei, housing various members of a leading Sienese family.

Right of the basilica is the

② **Oratorio di San Bernardino**, containing various artworks but, most importantly, an upper chapel filled with 1496-1518 frescoes depicting the *Life of the Virgin*.

Cross the piazza and walk up Via di Provenzano, passing the baroque, white marble **Santa Maria di Provenzano**, then veer right into Via del Moro to reach Piazza Tolomei. From here, walk south down Via Calzoleria and turn right into Banchi di Sotto, to skirt the **Torre di Roccabruna**, a once high tower cut short in the 16th century. Turn left into Vicolo di San Pietro by the 1417 **Loggia della Mercanzia**, to enter the immense and beautiful space of

③ **Il Campo**. On the likely site of the Roman forum, this was also the intersection of the city's *terzi* or 'thirds' when the Council of Nine planned a civic centre. It was completed in 1349 with nine symbolic

< Palazzo
Pubblico
from afar

segments marked in its paving. At the top of the piazza, flanked by *al fresco* cafés, is the **Fonte Gaia**, fed by a 500-year-old aqueduct and framed with recent copies of original reliefs by Jacopo della Quercia, who hailed from Siena. The gentle slope of the piazza draws the eye to
④ **Palazzo Pubblico**, which set the tone for Sienese-Gothic style. The Cappella di Piazza, the stone loggia on the front, doesn't match well; the council vowed to build it at the end of the terrible plague but funding was slow and architectural tastes had changed by its completion. Above the palazzo soars the magnificent campanile, the **Torre del Mangia**, the last building project before the Black Death struck. Its 500 or so steps can be climbed for stunning views over city and country.

Housed in the upper storeys of the palazzo is the somewhat ill-organised **Museo Civico**, visited not so much for its gallery pieces but for its amazing frescoes that decorate the council rooms. These include Simone Martini's wonderful *Maesta* and the famous equestrian portrait of the mercenary Guidoriccio da Fogliano, attributed to Martini, but the subject of much debate. Among the other glorious frescoes are those that make up Ambrogio Lorenzetti's *Allegories of Good and Bad Government*. These secular images, painted in 1338 and filled with details of medieval life, served as a moral guide for the council.

Leave the Campo by Via Rinaldini and turn right to skirt around **Palazzo Piccolomini**, which houses the city's archives. On the next corner is the **Logge del Papa**, created in 1462 at the orders of Pope Pius II, himself a Piccolomini. Walk up past this and cross Via del Porrione, one of the main streets of Roman Siena.

Take the narrow Vicolo delle Scotte, passing the synagogue in the heart of the Jewish Ghetto created by Cosimo I, and head down steps to Piazza del Mercato. Here you'll find several good trattorie with a view of Palazzo Pubblico's high loggia. The view south is over a surprisingly rural gully.

Zigzag into Via Giovanni Dupré, named after the 19th-century sculptor who was born at #35, to climb a steep hill. At the junction, there is a charming fountain to your left. Just up from this, turn left through the gates of the University Mensa (canteen) and follow the level path around the **Orti di Tolomei** for a wonderful panorama over the countryside. As you exit by a gate, look down the road to Porta Tufa, one of the city gates.

Turn right and head uphill. Soon, a gate on the left offers a detour to the peaceful ⑤ **Orto Botanico**, cunningly arranged on a steep slope and, once again, with views.

Further along on the right, set by a shady piazza, is the portico of

⑥ **Sant'Agostino.** This mostly 13th-century church has been deconsecrated and its airy interior now showcases a remarkable *Crucifixion* by Perugino, as well as paintings by Sodoma, Ambrogio Lorenzetti and others.

Continue up Via P.A.Mattioli, passing a fountain featuring a tortoise (the symbol of this area's *contrada*), and veer right along Via San Pietro to the

⑦ **Pinacoteca Nazionale**, housed in the 14th-century Palazzo Buonsignori. This collection traces Sienese art from the 12th to the 16th century, arranged in chronological order. It's well worth a visit if you can afford the time.

Continue heading north, now on Via del Capitano, to find yourself facing

⑧ **the Duomo**, built on one of the city's highest points. This is one of Italy's most beautiful cathedrals and you may well want to perch on the ancient ledge opposite to enjoy the view. The body of the duomo was completed in 1215 and the lower section of the façade—the work of Giovanni Pisano—by the end of that century. The Romanesque campanile was built in 1313. When the grand plans for the duomo's extension had to be shelved (you can see part of its frame to the right), the decision was made to further ornament the façade and improve the interior.

Inside is lavish by comparison with the duomo in Firenze, with whom the Sienese were competing. The floor is covered with 56 remarkable marble panels, worked in graffiti or intarsia techniques by 40 or so different artists from 1369 to 1547. Sadly, many panels usually remain covered for

Siena's Duomo >

Libreria Piccolomini

protection. Up high, 172 popes peer down at you: if you have binoculars, you'll find their countenances amusing. Nicola Pisano, the father of Giovanni, carved the pulpit in 1266–8, creating a medieval masterpiece.

A doorway in the cathedral leads to the **Libreria Piccolomini**, built in 1495 by Francesco Piccolomini, later Pope Pius III. He commissioned Pinturicchio to fresco it with images from the life of his uncle, Pope Pius II. The detailed pictures are wonderful; look for the storm in one scene.

Opposite the duomo is **Santa Maria della Scala**. In the 11th century, this *ospedale* or hospital was a shelter for the many pilgrims on the Via Francigena, the route from the north to Rome. As such, the institution grew wealthy and patronised the arts, which is why it now houses a major art collection. A series of frescoes depict the charitable work of the *ospedale* in fascinating detail.

Walk alongside the duomo to find the entrance of the **Museo dell'Opera**, housing artworks removed from the duomo. Among these are the original statues by Giovanni Pisano (those now on the duomo's façade are copies) and the famous *Maesta* by Duccio, a painting that influenced Sienese art for centuries.

Walk through the arch of the unfinished nave and descend the steps to find the ⑨ **Battistero** in an unusual location below the church. Inside is a hexagonal Renaissance font decorated with bronze panels by some of the era's finest sculptors: Donatello, Ghiberti and della Quercia. The walls here are also lavishly frescoed.

Cross Piazza San Giovanni and walk along Via di Diacceto, which affords a good view across to San Domenico. Veer left into Vie delle Terme, lined with some wonderful food shops. Turn left into the charming Via della Sapienza and peek into the **Biblioteca Comunale** at #5, a public library housed in ornate surroundings. At the next left, make a short detour downhill to visit the

A taste of Siena >

**Casa di Santa Caterina**, the home and sanctuary of St Catherine (1347-1380), patron saint of Italy, along with St Francis. Caterina took her vows as a child, and following mystical experiences, went out into plague-ridden Siena to give aid. She later played a role in religious politics and was canonised in 1460.

At the top of Via della Sapienza is the imposing Gothic church of ⑩ **San Domenico**, where Caterina performed miracles. Two of the chapels here commemorate her; one contains a portrait painted by her friend Andrea Vanni, another holds the saint's head.

Finally, walk up the flag-lined Via del Paradiso to regain Piazza Matteotti.

## OTHER EXCURSIONS

The **Basilica dei Servi**, near the Porta Romana, is yet another of Siena's major churches. From the Campo, take Via di Salicotto, then Via San Girolamo and Via dei Servi to arrive in the shady piazza of the basilica. The massive brick church contains a Renaissance interior and many fine paintings by Sienese artists, plus one by a Florentine, captured in battle and forced to paint for his release.

**Fortezza Medicea** (also known as Forte di Santa Barbara) is another outlying site

Fortezza Medicea

worth seeing, and a quiet place for a leisurely stroll. From Piazza Matteotti, walk up Viale Federico Tozzi and then through the Giardini della Lizzi to the entrance. Here you'll see signs for **Enoteca Italiana**, a cellar and bar which stocks every Italian wine.

Once in the fort, you can walk atop the walls. Built by Charles V after the terrible siege of 1555, it was torn down by the Sienese and then rebuilt by Cosimo I to garrison his troops.

---

### OPENING HOURS

| | |
|---|---|
| Oratorio di S.Bernardino | daily 10.30-1.30, 3-5.30 (Mar-Oct only) |
| Palazzo Pubblico | daily 10-7; Jul-Aug daily 10-11pm; Nov-March 10-6.30 |
| Torre del Mangia | daily 10-7; Jul-Aug daily 10-11pm; Nov-March 10-4 |
| Orto Botanico | Mon-Fri 8-5; Sat 8-noon |
| Sant'Agostino | daily 10.30-1.30, 3-5.30 (Mar-Oct only) |
| Pinacoteca Nazionale | Mon 8.30-1.30; Tue-Sat 9-7; Sun 8-1 |
| Duomo | daily 9-7.30 (in winter 7.30-1, 2.30-5) |
| Libreria Piccolomini | daily 9-7.30 (in winter 10-1, 2.30-5) |
| Santa Maria della Scala | daily 10-6 (in winter 10.30-4.30) |
| Museo dell'Opera | daily 9-7.30; Oct daily 9-6; Nov-March 9-1.30 |
| Battistero di S.Giovanni | daily 9-7.30; Oct daily 9-6; Nov-March 9-1;2.30-5 |
| Casa di S.Caterina | daily 9-12.30, 2.30-6 (in winter 9-12.30, 3.30-6) |
| Enoteca Italiana | Mon noon-8; Tue-Sat noon-1am |

# PERUGIA

The hill on which Perugia perches has seen more than its share of blood and turmoil. Visitors today will find there a charming city filled with ancient churches and medieval civic buildings, but dig a little and you'll uncover fortifications to control its own citizenry, tombs of murdered popes and street names with echoes of the violence committed there. Plus it has some wonderful cafés!

Early on, the Umbrii settled on the surrounding land but it was the Etruscans who established the hilltown as the most easterly of their 12 city-states. The city had a shifting relationship with Roma but fell under Roman domination in 310 BC when it was named Perusia. Waves of barbarian invasion seriously damaged the city but it survived to surface as a free *comune* under popular rule in the 11th century, growing in power over neighbouring towns, most prominently Siena.

Fighting between the city's nobles, the papal legates and the *priori* (representatives of leading guilds) caused havoc in the city's streets during the 14th century. Several *condottieri* or mercenary leaders exercised power but eventually the Baglioni family, a peculiarly immoral clan even by medieval standards, gained the upper hand. When their last ruler tried to assassinate the papal legate, Pope Paolo III besieged the city and in 1540 Perugia fell to the Papal States. The papacy ruled with a strong hand for three centuries and resisted the Italian Unification, when yet more blood was spilt.

Despite the culture of violence, Perugia produced a wave of Renaissance artists, notably Bernardino Pinturicchio and Pietro Vannucci, known as Perugino and renowned as the teacher of Raphael.

NOTES
Population: 157,000
Getting there: rail via Foligno or
  Terontola (and then local bus from
  station); bus from Roma or Firenze
Tourist Office: Palazzo dei Priori
  Tel: 075 5736458  Fax: 075
  5736828  e: info@apt.umbria.it
  www.umbria.turismo.it/perugia
Markets: below P. Matteotti, M-Sat am

Others—such as the monk Fra Angelico —came to work here. Their works can be seen in the Galleria Nazionale and on the frescoed walls of various buildings. A university town and host to many foreign language students, modern Perugia has a lively cultural scene, hosting the Umbrian jazz festival each summer.

To counter the difficulties of being such a large hilltop city, Perugians have built a number of *scala mobile*—huge escalators— taking pedestrians from various carparks and rail stations below. Much of Perugia now sprawls on the lower ground as ugly suburbs and industry. The main FS rail station lies amongst this but local buses make the trip up to Piazza Italia. Up high, Perugia is revealed as a wonderful medieval city, tumbling away from Corso Vannucci, the café-lined street where Perugians parade.

< Oratorio di San Bernardino

Corso Vannucci

## A WALK IN PERUGIA

*The strung-out hilltown of old Perugia demands a fair bit of footwork and step-climbing. If you are short of time or energy you might omit the excursion north or south.*

At the heart of Perugia lies the spacious ① **Piazza IV Novembre** on the site of a Roman reservoir. Taking pride of place is the recently restored **Fontana Maggiore**, designed in 1277 by the monk Bevignate and sculpted by the Pisano family. The lower basin is the father's work and depicts months of the year, signs of the zodiac and scenes from Aesop's fables, the Old Testament and Roman history. The son sculpted the upper basin with allegorical figures such as that of Perugia herself, bearing fruit.

The construction of the **Cattedrale di San Lorenzo** in the 14th century was interrupted by the Black Death and the pink stone façade still appears unfinished. The baroque interior warrants a brief inspection, but you won't see the Virgin's wedding ring, stored in 15 boxes-within-boxes and housed in the first chapel on the left, unless you're here on 30 July for its annual unboxing.

Opposite the cathedral is the **Palazzo dei Priori**, a fine building that dates from the 13th century. The façade features mullioned windows and, over the main entrance, a Guelph lion and a griffin of Perugia holding chains plundered from Siena. This entrance leads to the Sala dei Notari, the hall of the lawyers, in the oldest part of the palazzo. From another doorway in Corso Vannucci you can enter the Sala del Collegio della Mercanzia, where the merchants' guild met in a chamber decorated with 15th-century inlaid wood panelling.

A few doors further on is the **Collegio del Cambio**, the money exchange with a hall frescoed in 1496 by Perugino and his pupils, including the 13-year-old Raphael. The theme they depicted—the harmonious integration of classical and Christian cultures—was propounded by a humanist, Maturanzio. Perugino managed to slip in a self-portrait. As if this wasn't enough, the **Galleria Nazionale di Umbria** lies on the second floor of the palazzo, reached through an ornate doorway. This is an amazing collection tracing the development of Umbrian art, with masterpieces by locals Pinturicchio and Perugino, as well as by artists from outside, such as Duccio, Fra'Angelico and Piero della Francesca.

Walk a short way down Corso Vannucci and turn right through an archway into Via dei Priori. Pass Via della Gabbia on your right: the *gabbia* was a hanging cage in which prisoners were held. Pass the 13th-century Sant'Agata on the left and 17th-century San Filippo Neri on your right to walk below the medieval **Torre degli Sciri**, one of many that once rose above Perugia. Veer left before the Etruscan-Roman Porta Trasimena onto Via San Francesco to pass the tiny church of Madonna della Luce, which boasts an impressive altarpiece. Cross the grassy piazza, possibly lolled upon by art students from the nearby academy, to ② the **Oratorio di San Bernardino**, an extraordinary piece of polychromatic design.

< A doorway, Palazzo dei Priori

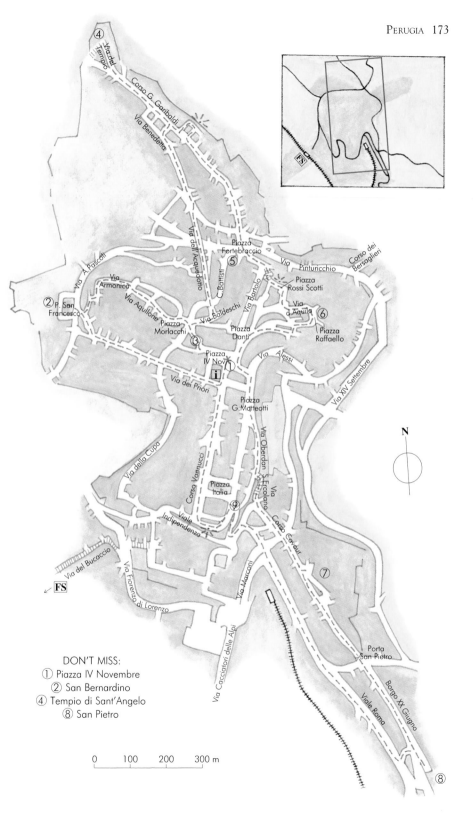

DON'T MISS:
① Piazza IV Novembre
② San Bernardino
④ Tempio di Sant'Angelo
⑧ San Pietro

0   100   200   300 m

Acquedotto Duecentesco

Created in 1461 by Agostino di Duccio, it is a delightful combination of bold effect and interesting detail, including San Bernardo's Bonfire of the Vanities in the lower frieze. Its simple interior is rarely open.

To the right of the *oratorio* are the ruins of the once-magnificent San Francesco al Prato, built in the 13th century but brought down by earth movement. Cross back over the road and turn left into the narrow Via della Siepe. At the end turn right to climb steps, then left to follow alongside an Etruscan wall on what becomes Via Armonica and pass the Palazzo Florenzi on your left. Zigzag into Via Aquilone and walk through Piazza Morlacchi and into Piazza Cavallotti. Here detour briefly to view one of the most picturesque medieval alleys: ③ the winding **Via Maestà delle Volte**, with its series of high-flying arches. Return to Piazza Cavallotti and turn right into Via Baldeschi but soon take steps left to cross Via C. Battisti.

Here you have a choice: you can save time by following Via Battisti along to Piazza Fortebraccio and skipping a few paragraphs. But to see Perugia's oldest church, continue on to the northern extreme of the old city by first climbing more steps to Via dell' Acquedotto, once an aqueduct, now a raised footpath. Follow this some 400 m to descend by the monastery of S. Benedetto and turn right to reach Corso G. Garibaldi. Turn left and walk along this to pass two monasteries on either side of the road, then veer right up Via del Tempio to the ④ **Tempio di Sant'Angelo**, in a tranquil setting surrounded by cypresses. This lovely circular church was built in the 5th century. The two rings of pillars inside its otherwise austere interior are from an earlier building, possibly a Roman temple on this site.

Retrace your steps and follow Corso G.

< Tempio di Sant'Angelo

Arco di Augusto >

Garibaldi south, detouring briefly along Via Canerino for views over the Parco di Sant' Angelo. Continue on to Piazza Forte-braccio, named after the 14th-century ruler 'Strong Arm'. On your right is the Palazzo Gallenga, the seat of Perugia's university for foreigners, established by Mussolini. Ahead is the

⑤ **Arco di Augusto**, which was the main entrance to the Etruscan city. The lower level is the work of 2nd century BC masons. The Romans added the upper arch; the loggia on top is 16th century.

Walk past the front of Chiesa di San Fortunato and along its side to the steps of Via delle Prome which lead up into the quarter of Porta Sole and to Piazza Rossi Scotti, where there is a magnificent view over the Umbrian countryside. From there, climb to Piazza Michelotti and take Via dell'Aquila to Piazza Raffaello and

⑥ **San Severo**, a chapel supposedly built on the site of an Etruscan temple to the sun. Inside this reworked church is an early work by the young Raphael. The panels below it were painted by an aging Perugino.

Head west, skirting another church, to the pleasant Piazza Danti where there is an Etruscan well that can be visited. Walk south back to Piazza IV Novembre and turn left into Via Calderini then right to pass the Palazzo del Capitano del Popolo, the home of the old law courts, and veer left into Via Oberdan. Steps on the left lead down by the octagonal Sant'Ercolano (on the site where Perugia's first bishop was beheaded by Goths) to busy Corso Cavour.

Turn left and follow this south to ⑦ the church of **San Domenico**. It has lovely stained glass and the tomb of the poisoned Pope Benedict XI, carved in fine Gothic style. The neighbouring ex-convent now houses the **Museo Archeologico**, with a good collection of Etruscan artefacts.

Continue on through the double arch of Porta San Pietro, built in 1147, and straight on Borgo XX Giugno to the 10th-century

⑧ **Basilica di San Pietro**, with its landmark pointed 15th-century bell tower. The entrance is tucked away in a courtyard. Inside the basilica is sumptuously decorated, with an excellent choir stall carved in the 15th century and paintings by Perugino and Caravaggio, some of which are hidden in the sacristy.

Nearby are the Giardini del Frontone, 18th-century gardens of great charm. Return to the city centre, for variation along Viale Roma. Where the road curves sharply continue straight on past the Tre Archi and left into Viale Indipendenza then sharp right to Via Marzia to remnants of the

⑨ **Rocca Paolina**, a huge 16th-century fortress built by Pope Paolo III Farnese in 1540 to control the city. The fortress incorporated an Etruscan archway that leads to a subterranean medieval street known as Via Bagliona. The stronghold was so hated that it was destroyed by the people of Perugia on Italian unification. The area was subsequently covered to create the gardens above and it was only during excavation for the contextually bizarre

< The view from the Porta Sole district

escalator that this section was unearthed. Take the escalator up to gain Viale Indipendenza once again. Turn left and skirt the Giardini Carducci for another good Umbrian view then parade with the citizens of Perugia down Corso Vannucci to complete the walk.

## OTHER EXCURSIONS

The **Ipogeo dei Volumni** is a wonderfully preserved Etruscan burial complex 3.5 km (2 miles) southeast of San Pietro. You could combine a walk there with the San Pietro leg of the main itinerary.

Continue on Borgo XX Giugno beyond the buildings of San Pietro and turn left down Via Benedetto then immediately right into Via San Costanzo, descending steeply. Veer left into Via Piscille Strada and, after the road curves, turn right on a road that takes you to Via Assisana. Turn left to follow this Assisi road for 500 m then turn left onto Strada del Cimitero. Follow this, ignoring a lane left and right and then keep left as the track curves around and passes under the *autostrada* to the site.

The hypogeum dates back to the 2nd century BC and contains the tombs of the Volumnio family. Entry is restricted to a few people at a time, so it remains an evocative place. To return to Perugia, walk west along Via Volumnia to nearby Ponte San Giovanni and catch a train to Perugia's station or a bus directly up to the city centre.

San Pietro

If you haven't yet had your fill of Perugia you could visit **Santa Maria di Monteluce** on the eastern wing of the upper city, beyond its ancient walls. From Piazza Fortebraccio, head east on Via Pinturicchio to pass through the Arco dei Tei and veer left along Corso Bersaglieri. Pass through Porta di San Antonio and turn left on Via Cialdini which leads past medieval workshops to Piazza Monteluce and the attractive 13th-century church with its pink-and-white stone façade.

| OPENING HOURS | |
|---|---|
| Sala dei Notari | daily 9-1; 3-7 |
| Collegio della Mercanzia | M-Sat 9-1, 2.30-5.30; Sun 9-12.30 |
| Collegio del Cambio | M-Sat 9-12.30, 2-5.30; Sun 9-12.30 |
| Galleria Nazionale | daily 9-7; closed first Monday of each month |
| Sant'Angelo | Tue-Sun 9.30-noon, 3.30-6.30 |
| San Severo | daily 10-1.30, 2.30-6.30 |
| Rocca Paolina | daily 6.15-1.45 |
| Museo Archeologico | M-Sat 9-1.30, 2.30-7; Sun 9-1 |
| Ipogeo dei Volumni | M-Sat 9-12.30, 4.30-6.30; Sun 9-12.30 |

# UMBRIAN HILLTOWNS

NOTES

Suggested base: Assisi

Getting there: rail from Perugia or Foligno; bus from Roma or Firenze

Tourist Office: P. del Comune, Assisi, Tel: 075 812534 Fax: 075 813727 email: info@iat.assisi.pg.it www.umbria.turismo.it

Maps: Kompass #663 1:50000 and IGM #131

Best Timing: spring and autumn

Dotting the landscape of landlocked Umbria are delightful hilltowns, often surrounded by a sea of olive groves and vineyards. Walking in this region is a very civilised affair: history and culture abound and there are the added benefits of the *tartufo nero* and *porcini* (black truffle and mushrooms) to be enjoyed, along with *Sagrantino* wine.

The 'green heart of Italy' has long been prized as fertile land and was settled by the 8th century BC by the Umbrii, a farming tribe described by Pliny as the oldest in Italy. Their successors, the Etruscans, built hilltowns that they could defend. In 217 BC they sided with Roma to defeat Hannibal under the walls of Spoleto. The Via Flaminia, built to connect Roma to Rimini, passed through Umbria, increasing its strategic importance and

prosperity; many Roman hilltowns were built along this road. Throughout the Dark Ages, Umbria was a battleground fought over by Byzantium, Goths, Lombards, the Papacy and Holy Roman Empire.

Christianity flourished early here—St Benedict, the father of monasticism, came from these parts—and Umbria's hills are dotted with sanctuaries. Assisi became renowned as a pilgrimage site when its monk Francesco (or Francis) was sanctified in the 13th century.

Our first walk is within and below the walls of Assisi, which has enough to keep you enthralled for a full day. Walk 2 visits the mountain hermitage of St Francis and heads over Monte Subasio to Spello, a charming Romanesque hilltown. Walk 3 follows the *Sentiero degli Ulivi*, 'the olive path', up and down terraced hillsides, past ancient sites between the hilltown of Trevi and Campello in the Vale of Spoleto. There is plenty more walking to be enjoyed in Umbria: further east lies the beautiful but less accessible meadowland of the Piano Grande.

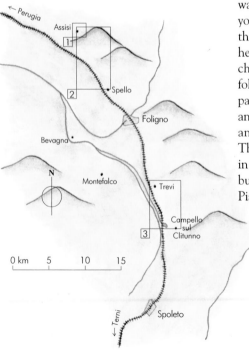

Ruins of San Cipriano, near Campello >

## WALK 1: AROUND ASSISI

*A focal point of Christian pilgrimage, Assisi is also an enticing town set on a foothill of Monte Subasio. Avoid Christmas and Easter and enjoy a walk around its medieval streets and down to the outlying San Damiano.*

Distance     9 km (6 miles)
Time         6 hours
Difficulty   easy
Start/Finish Assisi's Piazza del Comune

Assisi's origins date back long before the monk Francis lived here from 1182 to 1226. Occupied by the Umbrii and then the Etruscans, it became the Roman city of Assisium. Like many Italian hilltowns, the old town sits well above its nominal rail station, some 2 km (1.3 miles) below. A bus shuttles between the station and the terminal in Piazza Matteotti. This walk starts in the secular heart of the town, ① **Piazza del Comune**, fringed by a number of interesting buildings. The most eye-catching of these is the 1st-century-BC **Tempio di Minerva**, which has one of the most perfect Roman façades in all of Italy. It was converted to a church in 1529 and its 17th-century interior is less spectacular. The tower next door was built in the 13th century by Ghibelline supporters. Also in the piazza is the **Palazzo Comunale** which contains the *pinacoteca*. You can view excavations of the **Foro Romano** (Roman forum) which once lay here, accessed from Via Portica. (Leave these sites till later so you can view the basilica of San Francesco before the tour groups gain entry).

Leave the piazza along Via Portica. This becomes Via Fortini, then Via del Seminario as you pass an ex-seminary and then, once through an archway, Via San Francesco. On your left is the 13th-century Monte Frumentario and, further along, the ② **Oratorio dei Pellegrini**, a 15th-century building that served as a pilgrim hospice. Its walls are covered with exquisite frescoes.

Further down the road, on the right, is the 13th-century Casa dei Maestri Comacini, which housed the masons' guild and was so named because many of the basilica's builders were from Como. Dominating this end of town, on the old execution site known as the Hill of Hell (but since changed to the Hill of Paradise), is the monumental ③ **Basilica di San Francesco**, a somewhat odd tribute to a saint who espoused the simple life. Composed of two churches built one above the other between 1228 and 1253, it is an astounding medieval architectural feat. An earthquake in 1997 damaged some of the buildings and much effort was

< Assisi
from below

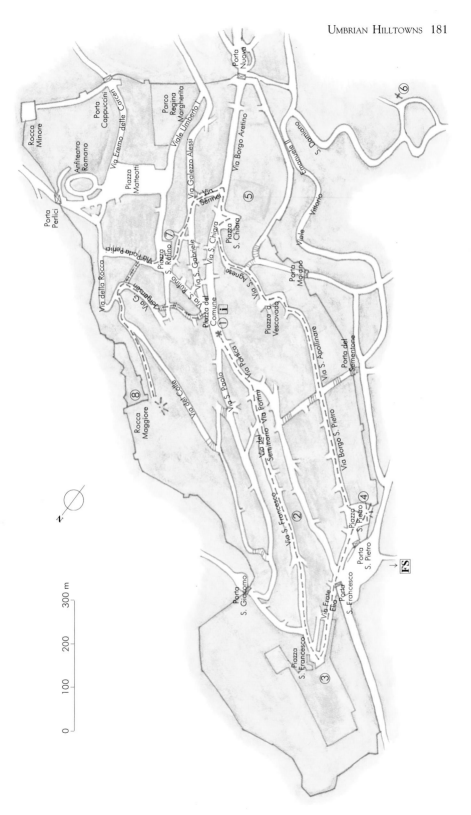

< Tempio di Minerva

Walk along Via Borgo S. Pietro which becomes Via S. Apollinare as it approaches the church of that name. Keep on to the Palazzo Vescovile and another Romanesque church, Santa Maria Maggiore, Assisi's first cathedral. Cross Piazza del Vescovado and turn right onto Via S. Agnese which winds along to the Gothic

⑤ **Basilica di Santa Chiara**. Chiara was a companion of Francis who rejected her wealthy background and founded the Order of the Poor Clares. Locks of her hair, which Francis symbolically cut off, are kept here and her body is in the crypt. The church, built between 1257 and 1265, was originally quite plain; the buttresses had to be added a century later to prevent collapse.

The interior was stripped of its frescoes in the 17th century and is now quite bare. A chapel from San Giorgio, the church that stood on the site previously, contains the cross that bowed to Francis and commanded that he rebuild the church (which Francis proceeded to do literally at San Damiano just out of Assisi). The 1997 earthquake caused damage here and the basilica may still be closed for repair.

Now is a good opportunity to detour to a lovely shrine below Assisi. Walk along Via Borgo Aretino to leave the town by Porta Nuova. Follow signs southwest through a carpark and descend through charming olive groves for just over 1 km to

⑥ **San Damiano**. This small 11th-century

spent repairing and fortifying them.

The lower church is Romanesque and relatively subdued, the upper one is light and airy. Both were frescoed by Italy's greatest 13th- and 14th-century painters: Cimabue, Giotto, Martini and the Lorinzetti brothers. Francis is buried in the crypt below, which remained concealed from outsiders until 1818.

Leave the basilica by the lower piazza and walk along Via Frate Elia and then Piaggia San Pietro to the pleasant Piazza San Pietro, from where there are excellent views over the Vale of Spoleto and of

④ **Chiesa di San Pietro**, with its tiered face and rose windows. The 13th-century church was originally Benedictine. Its spare interior is mainly Romanesque with Gothic touches in its vaulted ceiling and pointed arches.

A rose window, San Francesco >

< A distant view of Santa Chiara

fortress gains you entry to a museum of gruesome medieval implements, but the view outside its walls is worth the climb alone. You can see over Assisi and across the patchwork Vale of Spoleto to the Martani hills.

Return down the road to San Lorenzo and then turn right onto Via G. Jorgensen. Just before a church, S. Maria delle Rose, turn left down steps to cross Via S. Maria delle Rose and continue down the stepped Vicolo della Fortezza. This brings you back to the Piazza del Comune, where cafés offer well-earned refreshments.

church remains much as it was when St Francis wrote the *Canticle of the Creatures* here. St Clare founded the adjoining convent and died here in 1253.

Return to Santa Chiara and walk up Via Sermei. Continue over the road and up Via Dono Doni which brings you to the spacious Piazza San Rufino in front of the duomo or ⑦ **Cattedrale San Rufino**. Its substantial three-tiered façade dates from 1140 and is adorned with three rose windows. The sturdy Romanesque campanile competes with it for size. The interior was altered in the 16th century but it still houses the font used to baptise Francis, Clare and also Emperor Frederick II who was born nearby. This church too may be closed for repair.

Leave the piazza along Via Porta Perlici but soon veer left up the stepped Vicolo San Lorenzo, which climbs to join the Via della Rocca. Turn left onto this and follow it to climb all the way to the ⑧ **Rocca Maggiore** or the big fortress, to distinguish it from the smaller one on the western boundary. These were raised to assert papal authority in the 14th century, but there were probably fortifications around Assisi from long before. Visiting the

San Rufino and the Vale of Spoleto

| OPENING HOURS | |
|---|---|
| Foro Romano | daily 10-1; 3-5 or 7 |
| Pinacoteca | Tue-Sun 9-12, 4-7 |
| Oratorio | daily 9-12, 3-8 |
| San Francesco | daily 7-7 |
| Santa Chiara | daily 7-12, 2-sunset |
| San Damiano | daily 10-12.30, 2-6 |
| Rocca Maggiore | daily 10-sunset |

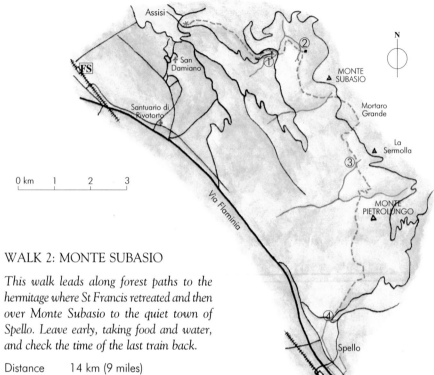

## WALK 2: MONTE SUBASIO

*This walk leads along forest paths to the hermitage where St Francis retreated and then over Monte Subasio to the quiet town of Spello. Leave early, taking food and water, and check the time of the last train back.*

| | |
|---|---|
| Distance | 14 km (9 miles) |
| Time | 7 hours |
| Difficulty | moderate (800 m ascent) |
| Start | Assisi |
| Finish | Spello |
| Transport | train and bus back to Assisi |

The route leaves Assisi from the Porta Cappuccini on the Via Eremo delle Carceri to the city's east. Outside the gate you immediately turn sharp left onto a red-and-white waymarked track (#50) which initially follows the city wall up to the Rocca Minore. Ignore a left diversion (#51) and ascend steeply a stony track for almost an hour with great views of the Vale of Spoleto to the right. The path levels and presently meets the hairpin Assisi/Monte Subasio road. Turn right and follow this downhill, and soon detour slightly to visit the
① **Eremo delle Carceri**. Set in a wooded gully, the hermitage, with its minute church hollowed out of the rock, became an occasional retreat for Francis and his followers. Since the 14th century the *eremo* has been a 'working' monastery and the

monks still live off the alms they receive, but Francis's tiny cell (*carcere* means 'enclosed space') has been preserved along with his stone bed and wooden pillow.

Back at the road, turn right and follow it uphill for 5 minutes then, at a sharp bend, turn left uphill on a waymarked woodland path. Later the path swings right and eventually meets a track and reaches the
② **Rifugio di Vallonica** (1059 m). Soon, you pass foundations and a water trough.

The path now becomes less distinct over treeless terrain; veer left over a saddle, following waymarks on poles. (A brief diversion is recommended: head towards a promontory marked by a cross for superb views over Assisi.) Head uphill towards communications towers to rejoin the road; follow this right briefly then veer left on trail #50. To the south are fine views of the distant Monti Sibillini, part of the Appennini range that forms the backbone of Italy.

Rocca Minore and the Assisi walls >

Presently the path skirts to the left of a smooth crater, the Mortaro Grande, and then swings right to meet up with another trail and regain the road. Cross the road, look for the path (which can be hard to find) and descend to reach ③ the **Fuente Bregno** at the 1000-m contour line where there are good views, a water hut and a picnic table.

Continue SE downhill and zigzag down to cross the gully and then contour the hill. The waymarking improves now as you descend through low scrub and there are superb views of Spello, the Vale of Spoleto and the distant Martani hills. The way becomes a broad stony path through olive groves and then a paved road which enters ④ the **Porta Montanara**, at the northern end of the elongated hilltown of Spello.

Spello, protected by its much rebuilt walls, rises gently out of the surrounding country-side. It has a Roman pedigree as Hispellium, built in the 1st century BC. This charming Romanesque hilltown is now a quiet backwater, but its six 12th-13th-century churches underline its former importance. While the entire town is worth exploring, the undoubted highlight is the **Cappella**

**Baglioni** in the church of Santa Maria Maggiore, where Pinturicchio's 1501 fresco sequence of Jesus's birth glows with detail.

To return to Assisi, leave the walled town by the southern Porta Consolare and walk along Via Ca'Rapillo to Spello's train station. From here you can catch a train north to Assisi's station and then a local bus up the hill to the town.

The Eremo delle Carceri

## WALK 3: TREVI TO CAMPELLO

*Visit the tourist-free hilltown of Trevi and then continue on a footpath past tiny hamlets and ruins to the lovely Fonti del Clitunno. Take provisions for the day.*

| | |
|---|---|
| Distance | 12.5 km (8 miles) |
| Time | 6 to 7 hours |
| Difficulty | moderate |
| Start | Trevi |
| Finish | Campello |
| Transport | train from Assisi and return |

If you are staying in Assisi, catch a train south to nearby Trevi rail station (from where there is the option of a bus up to the top of Trevi). Walk through Borgo Trevi, the district around the station, cross the Via Flaminia and begin the walk up to Trevi's lowest gate,

① the **Porta di San Fabiano**. Once inside Trevi's outer medieval wall, it is all uphill as you negotiate a wonderful maze of patterned cobblestone lanes. Trevi is most likely an old Roman town. Christianity was promoted here by the Armenian Emiliano, Trevi's patron saint who was martyred by being drowned in the nearby Fonti del Clitunno during the reign of Diocletian. The 12th-century church of Sant'Emiliano occupies the high point of Trevi. The narrow lanes radiating from the church are

< Umbrian olive oil is among the best

particularly atmospheric; the nearby Piazza Mazzini, Trevi's handsome and spacious centre, provides an attractive contrast.

Leave this piazza by the Via Roma and, from the piazza outside Trevi's walls, follow the Via Costa San Paolo then fork left up towards the Impantivi Sportivi. Proceed straight uphill through olive groves on a track waymarked #60 Costa S. Paolo. Keep looking back for the changing views of Trevi as you climb. When you reach a fork, take

< Sant'Emiliano in Trevi

⑤ **Tempietto di Clitunno**. The builders of this tiny church used recycled columns and it was long thought to be Roman. It probably dates from the 5th century and contains faded Byzantine frescoes from the 8th century, possibly Umbria's oldest.

Follow Via Flaminia south for 1 km to ⑥ **Fonti del Clitunno** where natural underground springs collect to form the source of the river Clitumnus. The Romans plunged animals in the *fonti* for purification prior to sacrifice, and Emperors Caligula and Claudius built villas and temples here of which nothing remains. Much later, the poet Byron and artist Corot found inspiration in the scene. Despite the nearby highway, the kiosk and the occasional tourist coach, the springs and willow-lined lake retain a romantic charm.

Follow the road south to a tourist office. If you plan to continue on to Spoleto the next day (see next page) you could stay off to the left in Campello. Otherwise, take the second road right to Campello sul Clitunno rail station in the Sette Camini district.

the right path and turn right at ② **a junction** just below **Costa San Paolo**. You now follow the *Sentiero degli Ulivi*, marked 'S.U.' in red on the map. Take a minor path to the right through woodland to join a wider track downhill to a clearing with a water trough. Continue downhill to reach the isolated Romanesque church of ③ **Sant'Arcangelo**. Proceed down between church and house on a narrow footpath. At a hairpin bend join a wider track and then turn left on a minor road down to a junction. Take the leftmost track uphill and at a Y-junction go right downhill, passing below a cemetery and La Cura church. Head downhill through Pigge and, keeping the village church on your right, regain the track at the corner of a communal wash house. This joins a minor road which eventually becomes a grass track and reaches ④ **Pissignano**. It is worth an uphill detour through the old gate to wander through the attractive narrow streets now occupied by numerous artists. The 13th-century *castello* is dangerously ruinous. From Pissignano take the road down to the highway; cross it and turn right onto a parallel road to soon reach the charming

Fonti del Clitunno

## OTHER WALKS IN THE REGION

### Campello to Spoleto

This route completes the *Sentiero degli Ulivi* above the Vale of Spoleto and could be added to Walk 3 to create a two-day itinerary. Take water and lunch provisions.

From the ruins of San Cipriano (where there is a tourist office) on the Via Flaminia, turn left gently uphill. At crossroads, turn left into Via Alighieri and wind uphill past attractive old villas. At a hairpin bend take a footpath up through woodland for 15 minutes. Turn left on a grassy path and right on a lane. Detour briefly past a sanctuary to the photogenic walled village of **Campello Alto**. A balcony nearby offers wonderful views over the valley.

At a junction take the right-hand road through Lenano then take a path right down through olive groves. Waymarking is poor: you should exit onto the Bianca/Silvignano road near a branch road to Poreta. Continue through **Poreta**, with its 14th-century *castello* towering above the hamlet, and take a footpath left at a shrine.

Ignore a path left (#11); continue past the wooded spur and enter olive groves. Turn left (east) to contour the base of the spur and then right (south). Cross the road near Santa Maria di Reggiano. Pass the church and go straight uphill at crossroads. Fork right to **Bazzano Superiore**, where you keep the church on your left and take the paved road right. There are delightful lanes along this section.

At the next hamlet take the lower path right past Santa Maria. Take a footpath by a wash house, cross an unpaved road and continue down. At a junction, continue down right and through **Bazzano Inferiore**, overlooked by its 14th-century *castello*. The village has a shop and a bus service to Spoleto. Turn left past the church and go left uphill at a fork through woods. At an olive grove, take a track left down to **Eggi**.

Descend to Eggi quarry, visible from a distance (the way is poorly waymarked).

Cross the quarry entrance and climb on a track to a clearing. Follow a track off to the right and very soon take a narrow footpath left which climbs steeply by a fixed rope. The path reaches a disused rail line which can be followed (through two short tunnels and over viaducts) to the outskirts of Spoleto. *Allow 6 to 7 hours.*

A sanctuary by Campello Alto

### Around Spoleto

Combine a visit to the town of **Spoleto** with a loop walk into beautiful nearby countryside. From Spoleto's Piazza Campello, skirt below the Rocca and cross the dramatic medieval aqueduct, Ponte delle Torri, some 80 m high. Pick up the path beyond it that climbs steeply to a church on **Monte Luco**, near the village of the same name.

From Monteluco, follow a minor road to the hamlet of Le Aie and then a path over a bridge. The path heads west, passing through a gallery (you will need a torch) and then north to the church of San Giuliano and then to San Pietro, from where a road walk takes you back to Spoleto. *Allow 4 to 5 hours.*

# ROMA

On a visit to Roma or Rome, there are two things that you must bring: a budding interest in history and a good pair of shoes. Over two millennia of historic evidence lies here, in a jumbled heap on both sides of the curving river Tevere.

The Romans arrived about the 9th century BC, settling on hills along the route of the important salt trade, and joined forces with nearby Etruscans. Centuries later, poets and historians created a legendary beginning: foundation in 753 BC by the wolf-suckled Romulus and Remus.

Roma was a kingdom until the tyrant Tarquin was killed in about 508 BC and it then flourished as a republic, extending its territory by conquering neighbouring tribes and expanding across the seas. The consular system of politics, always fraught, collapsed after the murder of Julius Caesar in 44 BC. Augustus ushered in Imperial Roma, building on a monumental scale funded by taxes from the provinces.

The Roman Empire's decline began in the 3rd century when it was split into East and West; soon after, Constantine moved the Empire's capital elsewhere. The fall came in the 5th and 6th centuries, when Goths and Vandals invaded.

The city regained status as the centre of Christian power. Early on, the bishop of Roma claimed primacy and, over time, the name pope was reserved for that role. The papacy gained control over a large

domain and immense influence as medieval pilgrims were drawn to the city. Various popes patronised the arts, particularly during the Renaissance, and this practice continued—after the sacking of Roma by Charles V—well into the 17th century, giving Roma much of its baroque splendour. Papal rule was once again interrupted by Napoleon and it came to a certain end when Garibaldi won the city in 1870 and made it the capital of unified Italy. Roma was then 'modernised' with the cutting of new roads, including one straight through the ancient fora.

Though much has been lost, much more remains and a visit can be both thrilling and daunting. A walk in Roma is filled with so many unexpected distractions—a stray column here, a Renaissance fountain there—that it is more of a discovery than an orderly tour. We've fashioned three walks, but you may well want to digress. There's a lot to see; fortunately, the weather this far south is usually fine and the city will invite you into its streets.

NOTES
Population: 2,644,000
Getting there: train from Fiumicino airport 30 km (18 miles) southwest; rail from Firenze and Napoli
Tourist Office: Via Parigi, 5
 Tel: 06 488991 Fax: 06 48899238
 www.romaturismo.com
Private agency: info@enjoyrome.com
Markets: mornings, Campo dei Fiori

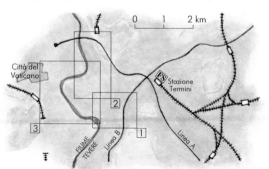

Fontana delle Tartarughe >

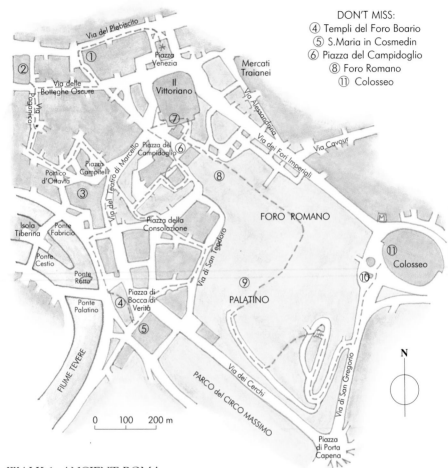

DON'T MISS:
④ Templi del Foro Boario
⑤ S.Maria in Cosmedin
⑥ Piazza del Campidoglio
⑧ Foro Romano
⑪ Colosseo

## WALK 1: ANCIENT ROMA

*This tour takes in many of the monuments of ancient Roma, including the artefacts in the Capitoline museums.*

This is a very full itinerary, albeit around a compact area. You might prefer to break it in two at Piazza Campidoglio. Start at Piazza Venezia, which is a hub for many bus routes. This spacious piazza is flanked to the west by the grand Palazzo Venezia, once home to Mussolini. To its south stands the massive white marble 1911 monument to Vittorio Emanuele II, first king of Italy.

Leave the piazza by the northwest corner and walk down Via del Plebiscito to the nearby 16th-century church of

① **Il Gesu,** an uninhibitedly baroque extravaganza with ornate illusionistic ceilings. This is the mother church of the Jesuits and it's an excellent example of counter-reformation architecture.

From the church, turn left along Via d'Aracoeli and then turn right on Via della Botteghe Oscure, street of 'humble workshops'. Pass the ruins of a temple to reach the Renaissance **Torre del Papito,** which stands at the corner of

② **Area Sacra di Largo Argentina.** This land contains some of the most ancient ruins in Roma, including those of four Republican temples, and is probably the site of Julius Caesar's assassination in 44 BC. The ruins were only discovered in the 1920s and are currently under excavation.

Cross the road and head down Via Paganica. **Palazzo Mattei di Paganica**, on the left, dates from 1541 and has a pretty courtyard that you can glimpse. Continue through Piazza Mattei, which features the delightful 16th-century **Fontana delle Tartarughe**, and along Via Reginella. Turn left into Via del Portico, the main street of the old Jewish Ghetto, to the excavations of the **Portico d'Ottavia**, built in 146 BC.

Just before the church of Sant'Angelo in Pescheria (so named because of the fish market held here in the Middle Ages), head up the narrow alley of the same name and turn right into Via Tribuna di Campitelli to reach Piazza Campitelli, lined with fine palazzi on one side and a baroque church on the other.

Turn right along a busy road to view the remains of the

③ **Teatro di Marcello**, a huge theatre begun by Julius Caesar and completed by Augustus. It was restored in the Middle Ages and used as a fortress by various rulers. The site, littered with columns and fragments of entablature, is currently closed for restoration work.

Turn first right and cross Lungo T. Pierleoni to get a riverside view of San Bartolomeo on the nearby Isola Tiberina. Follow the river south to view **Ponte Rotto**, or the 'broken bridge', which dates from the 2nd century BC. Cross the road once again and take a path down between the

④ **Templi del Foro Boario**, two beautiful and remarkably well-preserved temples from the 2nd century BC. The rectangular Tempio di Portunus was likely dedicated to the god of rivers and ports. The wonderful circular temple, built of solid marble and surrounded by 20 fluted columns, was probably dedicated to Hercules.

Cross the road to visit

⑤ **Santa Maria in Cosmedin**, one of the finest medieval churches in the city. The campanile and much of the decoration date from the 12th century. The mosaic pavement was created by the Cosmati, a Roman guild of marble workers. The portico shelters an ancient drain cover known as the Bocca della Verità or the Mouth of Truth. Folklore tells that the mouth will snap closed on a liar's hand.

Turn right out of the church and cross Piazza Bocca della Verità. Take steps up, left of the 4th-century **Arco di Giano** and

One of the Foro Boario temples >

< Bocca della Verità

of which now house museums. **Palazzo Nuovo** holds a collection of Greek and Roman sculptures; **Palazzo dei Conservatori** has a mixture of ancient sculptures and 17th-century paintings. Both demand a visit, though you might want to do so later, possibly at the end of Walk 3.

If you don't mind more steps, descend on Michelangelo's magnificent Cordonata staircase to climb the neighbouring one (or you could cheat by finding the upper rear entrance) to the 1250 church of ⑦ **Santa Maria in Aracoeli**. Its marble staircase was completed in 1348 in thanks for the end of the plague; it leads to an austere façade. Inside are 15th-century frescoes by Pinturicchio.

Leave the church by the rear to regain Piazza del Campidoglio. Descend the other side of the hill on a path passing the bronze statue of Romulus, Remus and the she-wolf. From a small balcony, there is a view over ⑧ the **Foro Romano**, a long stretch of ruined temples and civic buildings, and the core of political and religious life in ancient

along Via della Velabro. On your left is **San Giorgio in Velabro**, a 7th-century basilica. Veer left along Via di San Teodoro, skirting the walls of the Palatine hill. If the round church of San Teodoro is open, look in at the 6th-century mosaic in the apse.

Now turn into the narrow Via dei Fienili. Cross Via della Consolazione and head up the steps of Via di Monte Caprino. Turn right and climb more steps on Via di Tempio del Giove, passing first the hillock of **Rupe Tarpea**, from which traitors were once jettisoned, and then the temple dedicated to the god Jove.

Further along, skirt right around buildings for a wonderful view, then head up through an arch, an unorthodox entry to ⑥ **Piazza del Campidoglio**. The Capitoline Hill, overlooking the forum, was important to the ancient Romans and, centuries later, during the Renaissance. In the 16th century, Michelangelo was engaged to make improvements for a forthcoming visit of Emperor Charles V. The artist gave the piazza its lovely geometric paving and renovated the façades of the palazzi, both

The Foro Romano >

Roma. This is the earliest of the neighbouring fora; before a road was cut this area stretched north to encompass them.

Descend steps to enter the Forum (if this entrance is closed, walk around to Via dei Fori Imperiali and return to this point). Near the Campidoglio are the eight remaining columns of the **Tempio di Saturno** or Temple of Saturn, built in 497 BC and used as a treasury by Julius Caesar. Walk through the majestic **Arco di Settimo Severo**, erected in AD 203 in honour of Emperor Septimus Severus and his sons.

You are now on the Via Sacra, which runs right through the Forum. To the left is the **Lapis Niger**, a slab of black marble that legend says marks the tomb of Romulus. Beyond this stands the reconstructed **Curia**, the meeting place of the Roman Senate. On the right is the **Colonna di Foca**, which, in AD 608, was the last new monument raised in the Forum.

Further on, set off to the right, are the three remaining columns of a temple dedicated to Castor and Pollux. Next on the right is the area occupied by the **Tempio di Vesta** and the **Casa delle Vestali** or house of the Vestal Virgins, the six young women who tended the sacred flame in Vesta's temple. On the left are various temples converted over the centuries into churches, followed by the remains of the immense **Basilica di Costantino**, completed by Constantine in AD 315.

This brings you to the **Arco di Tito**, built in AD 81 following the sacking of Jerusalem by the Romans. In front of it, turn right to buy a ticket and enter ⑨ the **Palatino**, the city's legendary founding place and the favoured residence of wealthy Romans of the Republic. Head up the steps to the **Orti Farnesiani**, then veer left. Wander around the back of the museum building to the ruins of **Domus Augustana**, the emperor's private residence. Past this is the **Stadio**, probably the emperor's private garden or stadium. Take the steps beyond this and then descend a

The Colosseo

path to exit the complex near toilets. Turn left along Via di San Gregorio to pass the ⑩ **Arco di Costantino**, one of Imperial Roma's last monuments. It was erected in AD 315 to commemorate the newly-Christian Constantine's victory over his pagan co-emperor Maxentius. Most of the reliefs were purloined from earlier monuments.

You are now, of course, standing beside ⑪ the **Colosseo** or Anfiteatro Flavio, the huge amphitheatre begun by Emperor Vespasian in AD 72. It could hold at least 50,000 spectators, seated in four levels. They were witness to bloody battles between gladiators and against wild animals, as well as the occasional sea-battle. With the fall of the Roman Empire, the Colosseo was abandoned, damaged by earthquakes and finally pillaged for travertine and marble.

That ends this first walk in Roma. There is a Linea B metro station nearby or you could return to Piazza Venezia, via the **Mercati di Traiano** or Trajan's Market.

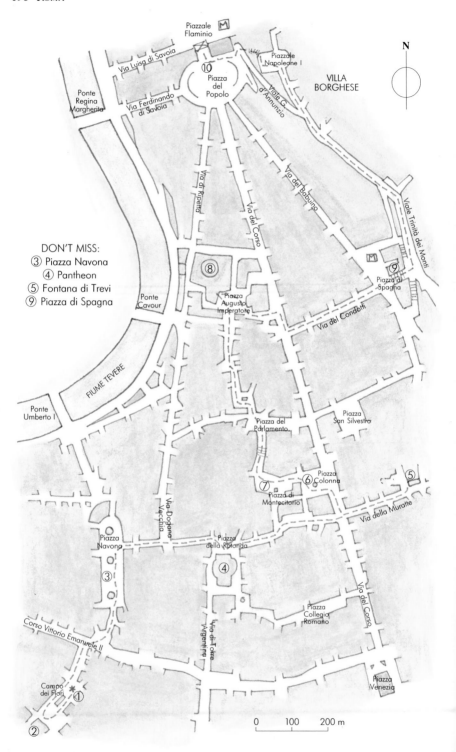

DON'T MISS:
③ Piazza Navona
④ Pantheon
⑤ Fontana di Trevi
⑨ Piazza di Spagna

## WALK 2: PIAZZAS OF ROMA

*Roma is a wonderful city for outdoor life, with its pleasing piazzas and public spaces. This walk takes in many of these much-loved sights.*

Begin at Roma's most appealing piazza, ① **Campo dei Fiori**, where a lively food market is held each morning. The origin of its name is unclear; possibly it was once a meadow or 'field of flowers' or it may have been named after Flora, mistress of Pompey. Standing here is a statue of Giordano Bruno, a philosopher and scientist who was burned for heresy on this spot in 1600.

First, make a short loop south along Via Baullari to view the façade of ② **Palazzo Farnese**. This fine Renaissance building was begun in 1514; Michelangelo had a hand in its design. It is now home to the French Embassy and rarely open to the public. A walk around the block lets you peek through the gate into its lovely garden. The twin fountains in Piazza Farnese are baths from the Terme di Caracalla.

Now walk up Vicolo Gallo and keep straight on alongside the handsome **Palazzo della Cancelleria**. (Glimpse through its gate, if possible, to see the double loggia in its lovely courtyard.) Head diagonally across Corso Vittorio Emanuele II to San Pantaleo, then up the narrow Via della Cuccagna to the long vista of ③ **Piazza Navona**, the city's most beautiful baroque piazza. Its elongated shape follows that of a 1st-century-AD stadium used for races. The fountain nearest you is the Fontana del Moro, named for the Moor holding a dolphin, a figure added by Bernini, Roma's great baroque architect of the 17th century. Bernini's design masterpiece is the central Fontana dei Fiumi, a 1651 fountain that embodies four great rivers: the Nile, the Plate, the Ganges and the Danube. At the far end of the piazza is the 19th-century Fontana del Nettuno, depicting Neptune fighting a sea monster.

Fontana dei Fiumi >

Make a near circuit of the piazza and then leave midway heading east. Cross Corso del Rinascimento and continue in the same direction along the side of **San Luigi dei Francesi**, which houses paintings by the great Caravaggio. Cross Dogana Vecchia and continue down Via Giustiniani to reach the bustling Piazza della Rotonda with its large fountain and, of course, ④ the **Pantheon**, a remarkable temple dedicated to all the gods and the best-preserved Roman monument. The structure dates from AD 118 when it was built, and possibly designed, by Hadrian. Even the massive Corinthian columns supporting the portico (each column is a single stone) can't prepare you for the interior. Construction of this vast dome remains an amazing architectural feat. Light enters from above through an opening or oculus. Some materials were pillaged from the building but it was rescued by being consecrated as a church in 608 and it houses the tombs of two kings of Italy and of Raphael.

You might want to walk around the back of the Pantheon to view Bernini's endearing **Elefantino**. The Egyptian obelisk supported by the white marble pachyderm dates from

the 6th century BC. Otherwise, leave Piazza della Rotonda on Via dei Pastini, passing the **Tempio di Adriano** on your right, then cross Piazza di Pietra and walk along Via di Pietra. Cross Via del Corso and walk along Via della Muratte, a pedestrian thoroughfare lined with bookstalls, to reach the
⑤ **Fontana di Trevi**, no doubt in the company of others. Designed by Nicola Salvi in 1732, this exuberant baroque fountain is built up against the Palazzo Poli. Its name probably derives from its location at the convergence of three roads or *tre vie*. Toss in your coin to ensure your return to the 'Eternal City'.

Return along Via della Muratte, turn right up Via del Corso briefly, then left into ⑥ **Piazza Colonna**, named for its centrepiece. Modelled on a column in Trajan's forum, this one was erected after the death of Marcus Aurelius in AD 180. It commemorates the Emperor's military exploits in a series of reliefs that spiral up the column. On the northern edge of the piazza is Palazzo Chigi, the official residence of the Italian prime minister.

*Detail, Colonna di Marco Aurelio >*

< Fontana di Trevi

Cross diagonally to the adjacent ⑦ **Piazza di Montecitorio**. Its obelisk was the needle of a giant sundial brought back from Egypt by Augustus. Pass the façade of the **Palazzo di Montecitorio**, designed by Bernini and the seat of Italy's Chamber of Deputies. Turn right to pass under an arcade and descend steps to walk between the Camera dei Deputati and a carpark. Cross Piazza del Parlamento and walk up Via di Campo Marzio. Take the second alley left to the tiny but charming Piazza della Torretta and continue up the *vicolo* of the same name. Cross Largo Fontanella Borghese and walk up Via di Monte d'Oro to the Piazza Augusto Imperatore, which hosts a small fruit market. Beyond this, and somewhat overlooked, is the
⑧ **Mausoleo di Augusto**. This massive circular monument was commissioned by Augustus as his tomb. Though its travertine covering has long gone, now replaced with weeds, it was Roma's most impressive burial site when Augustus died in AD 14. Its entrance was flanked by two obelisks, inscribed with the emperor's achievements. Restoration work is underway on this and the nearby **Ara Pacis**, a monumental altar erected around 10 BC to mark the

state of peace attained by the Empire under Augustus. It features remarkable reliefs and will soon be on full display.

Take the narrow street to the right of Santi Ambrosio e Carlo al Corso and then turn right down Via del Corso, then immediately left along Via dei Condotti. This pedestrian (save for taxis and mopeds) thoroughfare is lined with luxury shops and leads to the beloved ⑨ **Piazza di Spagna**, named for the nearby palazzo built for the Spanish Embassy. The famous **Spanish Steps** were built in the 1720s and paid for by French expatriates to link the piazza to their church above. This area has long been the haunt of foreign visitors to Roma; on the right, as you face the steps, is the house where Keats died in 1821, now a museum honouring English Romantic poets. The boat-shaped fountain, named **Fontana Barcaccia**, was designed by Bernini's father Pietro.

Climb the steps, which are bedecked with azaleas in April, to the 16th-century French church of **Trinità dei Monti** and then turn left along the *viale* of the same name. This passes the 16th-century Villa Medici, home to the French Academy for artists and musicians, and continues along the edge of the extensive gardens of **Villa Borghese** (see the end of the chapter). Take steps up on the right to walk along Viale del Belvedere, which does indeed offer wonderful views, as does the Piazzale Napoleone I, which you soon reach.

Leave this grand balcony by a footpath leading to Salita del Pincia and descend the Pincio hill to the equally grand ⑩ **Piazza del Popolo**. This vast space near Roma's northern gate was laid out in the 16th century as the 'people's piazza'; it has been recently restored to its full glory. In the centre is an Egyptian obelisk, another of Augustus's trophies. The neoclassical fountains date from the early 19th century. The 'twin' baroque churches that frame the Via del Corso have subtle differences.

Make a point of visiting the Renaissance church on the northern edge of the piazza:

Piazza di Spagna

**Santa Maria del Popolo.** Built on the site where Nero was buried, this was rebuilt during the early Renaissance and its interior later remodelled by Bernini. It holds a wealth of art, including lovely frescoes by Pinturicchio, two paintings by Caravaggio and the Cappella Chigi, designed in 1516 by Raphael but completed later.

To reach the nearby Flaminio metro station (on Linea A), walk through the **Porta del Popolo**, pierced in the city walls in the 3rd century.

Piazza del Popolo

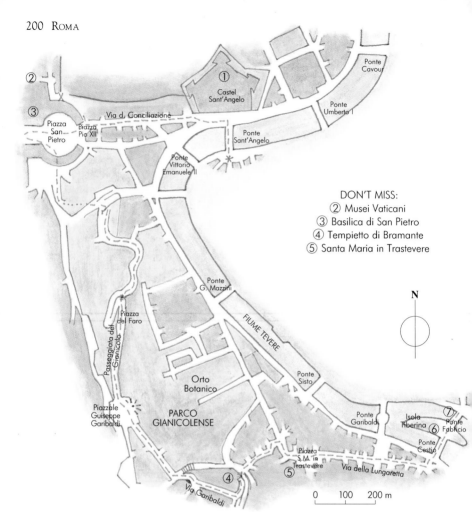

**DON'T MISS:**
② Musei Vaticani
③ Basilica di San Pietro
④ Tempietto di Bramante
⑤ Santa Maria in Trastevere

## WALK 3: TRASTEVERE

*Many of Roma's ecclesiastic riches are west of the Tiber or Fiume Tevere, but this bank also conceals a residential area of great character.*

Advance warning: if you plan to visit San Pietro (St Peter's), don't wear shorts and do have something to cover bare shoulders; this dress code is strictly enforced!

Today's walk begins at the **Ponte Sant' Angelo**, a charming pedestrian bridge lined with statues of angels, sculpted by Bernini and his pupils. Cross over to the imposing ① **Castel Sant'Angelo**. Built by Hadrian as an imperial mausoleum, this massive and imposing structure was later fortified for the use of the pope; Pope Clement VII took

refuge here while the troops of Charles V sacked Roma in 1527. It now houses an art and military museum and there is a wonderful view from the battlements.

Walk west along the broad Via della Conciliazione, which leads to Piazza Pio XII. The area ahead of you was once the site of Nero's Circo Vaticano where San Pietro was martyred in the 1st century. Christians have marked it ever since as a place of veneration and Constantine built a basilica here in 326. From then on it was the stronghold of the papacy and, following an uneasy standoff between church and state during Unification, Mussolini signed the 1929 Lateran Treaty giving the pope sovereignty over the

The view from San Pietro

Città del Vaticano, or Vatican City, and over several major basilicas in Roma.

Before you enter the even grander Piazza San Pietro, a lengthy detour right takes you to the entrance of the
② **Musei Vaticani** or Vatican museums. Housed in the Renaissance palaces of previous popes, these various museums contain hectares of classical antiquities, early Christian artefacts, paintings from the 11th to the 19th centuries, mementos from missionary expeditions, Egyptian and Etruscan artefacts, a map gallery and lavish apartments. Of great note is the **Cortile Ottagono** or Octagonal Courtyard with its wonderful statuary, and the **Cappella Sistina** or Sistine Chapel, featuring Michelangelo's ceiling. Pick up a floor-plan that maps out four colour-coded itineraries, ranging from 90 minutes to 5 hours.

Return to enter the colonnaded **Piazza San Pietro**, designed in majestic style by Bernini in 1656. Ahead are steps to the
③ **Basilica di San Pietro**, or St Peter's Basilica. In the 15th century the decision was taken to replace Constantine's basilica and most of it was demolished, including Byzantine mosaics and frescoes by Giotto. The new basilica took two centuries to complete and various architects, Bramante and Michelangelo included, had a role.

In the centre of the façade is the balcony from which the Pope gives his benediction. Once through the Renaissance doors, the interior is huge, mostly decorated by Bernini. Look for his monument to Pope Alexander VII, and also for Michelangelo's *Pieta*. You can climb to the roof, into the dome, or even to the top of the dome for the most amazing views; entry is to the right of the basilica's atrium.

Leave the basilica and then its piazza by the first exit south, heading through the colonnades and along the road to Porta Cavalleggeri. Before you reach the busy road, which sweeps into a tunnel, take the pedestrian ramp down and turn sharp left to go up mobile walkways and into the Vatican carpark. Keep right to soon exit this and then walk uphill on Via del Gianicolo, passing **Sant'Onofrio**, where the 16th-century Italian poet Tasso is buried, and then past the Jesuit children's hospital.

< Roma from the
Janiculum Hill

Soon after, steps at the left cut off a loop of road. You reach Piazza del Faro (a *faro* is a beacon), atop the Janiculum Hill, where there is a small bar plus panoramic views sweeping from Castel Sant'Angelo around to the hills southeast. Keep on through the parkland to **Piazza Giuseppe Garibaldi**, featuring monuments to both Giuseppe and Anita Garibaldi, then take the lower left-forking road. Ignore steps right and reach, on your left, the 1608 **Fontana Paola**. From here, head left downhill on Via Garibaldi, passing a monument to those killed in a battle here between Garibaldi's troops and the French.

Further down on the left is the late 15th-century church of **San Pietro in Montorio.** Of more interest, however, is the ④ **Tempietto di Bramante**, tucked away in the cloister beyond the church's elegant façade. This diminutive masterpiece of classical design was created by Bramante in 1502. Its circular shape derives from the chapels that early Christians built on the site of a martyrdom; this one incorrectly marks the site of St Peter's crucifixion. Walk around the little temple to view the stairs, added by Bernini, to the crypt.

Head through a gate and down the steps of the Via di S.Pietro in Montorio. Cross the road below and veer left to descend more steps at a road bend, by a parking sign. You are now entering the heart of the Trastevere district, formerly a working class neighbourhood but lately fashionable. Walk down Vicolo del Cedro, which winds through a lovely district, and turn right into Piazza di San Egidio, then left into Via della Paglia to soon arrive at the basilica of ⑤ **Santa Maria in Trastevere**. This was built in 1138 on the site of an earlier church, possibly Roma's first. Its Romanesque façade features a stunning mosaic of the Virgin feeding the baby Jesus, flanked by 10 lamp bearers. Inside are 21 ancient Roman columns and more lovely 1140 mosaics. A Byzantine painting of the Madonna is displayed in a chapel.

Leave the piazza, which features a fountain of Roman origin, by its northwest corner and walk along Via della Lungaretta, which crosses Viale di Trastevere and goes straight on. At Piazza in Piscinula, veer left across the Lungotevere del'Anguillara and walk over the Ponte Cestio, built in 46 BC but rebuilt in the 19th century, onto a tiny island of volcanic rock, ⑥ **Isola Tiberina**. A temple dedicated to Aesculapius, the Greek god of healing, was founded here in 293 BC and the island still hosts a hospital. Also here is the church of **San Bartolomeo**, which has suffered flood damage on several occasions.

Cross to the other side of the Tevere on ⑦ **Ponte Fabricio**, built in 62 BC and the only Roman bridge to remain intact. Just south are the ruins of the older Ponte Rotto, destroyed in the flood of 1598.

## OTHER EXCURSIONS

The **Villa Borghese** is a beautiful park in the north of the city on the Pincio hill. It is the former estate of the pleasure-loving Cardinal Scipione Borghese, who, in 1614, built the Villa Borghese, which now houses the **Museo e Galleria Borghese**, the cardinal's extraordinary collection of paintings and sculptures.

Also in the park, set further west, is the Villa Giulia, built in 1550 as a retreat for Pope Julius II and now the home of the **Museo Nazionale Etrusco**, a collection of pre-Roman antiquities. Between the two buildings lies the shaded lake and folly of the **Giardino del Lago**, a pleasant place to relax. The nearest metro stations to the park are Spagna and Flaminio.

South of the city centre are several ancient sites well worth a visit. The **Terme di Caracalla** were completed in AD 217 and served as public baths until the 6th century. They could accommodate 1,600 people and were sumptuously decorated. Their fascinating ruins can be reached by bus #118 from the Colosseo, or #160 or 628 from Piazza Venezia.

Some 4 km (2.5 miles) further southeast, along the Via Appia Antica, are several sets of **catacombs**. These vast warrens of underground cemeteries used by early Christians can be toured with a guide. From the Terme di Caracalla, walk right to Piazzale Numa Pompilio and southeast on Via di Porta San Sebastiano. Visit the Museo delle Mura and walk along the ramparts of the Mura Aureliane. Continue through the Porta San Sebastiano and walk the busy and narrow Via Appia Antica. At the junction with Via Ardeatina, take the parallel private road (closed Wed) for 2 km past the Catacombe di San Callisto to reach the Catacombe e Basilica di San Sebastiano.

On Sundays, the cypress-lined Via Appia Antica is closed to traffic, making it ideal for the walk from the baths to the catacombs; you could then catch a bus back.

Tempietto di Bramante

OPENING HOURS

| | |
|---|---|
| Musei Capitolini | Tue-Sun 10-9 |
| Foro Romano & Palatino | daily 9-1 hour before sunset |
| Colosseo | daily 9-1 hour before sunset |
| Mercati di Traiano | Tue-Sun 9-4.30 (or 6.30 in summer) |
| Pantheon | Mon-Sat 9-6.30; Sun 9-1 |
| Musei Vaticani | Mon-Fri 8.45-4.45; Sat 8.45-1.45 |
| Museo e Galleria Borghese | Tue-Sat 9-7; Sun 9-8 |
| Museo di Villa Giulia | Tue-Sat 9-7; Sun 9-8 |
| Terme di Caracalla | Tue-Sun 9-1 hour before sunset; Mon 9-2 |
| Catacombe di S. Sebastiano | Mon-Sat 8.30-12, 2.30-5 |

# THE MAIELLA

The Maiella, along with other areas in the heart of the Abruzzo region, is sparsely populated and seldom explored by foreign tourists. This is their loss for the mountainous hinterland contains some of Italy's wildest landscapes, dotted with grottoes and sanctuaries, and with villages little changed over the centuries.

An extraordinary 30 percent of Abruzzo is environmentally safeguarded by national parks and smaller reserves. We've focused on the Parco Nazionale della Maiella, one of Italy's newest, which protects 80,000 hectares of the Montagne della Maiella, one of the highest mountain groups of the Appennini. On the massif are many high, karstic plateaux and on its western flanks, steep scree slopes suddenly give way to superb beech forest.

Over 1,800 plant species have been recorded here, a third of Italy's entire flora. Above the treeline, high meadows bloom with summer wildflowers. Remote areas harbour rare fauna: the Abruzzo chamois, Appenine wolf and Marsican bear. You're more likely, though, to chance upon a wild boar or the red and roe deer.

For over 3,000 years and until quite recently, most Abruzzese lived in sheep-farming communities. The twice-yearly

NOTES
Suggested base: Campo di Giove
Getting there: rail from Roma & Sulmona
Tourist Office: Corso Ovidio 208, 67039
    Sulmona  Tel/Fax: 0864 53276
    email:iat.sulmona@abruzzoturismo.it
    www.abruzzoturismo.it
Map: CAI  Gruppo d. Majella 1:25000
Best timing: April-May; Sept-Oct

transhumance or movement of sheep took place between the high summer pasture of the Maiella and the winter pasture of lowland Puglia, hundreds of kilometres south along legally protected drove routes or *trattori*. Along these routes sprang up towns, villages and isolated chapels. Religion went hand in hand with farming: Cistercian and Benedictine monks established a network of farm-monasteries and, in the Middle Ages, Abruzzo was Europe's leading wool producer. The isolation also suited others; most famously, Celestine V, the 13th-century 'Hermit Pope' who abdicated the papacy, spent his life alone and deep in the Maiella.

Campo di Giove, a high village beneath the imposing ridge of Monte Porrara, makes a charming base for walking. It serves as a modest ski centre in winter and has hotels which are little used in other seasons. Walks 1 and 2 lead in the footsteps of shepherds and, though sheep farming has declined, you may still encounter a herd of animals, grazing under the watchful eye of their keeper. The final walk takes you to a remote pilgrimage sanctuary and ends with a vertiginous traverse of Monte Porrara.

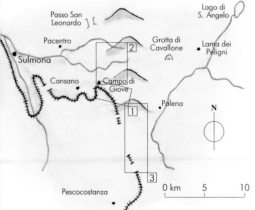

A rest at Fondo
di Maiella >

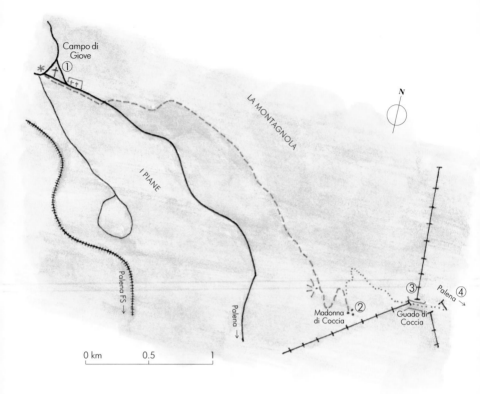

## WALK 1: ABOVE CAMPO DI GIOVE

*A short walk leads to the ruins of a tiny chapel with a lovely viewpoint. From here you can return to Campo di Giove, or you could cross over the pass of Guado di Coccia and descend to Palena on an extension.*

Distance       7.5 km (4.6 miles)
Time           3 hrs to M.d.Coccia & back
Difficulty     easy
Start/Finish   Campo di Giove

From the main piazza of Campo di Giove, walk east to the adjacent piazza where there is a bus stop and where the outdoor market is held. Walk towards the pretty church of ① **Sant'Eustachio**, said to stand on the site of a temple dedicated to Jove. Eustachio is the protector of shepherds; a celebration is held in the saint's name on 20 September, when the flocks were brought down from the mountains.

Just before the church, turn right on the road to Palena. Pass the cemetery, which has a tap outside, and soon bear off left uphill on a track marked as P1. Ignore a minor track forking left to a small quarry and keep right further on. The track narrows. At a junction, turn right onto a broad jeep track marked 'Parco Nazionale – Il Sentiero della Libertà' and very soon turn left on a footpath marked 'MC'. Expansive views open up as Campo recedes.

Approximately 1 hour 15 minutes from Campo, you enter the shade of beech woodland as you zigzag uphill. At a fork, take the lower right footpath marked 'MC'. After a small clearing, you reach the ruins of ② **Madonna di Coccia**. This little church or *chiesetta* was built against the rockface in 1748 and its position offers a good view back to Campo di Giove. Church buildings like this one offered shelter for those crossing the nearby mountain pass. The path winds behind the *chiesetta* and a rough bench there offers a shady place to rest.

From here you can return downhill along the same route, which should take only an hour or so. Alternatively, an extension takes you up to the nearby mountain pass and down to Palena, but as there's no bus connecting Palena to its nominal rail station 10 km south, you'll need to arrange transport or allow time for the road walk.

**Extension:** From Madonna di Coccia, retrace your steps to the last path junction (where 'MC' is painted on a rock) and take the good but unwaymarked path right uphill. This winds up through delightful woodland and brings you to a spur near an ugly ski run. Head uphill, staying on the higher ground left of the ski run to reach ③ **Guado di Coccia** where there's a seasonal *rifugio*. This saddle (a *guado* is a ford) sits between the peaks of Tavola Rotonda (2403 m) to the north and Monte Porrara (2137 m) south.

Now on path #I1, walk to the area between two ski lifts, crossing the saddle on the lowest ground. Keep on between the

Looking back to Campo di Giove

bases of two more ski lifts to pick up a stony jeep track heading downhill. You leave behind the ski intrusions to descend the Vallone di Cocci with a fine view of Palena and beyond to distant craggy mountains. Keep right on the track where it curves (the Sentiero della Libertà veers left) and pass ④ **a water trough** for livestock. On the left a gully, the Vallone di Cocci, opens up. The track forks: keep left on a stony path, then leave this to cross the gully at a break in the crags. Now continue downhill with the gully your right to eventually regain the path, sporadically marked with posts marked 'I1', as it heads towards Palena. At a large pipe, keep right of a fence (or you'll end up in someone's property) to reach a farm lane and then the road. Turn right and descend gently into the town of Palena, some 2 hours from Madonna di Coccia.

Ask in Palena's main bar and you may get a lift to the rail station, which is 10 km on the road south.

< Madonna di Coccia

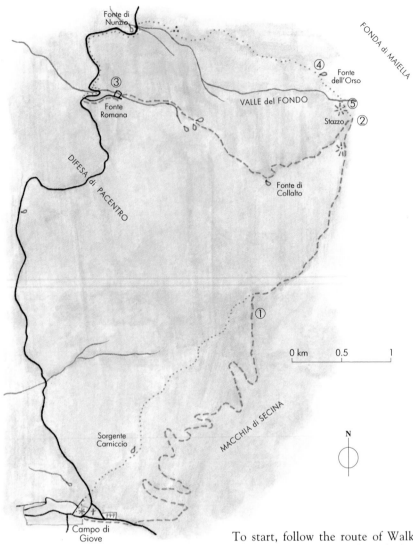

Fonte di Nunzio

FONDA di MAIELLA

④ Fonte dell'Orso

③ Fonte Romana

VALLE del FONDO

⑤
Stazzo ②

DIFESA di PACENTRO

Fonte di Collatto

①

0 km   0.5   1

MACCHIA di SECINA

Sorgente Carniccio

N

Campo di Giove

## WALK 2: FONDO DI MAIELLA

*This route climbs to a stunning amphitheatre of high crags and descends to the pretty woodland of Fonte Romana, from where you can return along the road. A longer variant, returning via a second ascent, will require more time and energy. Bring lunch!*

| | |
|---|---|
| Distance | 20.5 km (12.7 miles) |
| Time | 6 hours (9 for longer variant) |
| Difficulty | moderate |
| Start/Finish | Campo di Giove |

To start, follow the route of Walk 1, following P1 signs. On reaching the broad jeep track, however, you part company with Walk 1 and turn left instead of right.

The track (#13) loops steadily uphill and approximately 1 hour from Campo, you enter beech woods. The jeep track ends at ① **a clearing** with some concrete buildings and a trough. Head beyond it, along a narrow track, to a yellow post. At the next yellow post, a variant track (marked by a yellow dash on a rock) enters from the left; you should make a mental note of this if you plan to return by the longer variant.

Continue on the level path which is narrow but clear. At a post, the path forks: ignore the uphill red-and-yellow #1E path and stay on the level path. Low, prickly bushes encroach on the path along this section. As you leave the woods to cross open grassland, look left to sight the elongated hilltown of Pacentro on a ridge below Monte Mileto. The larger town of Sulmona lies on the plain beyond. Soon, the words 'Fonte Romana' painted on ② **a large boulder** direct you to fork left. Before you do so, pause to enjoy the natural amphitheatre of Fondo di Maiella. Up to your right is a junction signpost at a spot named Stazzo (1836 m) which means 'sheep-fold'. Above, loom crags which obscure the upper slopes of Monte Amaro. Just beyond this ridge is a high plain with the ominous name of Valle di Femmina Morta. Birds of prey can often be seen circling in this place of great atmosphere.

From the boulder, your path (#13A) descends into extremely pleasant beech woods on a path with red-and-yellow waymarks. Signs of wildlife—most likely wild boar and pine marten—are evident on

The old bridge, Fonte Romana

Monte Mileto from Stazzo

Monte Porrara behind Campo di Giove

the ground. After 20 minutes of descent, you reach a welcome *sorgente*, or spring, with a handy spout. Soon after, you join a broader track downhill. Immediately after a second *sorgente* (without a spout), turn sharp left off the track, following a red-and-yellow arrow on a footpath which follows the course of the emergent stream downhill. Eventually, your path crosses the stream to reach the

③ **Fonte Romana**, a popular picnic spot which boasts a bar/restaurant and a seasonal *rifugio*. Take the car track below the *rifugio* to the road. For a direct return to Campo di Giove, turn left and follow the winding but gradually descending road for 5.6 km back to the town.

Those with plenty of energy and time might consider a return via a different route up to the Fondo della Maiella and the variant path back down, a walk of some 4 hours. Turn right to pass the ruins of an old bridge and follow the road north for 1.4 km. After a small bridge above a *sorgente*, turn right at a CAI notice onto the broad

#13 trail. The track passes right of a quaint ruined stone building and then winds uphill. Footpaths with red-and-yellow waymarks short cut loops of the track. As you climb, you gain a good view of the shapely Monte Mileto to the northwest. A long steep climb through beech woods brings you to

④ **Fonte dell'Orso** at a height of 1706 m. Continue over open ground, along a ledge and up to a spur with a fireplace: a good place to enjoy the panorama and to recover!

A short climb further brings you to the signpost at

⑤ **the Stazzo junction.** Turn right downhill on a path signed to Fonte Romana, but make sure you turn left at the boulder just below; having completed the loop, you don't want to do it twice! Retrace your steps of this morning until you reach the turn-off right downhill on the variant path (before the large clearing with buildings). This path, marked in yellow, heads more directly down to Campo di Giove, passing a round water pool, then various water supply buildings, to reach a driveway. Cross the road and walk straight on to reach the main piazza.

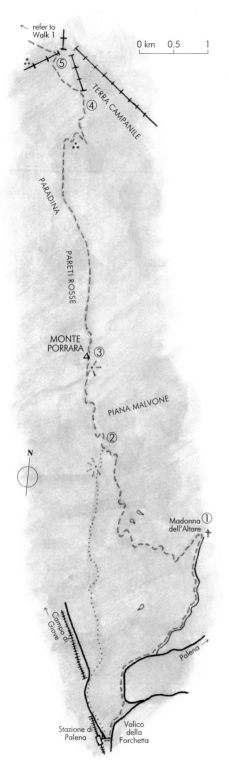

refer to
Walk 1

0 km   0.5   1

⑤

TERRA CAMPANILE

④

PARADINA

PARETI ROSSE

MONTE
PORRARA   ③

PIANA MALVONE

②

N

Madonna ①
dell'Altare

Campo di
Giove

Palena

Stazione di
Palena

Valico
della
Forchetta

## WALK 3: MONTE PORRARA

*A visit to the sanctuary of Madonna dell' Altare is followed, first by a delightful forest walk, then by a panoramic traverse of Monte Porrara and a scramble down its slopes.*

| | |
|---|---|
| Distance | 19.5 km (12 miles) |
| Time | 8.5 to 9 hours |
| Difficulty | demanding |
| Start | Palena rail station |
| Finish | Campo di Giove |
| Transport | train from Campo to Palena |

The full route of this walk is long and strenuous and the traverse should only be undertaken by the sure-footed with a head for heights. Less ambitious walkers could create a shorter walk, either to Madonna dell'Altare and return to Palena station, or up as far as Piana Malvone and return to the station by a direct route. Take lunch supplies and plenty of water with you.

Catch an early train to Palena station, then walk the short station lane and turn left uphill. At the top of the hill, by the 'Valico della Forchetta' sign, veer left off the road, below a building, to cross open ground and enter woods just to the left of a power line. Keep on down through the woods to regain the road at a bend, having cut out a switchback. Turn left and continue down the road.

Just past a forestry nursery, turn left on the paved lane to Madonna dell'Altare. This rises gently for just over 2 km through beech forest to reach, at the lane's end, the ① **Santuario della Madonna dell'Altare** and Eremo Celestiniano, by a spring. The small 14th-century convent was built where Pope Celestine V first lived as a hermit.

Across the lane is a grassy hillside, well-supplied with fireplaces. Climb to the very top and then descend the other side to a track; turn right uphill. This soon peters out, but you continue in the same direction uphill to reach a level forest track. Turn left and soon join a rising track waymarked

Eremo Celestiniano

with yellow '14' posts. Continue winding uphill as forest path I5 joins from the left.

A worthwhile short cut follows: just after a yellow post, and with red-and-white tree waymarks on both sides of the track, turn left uphill and follow the red-and-white tree waymarks. At a meadow, you gain a good view east of windsails and jagged Monti dei

The knife-edge ridge of Monte Porrara

Frentani beyond Palena. Now look for waymarks on rocks which guide you up to re-enter dense woodland by a marked tree. Follow more tree waymarks uphill and turn left onto the broad track once again.

After 250 m or so, a yellow '14' post and a red-and-white waymark guide you off on a right-forking footpath heading uphill. Shortly after some exposed crags, a large boulder marks
② **a major path junction** at a height of around 1850 m. Detour left for a few minutes to enjoy a sweeping view over the long plain to the south. If the weather has turned bad, you should head down this path #12 to reach the Campo-Palena road that leads south for 1 km to Palena rail station or north for 12 km to Campo di Giove.

All being well, return to the junction and take the exposed path, signed to Monte Porrara. Follow various waymarks (red poles, red-and-white stripes, plus some grey marks) over the high ground of the Piana Malvone. There are several false peaks before attaining the summit of
③ **Monte Porrara**, the walk's high point, crowned by a metal cross at 2137 m. The views are wonderful in all directions: east,

beyond the Monti dei Frentani, you might see the Adriatic; west are the forrested slopes of the Bosco di San Antonio. The path descends 100 m and then later climbs once more. It continues to follow the knife-edge ridgeline, leaving it only to skirt the occasional rocky outcrop.

Directly above the ruins of a hut, veer right downhill on a narrow looping path; this route is necessary because the ridge ends abruptly in a steep scree slope. Your path skirts above woods and then becomes a steep descent with loose stones, so take care. When facing a steep drop, look left to a cairn of stones, marking a negotiable route. Zigzag slowly down to a red post in the high pasture of

④ **Terra Campanile**, a pleasant saddle in which to rest awhile. Continue up the opposite slope along a furrow and by sporadic red posts, staying left of a small hilltop. Head for a series of tall metal poles and then follow red posts down towards ski buildings at

⑤ **Guado di Coccia**. Turn left to follow the broad stony ski run downhill away from the buildings but soon take a narrow footpath to the right of the track. Where the ski run veers left, you keep right by a ditch and, at rocks, pick up an unmarked but quite clear footpath which leads down through lovely woodland. This zigzags down to reach a broader path (the one to Madonna di Coccia): turn right downhill towards Campo di Giove. From here, you should refer to the map for Walk 1. At a broad track, turn right then very soon veer left on a footpath. Continue down this to the road and turn right to follow it into Campo di Giove.

## OTHER WALKS IN THE REGION

### Pescocostanza

This is a well-preserved Abruzzo mountain village (1400 m) with a Renaissance character, an 11th-century church and artisans who produce fine metalwork and lace.

Sant'Eustachio in Campo di Giove

Catch a train from Campo di Giove to Rivisondoli-Pescocostanza station. Take the road from the station, then turn right and follow the signs for the village which is almost 2 km northwest. *Allow 3 hours.*

### Grotta del Cavallone

This ascent to one of Abruzzo's fascinating caves starts and ends in Lama dei Peligni This town is not on the rail line so you will need a car to reach it.

From the carpark of the picnic area at Lama dei Peligni, pick up yellow-and-green waymarks along a mule path. Cross meadowland and ascend to the *rifugio* at Tarì (1540 m), where there is a fountain. This hut overlooks Valle di Taranta, rich in birdlife and visited in cooler weather by chamois. At 1610 m, the steep path reaches the Grotta del Cavallone, open to the public. A short distance further on, turn left on a path descending Valle di Taranta to the road. Turn left and follow it through a short tunnel and then 2.5 km back to Lama dei Peligni. *Allow 5 to 6 hours.*

# NAPOLI

Napoli or Naples is a city with something of a bad reputation. While petty crime and signs of poverty may not be the stuff of a tourist dream, they are a reality of southern Italian life and Napoli shouldn't be dismissed if it has a full share. There's a vitality about Napoli that you won't see in Milano. There's also a wealth of historic treasures here—many of them in the city's archaeological museum—and the old centre is packed with fascinating churches and art treasures. On top of this, the Golfo di Napoli provides a marvellous setting, with the sleeping volcano Vesuvio nearby.

Napoli has a long history. There was a settlement here named after the siren Parthenope back in the 9th century BC. Greek colonists arrived in 750 BC and gave the settlement the name of Neapolis. The city thrived and when it came under Roman rule it was a popular holiday destination for the elite. There were incursions by the Goths but the city resisted invasion by the Arabs and it was an independent dukedom until the arrival of the Normans in 1139.

From then on, Napoli fell into the hands of various dynasties, whose contribution to the city was not always beneficial. The German Hohenstaufens who quickly followed the Normans did create a university. The French Angevins gained control after beheading the 16-year-old King Conradin in Piazza del Mercato. One of the Anjou line was Robert the Wise who cultivated the arts in Napoli. Alfonso of Aragon won the city in 1422 and the Spanish ruled through viceroys for some 300 years until the French Charles of Bourbon arrived in 1734.

In the following centuries the city's population swelled and its prostitution

NOTES

Population: 1,002,000

Getting there: bus from Capodichino airport 4 km (2.5 miles) northwest; rail from Roma or Sicilia

Tourist Office: Piazza del Gesù 78 and also Piazza dei Martiri 58

Tel: 081 405311 Fax: 081 401961

Markets: La Forcella, near P. Garibaldi

trade brought it an influx of travellers. When Unification was achieved it was a contender for capital of the nation. In WWII it was heavily bombed and a 1980 earthquake wrought further havoc.

While Napoli is a sprawling city, the *centro storico*, or historic centre, is quite manageable, bounded on the west by Via Toledo (sometimes called Via Roma), on the east by the Porta Capuana, north by the hills of Capodimonte and south by the sea. Two parallel roads—Via Tribunali and Via San Biagio—follow the route of ancient Roman roads to bisect this; the surrounding district is known as Spaccanapoli, literally 'split Napoli'.

Traffic in Napoli seldom seems to obey rules and you'll need to be on your toes when crossing roads. To reduce the chance of theft, don't carry loose bags and watch your possessions in a crowd.

< Vesuvio across the Golfo di Napoli

The city from Vomero

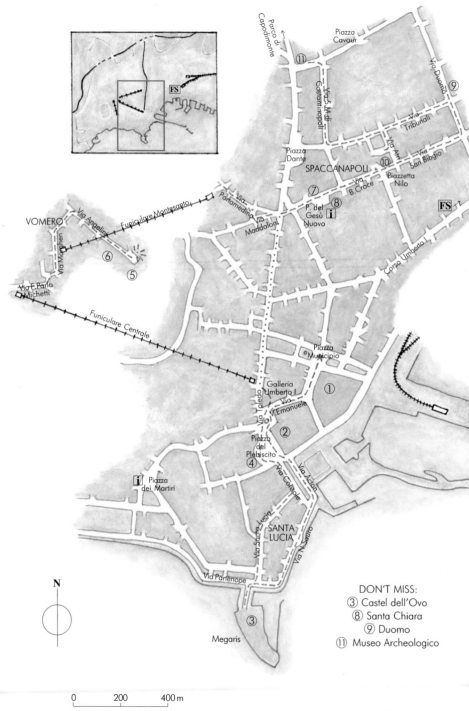

Parco di Capodimonte

Piazza Cavour

Via S. M. di Costantinopoli

Via Duomo

⑪

⑨

Via Tribunali

Via Anni

Via San Biagio

Piazza Dante

SPACCANAPOLI

⑩

Piazzetta Nilo

FS

⑦

Via B. Croce

⑧

Via Portamedina

Via Maddaloni

P. del Gesù Nuovo

VOMERO

Via Angelini

Via Morghen

Funiculare Montesanto

Corso Umberto I

⑥

⑤

Via F. Parla Michetti

Funiculare Centrale

Piazza Municipio

①

Galleria Umberto I

Via V. Emanuele

②

Via Toledo

Piazza del Plebiscito

④

Via Acton

Via Chiaia

Piazza dei Martiri

Via Console

SANTA LUCIA

Via Santa Lucia

Via N. Sauro

Via Partenope

N

③

Megaris

DON'T MISS:
③ Castel dell'Ovo
⑧ Santa Chiara
⑨ Duomo
⑪ Museo Archeologico

0    200    400 m

Castel Nuovo >

# A WALK IN NAPOLI

*Our route gives you a sense of Napoli as a lively coastal city and leads you by its impressive castles and its ancient churches.*

This excursion starts in Piazza Municipio, almost 2 km (just over 1 mile) southwest of the rail station, in the financial and governmental centre of the city. Head down Via Vittorio Emanuele to the entrance of the imposing

① **Castel Nuovo**. This crenellated castle was built from 1279–2 for Charles of Anjou when he relocated to Napoli; hence it is 'newer' than Castel dell'Ovo. It was altered by the Aragonese in the 15th century who added the elaborate triumphal arch at the entrance. In classical style, it commemorates the entry of Alfonso I into Napoli. The Museo Civico inside the castle displays art related to the city.

Further down Via Vittorio Emanuele, on the same side, is the

② **Palazzo Reale**, a complex of buildings dating back to 1600, when it was built for the Spanish viceroys. Napoli's royal palace was extended by later residents but was badly damaged in WWII. In the courtyard, stairs lead to a museum in the apartments.

On the ground floor is the Biblioteca Nazionale, boasting the Farnese collection of ancient manuscripts. A ramp in the garden leads down to the old stables. Adjoining the palazzo to the north is the **Teatro di San Carlo**, the largest theatre in Italy, with a magnificent interior fashioned in wood and stucco for perfect acoustics.

Cross the vast Piazza del Plebiscito and walk down Via Acton with glimpses over the nearby marina. Along Via N. Sauro there are even better views of Vesuvio across the Golfo di Napoli. Pass the 17th-century Fontana dell'Immacolatella and then the boats in Porta Santa Lucia and cross the causeway to the island of Megaris. This was the site of a Roman villa, but in the 12th century the Normans built the

③ **Castel dell'Ovo** to defend the coastline. *Ovo* means 'egg': there is a tale that Virgil concealed an egg below its walls and if the egg breaks, Napoli falls, but as Virgil was born in 70 BC this theory seems to be flawed. It's possible to walk the lanes of the island but the castle only opens for exhibitions.

Cross Via Partenope (which continues to sweep around the bay to the district of Mergellina) and walk up Via Santa Lucia, along the base of a high wall. This district,

Castel dell'Ovo

once home to lively fish markets, now includes expensive hotels. Turn left up Via C. Console to regain Piazza del Plebiscito and briefly visit the somewhat pompous ④ **San Francesco di Paolo.** Begun in 1816 by Ferdinand I, the neoclassical church is modelled on the Pantheon in Rome and is a popular spot for Neapolitan weddings. Canova sculpted the equestrian statues of Ferdinand I and Charles III of Bourbon which guard the front.

Cross the nearby Piazza Trieste e Trento and Via V. Emanuele and walk through the Galleria Umberto I, an elegant 1890 arcade, modelled on Milano's Galleria Emanuele. You exit on the busy Via Toledo where, if you have time, you can make a trip up to the Vomero district. If you would prefer to shorten the walk, head straight up Via Toledo and skip a few paragraphs.

To visit the well-off quarter of Vomero, cross Via Toledo and catch the Funicolare Centrale, a 10-minute ride to the upper station. Climb the steps to the right of the exit and walk up Via F. Parlo Michetti, then

turn left into Via Morghen, past another funicular station, and then right into Via Angelini to gain wonderful views of Napoli, split by its Roman road. At the end of the street are the church and monastery of ⑤ **San Martino.** Established in the 14th century, this Carthusian monastery was rebuilt in the 17th century. Inside is a museum with a strange coverage including a display of *presepi*, the elaborate nativity scenes which are so popular in Napoli. The terrace offers wonderful views over the bay and the cloisters are quite lovely.

A short way back up the hill are the high ramparts of ⑥ **Castel Sant'Elmo,** a star-shaped fortress built in the 16th century on a 14th-century structure. For much of its life it served as a prison but is now open to the public.

Retrace your steps to the station for Funicolare Montesanto and descend on this line. From the lower station, head downhill on Via Portamedina and then along Via Pignasecca, then turn left into the long,

Galleria Umberto I >

straight Via Maddaloni to cross Via Toledo and follow the route of the Roman road into Spaccanapoli, the heart of the old city.

Continue along this narrow pedestrian (and inevitably moped) street lined with vendors of various wares to Piazza del Gesù Nuovo, where stands a *guglia*, an 18th-century obelisk raised after salvation from plague. The 16th-century Jesuit church of ⑦ **Gesù Nuovo** is on your left. The church was built from an existing palazzo, which contributed its Renaissance façade in dark embossed lava-stone. Its interior was redecorated in baroque style following a fire.

Almost opposite is the church of ⑧ **Santa Chiara**, built in the early 14th century. It was embellished heavily in later centuries but damage suffered in WWII revealed much of its original state and it is once again a beautiful Provençal-Gothic building. Memorials to the Anjou dynasty adorn the chancel. Behind the church are the lovely cloisters of the related convent, established by the wife of Robert the Wise. Its walkways are decorated with brightly painted ceramic tiles depicting rural scenes.

Further on, the area becomes a bazaar of *presepi* stalls, selling elaborate crib scenes or the intricate components for the DIY crib-maker. Set behind a *piazzetta* on the left is the 14th-century San Domenico Maggiore with a 19th-century Gothic interior. On your right is Piazzetta Nilo,

featuring a Roman sculpture of the personified river Nile. Continue on until Via Duomo, where you turn left and cross the road to soon reach ⑨ the **Duomo**, dedicated to San Gennaro and in proud possession of his head and two vials of his blood. Originally a temple to Neptune stood here, followed by various churches before the cathedral was built in 1294-1323. It was damaged badly by an earthquake in 1456 and much reworked: the façade is late 19th-century. Inside, a passage leads from the left aisle to the much older Basilica di Santa Restituta. From here you can access excavations of Greek and Roman urban ruins and also a 5th-century baptistry which still bears fragments of contemporary mosaics.

Return a little way down Via Duomo and turn right down Via Tribunali. On your left is San Lorenzo Maggiore, a 14th-century Franciscan church with an 18th-century façade and a spare Gothic interior. On the right is Chiesa di San Paolo Maggiore, built on the ruins of a Roman temple. Turn left down Via Atri and then right on the narrow Via de Sanctis to ⑩ **Cappella di San Severo**. This small 16th century chapel has an exuberant baroque interior. Now a museum, it contains some wonderful pieces of 18th-century sculpture, including Sammartino's amazing figure of Christ veiled with a thin shroud. In the crypt

< Chiesa di Gesù Nuovo

are the gruesome anatomical experiments of an eccentric alchemist, Prince Raimondo.

Head south again on Viale del Sole and at Piazza Miraglia turn left back into Via Tribunali. If you still have time and energy to continue, turn right at Via S.M. di Costantinopoli to the

⑪ **Museo Archeologico Nazionale.** This museum has the most important collection of Greco-Roman artefacts in the world. It's housed in 16th-century barracks, converted in 1790 to store the Farnese collection of classical sculpture and treasures excavated from Pompeii and Ercolano (Herculaneum). Also here is the Borgia collection of Etruscan and Egyptian finds.

This collection should not be missed but you might leave it for the next day and combine it with the excursion below. If so, simply head on now to Piazza Dante, which lies on the main north-south road.

## OTHER EXCURSIONS

In the hills north of the city lies the **Parco di Capodimonte**, the grounds of an 18th-century palazzo begun for Charles of Bourbon. The palazzo, recently restored, houses a museum and gallery which includes the Farnese art collection. To get there, head directly north from the Museo Nazionale on Via S. Teresa degli Scalzi. A lift takes you from the Sanità district up to Corso Amadeo di Savoia, which leads to

The duomo's baptistry mosaics

Capodimonte. Alternatively, buses leave from Piazza Dante.

South of the palazzo are the **Catacombe di San Gennaro**, catacombs dating from the 2nd century AD. The entrance is on Via di Capodimonte and inside, on two levels, are spacious chapels carved into the tufa and frescoed by the early Christians.

Napoli is a good base from which to visit **Vesuvio** and **Pompeii**: see 'Other Areas for Walking' at the back of the book.

---

OPENING HOURS

| | |
|---|---|
| Castel Nuovo | Mon-Sat 9-6 |
| Museo del Palazzo Reale | Tue-Sun 9.30-1.30; weekends also 4-7.30 |
| Teatro di San Carlo | opening times vary |
| San Martino | Tue-Sun 9-2 |
| Castel Sant'Elmo | Tue-Sun 9-2 |
| Santa Chiara cloisters | daily 8.30-12.30; 4-6.30 |
| Duomo | daily 9-noon; also Mon-Sat 4.30-7 |
| Cappella di San Severo | Mon, Wed-Sun 10-5 |
| Museo Archeologico | Tue-Sat 9-2, Sun 9-1; open late in summer |
| Palazzo di Capodimonte | Tue-Sat 10-7, Sun 9-2 |
| Catacombe di S. Gennaro | guided tours throughout each morning |

# COSTIERA AMALFITANA

NOTES
Suggested base: Sorrento
Getting there: Circumvesuviana train
   from Napoli; bus from Napoli airport
Tourist Office: Via L. de Maio, Sorrento
   Tel: 081 8074033 Fax: 081
   8773397 www.vol.it/sorrento
Map: Monti Lattari (CAI) 1:30000
Best timing: avoid June-August

The undoubted charms of the Costiera Amalfitana, or the Amalfi Coast, draw many travellers, yet it remains a place of great natural beauty where you can quickly escape the tourist centres on foot.

This chapter should perhaps be named Monti Lattari after the chalky mountain range that spills down into the Tyrrhenian to form the Penisola Sorrentina and, at its tip, the isle of Capri. The peninsula's sedimentary coastline is dramatic in the extreme: ravines tumble between jutting cliffs studded with picturesque towns and villages. The scenery has always drawn visitors: the Greeks were inspired to set legends here. Capri was the playground of Roman emperors and, for Tiberius, the main office. Centuries on, the town of Amalfi was a great maritime power before most of it collapsed into the sea in 1343. In the 19th century, English and German literati and artists discovered the area and reinvigorated the tourist trend.

Sorrento, a resort town with an air of faded elegance, is situated on the west of the peninsula. It makes a good travel base as frequent ferries depart from here to Capri and a bus service runs along the southern flank of the peninsula, through Positano, to Amalfi. If you wish to do more walking in the vicinity of Amalfi, Positano would be a good alternative.

The three walks detailed here will give you a real sense of 'the lie of the land' and a taste of both well-touristed towns and nearby but nonetheless remote villages, where vines and lemon groves are the local mainstay. The first walk takes you to Punta Campanella at the very tip of the peninsula, the second is a short walk on beautiful Capri, and the third is a more demanding hike above Positano, with stunning views right along the Costiera Amalfitana. All of these involve ascents and descents, which is why you may find yourselves blissfully alone!

View of the mainland from Capri >

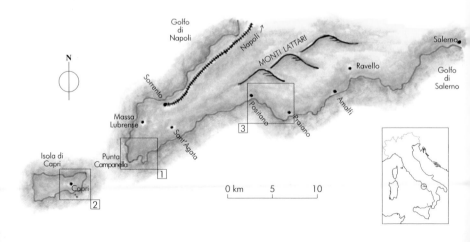

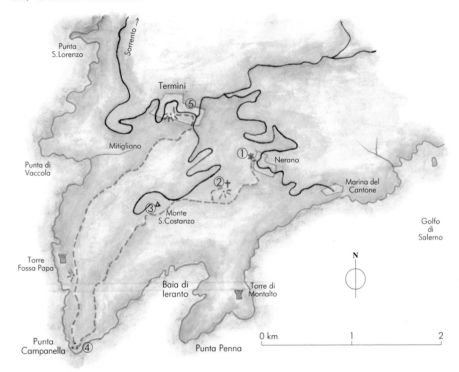

## WALK 1: SORRENTO PENINSULA

*This coastal walk leads you along the rocky shores where legendary sirens lured hapless sailors to their doom. There's no doubt that the natural beauty hereabouts is distracting.*

| | |
|---|---|
| Distance | 7 km (4.4 miles) |
| Time | 4 hours |
| Difficulty | moderate; some rough terrain |
| Start | Nerano |
| Finish | Termini |
| Transport | bus from Sorrento and return |

The terrain at the southern tip of the Sorrento Peninsula is less rugged than the coastline further east, making this a good introductory walk for the region. To reach the start, catch the SITA bus from outside Sorrento's train station to the small village of Nerano. If you miss the stop, the bus continues down to the pretty Marina del Cantone and then returns, so you can disembark at

① **Nerano's** several shops. A short distance down from the shops, take a right forking path called Via Ieranto and waymarked CAI 2 and E3 with red and white. Head through a gate and then diverge right on a path that zigzags uphill through woodland. The overgrown path climbs to the top of a coastal ravine at a stone building.

The path levels to contour the hill above two more buildings, giving you views down over Punto Montano and Punta Penna. The route becomes less clear: follow markers to climb uphill to trees and a path junction featuring a plaque. A 5-minute detour right will take you to

② **San Costanzo**, a whitewashed church on the site of a Greek temple, which offers wonderful views in all directions. Back at the junction, take what would have been a left turn, heading west. The path touches the road for 50 m or so until it curves. Diverge left at a splash of green paint and follow overhead wires up the hill. This is as close as you get to the top of

③ **Monte San Costanzo**, which is crowned by a military zone. The route skirts below the zone's fence and then diverges to continue towards the point. This terrain is stony and difficult so descend carefully, following the red-and-white marks on the limestone rocks. When you reach an old cement footpath, a short detour left takes you to a disused winch, from where there is a wonderful view of the Baia di Ieranto, a sheltered bay with beautiful azure waters.

Backtrack on the cement path, which soon deteriorates and then turn left onto a broader track, to reach the buildings at ④ **Punta Campanella**, which comprise a lighthouse, the ruins of what was reputedly a temple to Minerva, and even less distinct, the rubble of a Roman villa. The name of the point derives from the large bell that was rung to warn the nearby villages of impending raiders. Nearby, steep steps lead down a narrow ravine where waves crash dramatically against the rocks.

Retrace your steps up the track and continue to follow this uphill, passing above Torre Fossa Papa, one of the many towers built by the ruling Spanish in the 16th century to guard against Ottoman raids.

From the track you have a good view out to the islands of Capri and Ischia before

Monte San Costanzo

heading between olive groves, by a plaque memorial to victims of a rockfall, past a track to the hamlet of Mitigliano, and into the outskirts of ⑤ **Termini**, an agricultural town. Turn left at a paved road to reach a church. A left turn takes you to the centre of this small town, where there is a limoncello 'factory' and a SITA bus stop at the terrace, with more sweeping views.

Baia di Ieranto

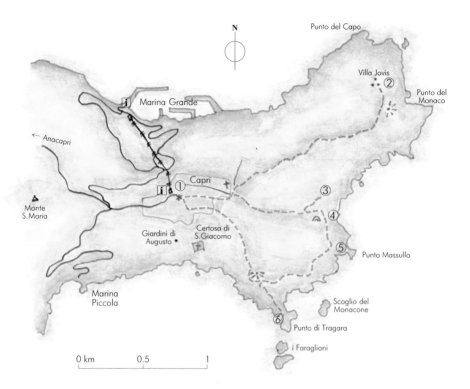

## WALK 2: THE ISLE OF CAPRI

*Escape from the born-to-shop tourist throng and enjoy the natural beauty of this stunning island. This route, which is all on public footpaths, takes you to the ruins of Villa Jovis and past the spectacular Faraglioni rocks.*

| | |
|---|---|
| Distance | 7.5 km (4.7 miles) |
| Time | at least 4 hours |
| Difficulty | easy, but lots of steps |
| Start/Finish | Capri, the town |
| Transport | ferry to Capri from Sorrento |

The island of Capri lies three nautical miles off the Sorrento Peninsula, of which it is the geological extension. Much of its 10-square-kilometres is accessible only by narrow, car-free alleys, making it ideal for relaxed walking. The island is also unusually rich in flora, with some 850 species of plants crammed onto its limestone shelves.

< Capri from Punta Campanella

From Capri's Marina Grande, where you disembark from the ferry, you can catch a funicular or climb various (and many) steps to the town of Capri. The top funicular station is beside a Tourist Office in the ① **Piazza Umberto I**, where you will also find the church of San Stefano. This was built in 1685 on the site of a Benedictine monastery and the floor of its altar is paved with marble taken from Villa Jovis.

Leave the piazza on Via le Botteghe, a narrow, shop-lined alley on the right of the Municipio. At the end of the shops the alley broadens and climbs. Keep straight on at a cross-junction, now on Via Tiberio and continue up past the small church of San Michele della Croce.

Follow the signs to Villa Jovis. As you pass a vineyard growing grapes for the famous *Lacrimae Tiberii*, there are excellent views across to the volcanic islands of Ischia and Procida. The path climbs between

Roman brickwork at Villa Jovis

parkland: Parco Astarita on the right is an essential detour with fine views northeast to the Penisola Sorrentina and glimpses south of the Faraglioni. Soon reach ② **Villa Jovis** (open daily, 9 to one hour before sunset). This was the largest of some

12 imperial villas on Capri and Tiberius retired here to rule the Roman Empire from AD 27 to 37. It was the scene of much debauchery and paranoia: slaves were retained for unusual sexual practices while enemies were reputedly tossed over the sheer cliffs. The site has been pillaged for materials but you can gain an impression of the complex's layout from what remains. Nearby is the Faro, the ancient lighthouse which passed signals to the mainland.

Retrace your steps (though for variation you could go down Via Moneta) to the junction below S. Michele della Croce where you turn left onto Via Matermania. At a shrine, fork left. Continue past the terrace of a trattoria and then descend steps to reach the striking formation of the ③ **Arco Naturale**, all that remains of a large grotto, carved out when the sea was at this level. Return to the trattoria and then take the steps left which lead down to ④ **Grotta di Matermania**, a once richly decorated cavern where the earth goddess Cybele (or Mater Magna) was energetically worshipped in the Roman era. Continue

Capri from the eastern tip

The Faraglioni, on Capri's southeast

along the path, which passes a spur and then climbs to give a good view over
⑤ **Villa Malaparte**, which straddles Punto Massullo. The distinctive red roof of this modern building was designed with the hammer and sickle in mind.

A short distance further on, where steps cross the path, you can detour down to Localita Faraglioni, a popular swimming and sunbaking spot at the base of spectacular rocks known as
⑥ **I Faraglioni.** These sheer limestone pinnacles are a refuge for birds and other wildlife including a rare blue lizard. Back up the hill, the main path contours up to the **Belvedere di Tragara**, a lovely terrace offering views of the Faraglioni, Marina Piccola and Monte Solaro. Walk along the pretty Via Tragara and back into Capri.

A possible extension to this walk is a visit to **La Certosa**, a Carthusian monastery founded in 1371, and to the nearby ancient gardens of Augustus. The monastery is open from 9-2 daily except Mondays so you might consider walking the route in reverse, visiting La Certosa first and then heading past the Faraglioni.

The dramatic Arco Naturale

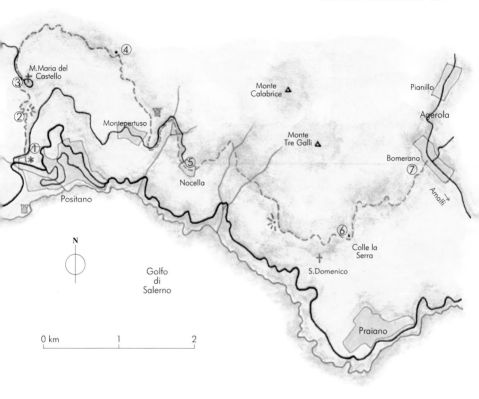

## WALK 3: ABOVE POSITANO

*The exact route of the renowned Sentiero degli Dei or 'Path of the Gods' differs according to your source but this walk certainly warrants the name, with spectacular views from high above the Costiera Amalfitana.*

| | |
|---|---|
| Distance | 12 km (7.5 miles) |
| Time | 6.5 hours |
| Difficulty | demanding |
| Start | Positano |
| Finish | Bomerano |
| Transport | bus from Sorrento and return |

Catch a SITA bus from outside Sorrento's train station and alight at the start of Positano; the ride along the coastline is unforgettable. Positano is a popular town which you may find brimming with tourists. A visit down to its grey beach is fascinating, if only for the contrast of fashion boutiques

< A divine view of the Amalfi coastline

and luxury hotels with what you will see later in the day. Take lunch and water.

① From the bus stop at the western edge of **Positano**, walk up Via Chiesa Nuova to the small piazza beside the church. Further along the alley you climb steps, cross a road and climb more steps. A CAI plaque and faint signage to Santa Maria dell Castello show the way. A stone-laid mule path zigzags up the steep hillside and you gain ② a clear view of **Montepertuso**, a nearby mountain breached by a large hole. Local legend claims this was formed by the Virgin Mary who walked through the solid hillside to win a bet against the bragging Devil.

Continue climbing steadily up the hill; eventually the path leads through pasture and along a lane to reach the road at ③ the hamlet of **Santa Maria del Castello**. Turn left down the road, past a bar. Some 5 minutes or so further on, turn right

The path above Positano

downhill on a concrete road marked Via della Canocchia and Sentiero degli Dei. Once past some small farms there is a good view down the lovely Pozzo gully.

The path now weaves pleasantly through cypress groves. Soon after you gain a good view of the town of Praiano on the coast, take a right fork (marked #3) down to the ④ **Caserma Forestale**, or Forresters' Barracks, some 40 minutes from Santa Maria del Castello. Continue down the steps in front of this stone building and through woodland to pass a shrine. Descend to the road near the village of Montepertuso and turn left, following the road to a bridge over a steep ravine. Just after crossing the bridge, fork right onto a well laid footpath. Until recent roadworks, this path was the only means of reaching ⑤ the charming hamlet of **Nocella**. Walk along the narrow alley of Via Nocella. At a shrine and water spout (non-potable) turn left up steps to leave the small village. The path now contours the lower slopes of Monte Tre Galli, its exposed rock faces

interspersed with woodland. There are spectacular views in both directions along the coast; looking west you can see the distant Faraglioni rocks off Capri.

The path passes above ruins and beneath cliff shelters. A herd of goats on the nearby ridge are guarded by some assiduous dogs, so take care here. Where the path reaches a stone wall between vineyards, take a left fork uphill to pass below a house. At ⑥ **Colle la Serra**, there is a path junction (careful navigation is needed) where you turn left up the steps onto a better marked path heading north. You soon pass directly beneath tall rock spires. The track shortly becomes a concrete road and passes ⑦ **Grotta Biscotta**, an overhang featuring shelters in the rockface. Stay on the road and then turn left onto a road which leads into the well settled Bomerano, a district of Agerola. The bus stops at the junction opposite a general store. From here you can catch a SITA bus which zigzags down to Amalfi and from there, another SITA bus back to Sorrento or Positano.

Pencil pines near the Caserma Forestale

## OTHER WALKS IN THE REGION

### Above Sorrento

This mostly downhill route leads through old villages between Termini and Sorrento and offers excellent views. Catch a bus to Termini's piazza (see Walk 1). Follow Via delle Tore and climb steps right, following waymarks. Cross the hill of Le Tore and turn right onto the road. After 100 m, turn left on a path down to the village of Schiazzano. From its church take Via S. Maria and continue down to the village of Santa Maria. Turn right to pass the church and descend wide steps then head left, following waymarks through olive groves. Continue straight on, along Via S. Antonio then take the road right into Massa.

After a rest in Massa, continue straight past the Vespoli palazzo but soon veer left on a track to Molini. Continue on and then turn right to La Rorella. Fork left onto a path which passes between Monte Corbo and Priora and descends to cross the winding Via Nastro Verde. Continue downhill to join a minor road which zigzags downhill. Turn right onto Via Capo and then left on a path to skirt the parking area. Continue along Via Fuoro and then Via S.Cesareo to reach Sorrento's Piazza Tasso. *Allow 3.5 hours.*

### Valle delle Ferriere

This superb but demanding walk (there are many steps) leads you up a valley enclosed by limestone cliffs and terraces. Start in the lovely Piazza Duomo in Amalfi. Walk up Via Lorenzo d'Amalfi; just before a short tunnel, turn right up steps. Fork right at a wall mural. Climb flights of steps to Pontone. Continue up steps, past a good viewpoint and left up more steps to Minuto, and up to a sharp bend in the road (with a view over Ravello). Climb steps to the left.

At a junction, turn left on a level path then descend gently into pine forest. Head past a fountain and through a tunnel, then contour below a huge tank to gain stunning views of limestone cliffs. The path (#57)

contours the base of cliffs (popular with rock climbers) to reach the head of the valley.

Cross the stream and follow the path (#01) back along the bank. Cross a smaller stream and follow waymarks uphill (still on #01) out of woodland. The path levels and crosses another stream. At a waymarked junction, fork left downhill on #59. This winds along hillside and eventually leads down to Pogerola. From here several paths wind down to Amalfi. *Allow 6 hours.*

The harbour at Amalfi

### On Capri

This route explores the high ground of Capri, from where sweeping views can be gained. From the town of Anacapri, catch the chairlift up to Monte Solaro, the highest point on the island. Walk via La Crocetta to S. Maria a Cetrella. Retrace the route past La Crocetta and then walk along Via M. Solaro and then along Via Axel Munthe to Villa S. Michele (now a fascinating museum). Head back along Via A. Munthe and then Via Capodimonte to Piazza Vittoria in Anacapri. *Allow 3 hours.*

# PALERMO

Palermo is one of those cities which affects any visitor, particularly those who walk through it. Life is very much lived on its streets: in the lanes where street vendors proffer everything from marzipan *frutti alla martorana* to swordfish, in the busy thoroughfares where cars and scooters engage in combat, and in alleys where children play football. All this activity can be a little daunting at first, but there's always the chance to pause and watch a game of cards in the piazza.

The city lies at the end of a fertile valley known as the Conca d'Oro or 'Golden Conch' and at the base of the limestone promontory of Monte Pellegrino. Its strategic position in the Mediterranean made it a successful trading post established by the Phoenicians, conquered by the Romans, occupied by the Vandals, and brought back under Byzantine rule. It wasn't until the Saracens conquered the city in 831, however, that it began to

NOTES
Population: 730,000
Getting there: bus from airport 30 km
   (19 miles) west; rail from mainland;
   ferries from Napoli and Cagliari
Tourist Office: Piazza Castelnuova, 35
   Tel: 091 6058111 Fax: 091 582788
   email: info@aapit.pa.it
   www.aapit.pa.it
Markets: Vucciria, Capo & Ballaro, daily

flourish and became one of the centres of the Arab world. The Normans won this prize in 1072 and built further on the foundations, adapting earlier forms to create such masterpieces as the Cappella Palatina and the cathedral at Monreale. By the 12th century, Palermo was one of Europe's most magnificent cities.

Its fortunes stumbled somewhat once it passed to the German Hohenstaufens and then to the French Anjou line and slipped into full decline after that. It suffered severe bombing by Allied forces during WWII and portions of the city, notably La Kalsa district, remain bombsites.

This tumultuous history has made Palermo a rich fusion of architectural styles. As a general rule, the outside of a Palermitan church belies its interior. This is particularly true of the cathedrals: Palermo's, with its fascinating Arab-influenced exterior, and Monreale's, from the appearance of which one would never guess at the treasures displayed inside. The generalisation can also be applied to many of the lesser churches that fill the city. There is plenty to please lovers of the baroque, as many churches are decorated with elaborate stucco work. Others will draw greater pleasure from the breath-taking mosaics executed centuries earlier during Palermo's Norman period.

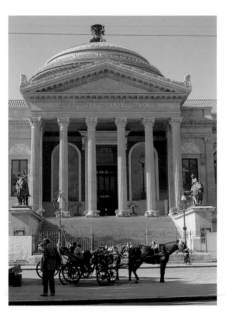

Teatro Massimo

The cloisters of Monreale's duomo >

DON'T MISS:
② outdoor markets at
Capo, Ballaro or Vucciria
⑤ La Martorana
⑧ San Giovanni
⑨ Cappella Palatina
⑩ Monreale Duomo

⑩
△

↑ Monte Pellegrino

Via Francesco Crispi

Politeama

Piazza
Castelnuova
★

i

Via Ruggero Settimo

Via Roma

Via Cavour

Piazza
Verdi
①

Via Volturno

La
Cala

← Zisa

C. Finocchiaro
Aprile

P. San
Domenica ③
② 

Via Bandiera

CAPO

VUCCIRIA

Via Maqueda

Quattro
Canti
④

Via Vittorio Emanuele

⑦

⑤
⑥

Via Roma

V. dell'
Università

BALLARO

FS

Villa
Bonanno

Porta
Nuova

← Monreale

N

⑨

V. del Gasthine

Piazza
Independenza

⑧

V. dei Benedettini

0    100    200    300 m

# A WALK IN PALERMO

*This is your chance to soak up the wealth of Arab-Norman art and architecture which makes Palermo and its outlying town of Monreale so fascinating.*

Our route starts in Piazza Castelnuovo which is dominated by the Politeama Garibaldi on its eastern side. This solid theatre building also houses the modern art gallery. Walk down the broad Via Ruggiero Settimo to

① **Teatro Massimo**, another monumental but more attractive theatre, built in Neoclassical style towards the end of the 19th century. It boasts one of Europe's largest theatres and has recently undergone a drawn-out renovation.

On the other side of Via Maqueda, a detour down Via Bara all'Olivella would take you to the **Museo Archeologico Regionale** with its major collection of historic finds, including sculptures from Selinunte. This, however, demands time and you might want to dedicate a few hours to the museum on another occasion.

Continue along Via Maqueda and head left down Via Bandiera to taste a small section of the

② **Vucciria outdoor markets** which make Palermo so vibrant. The city has several labyrinths of such alleys lined with vendors selling foodstuffs and bric-a-brac. At the end of this street, cross Via Roma to Piazza San Domenico and, at its far end,

③ **Chiesa di San Domenico**. This pale baroque church was rebuilt in 1640 and the façade added in 1726 when the piazza was created. It holds the tombs of many noted Palermitans. Behind the church is the charming **Oratorio del Rosario**; the custodian is located at the nearby Via dei Bambinai 16. The oratorio is decorated with stucco work by the master Giacomo Serpotta and its altar bears the *Madonna del Rosario* painted by Van Dyck in 1628.

Retrace your steps a little and turn left onto Via Roma and then right up Via Vittorio Emanuele to reach the central (and chaotic) crossroads known as Quattro Canti, literally 'four corners'. Created under Spanish rule in 1620, each corner bears a season, a Spanish king and one of Palermo's patron saints. One corner also features the church of San Giuseppe, but unless you are fanatical about baroque architecture, cross to the opposite side of Via Maqueda to

④ **Piazza Pretoria** which features the massive 16th-century fountain known as the **Fontana Pretoria** (currently being restored). Pass the fountain and also the Palazzo Pretorio and Santa Caterina (also under restoration) to reach the more intimate Piazza Bellini. Opposite are two churches: the one on the left is officially named Santa Maria dell'Ammiraglio but is more commonly known as

⑤ **La Martorana**. This Norman church was built in 1143 by an admiral of King Roger II. The façade overlooking the piazza is a later addition but the square campanile is original. The beauty of La Martorana,

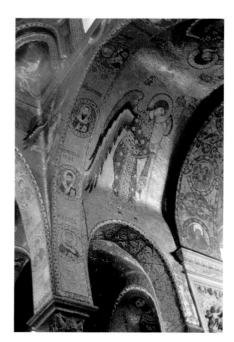

*La Martorana's mosaic interior*

however, lies not in its exterior but inside, where exquisite mosaics cover its upper walls. The style is pure Byzantine and depicts Christ, the Virgin and major New Testament scenes.

Immediately next door is another church of the 12th century:

⑥ **San Cataldo**. Here the original Arab style architecture is more clearly visible in its square forms and three-domed roof. The walls of the rectangular interior were never decorated and the simple effect is in sharp but pleasing contrast to that of La Martorana.

Descend the steps facing the two churches and cross Via Maqueda at a slight angle. Head down Via dell'Università, often congested with students' motor scooters stacked deep. Turn right, climb the broad steps of Salita Raffadali, and continue straight on to reach Via Vittorio Emanuele. Turn left and head uphill, past the *biblioteca* or library which occupies an old Jesuit college on the left, to arrive in front of

⑦ the **Cattedrale**, an exuberant complex which combines a bizarre mix of architectural styles. Built as a Christian edifice in 1184 on the site of a basilica, it was adapted by the Arabs as a mosque and then restored by the Normans. Minor details were added from the 14th to 16th centuries, then major structural changes were made at the end of the 18th century. The result is an intriguing jumble of mullioned windows, Muslim inscriptions, crenellations and Gothic arches, all topped by a baroque dome. Inside is a somewhat cold expanse, with one chapel dedicated to the tombs of Norman kings and Hohenstaufen rulers.

Back outside, cross Via V. Emanuele and then veer left to cut diagonally across the tropical gardens of Villa Bonanno. Just before you reach the tiered statue of Filipo V, descend on steps and turn right into Via del Gasthine, walking under the massive walls of the Palazzo Reale. At a busy inter-

< San Giovanni degli Eremiti

Palermo's Cattedrale

section, turn left into Via dei Benedettini and on your right is the entrance to

⑧ **San Giovanni degli Eremiti**. The church, dedicated to St John of the Hermits, was built at the command of Roger II in 1136 on the site of a Gregorian monastery. In this case it is not an elaborate interior that draws the eye; indeed the inside of the church is unadorned apart from the peeling remains of a 12th-century fresco. Instead it is the distinctive Arabic architecture of square structures and red domes that is so pleasing, particularly as the church is set in a small but beautiful garden replete with a miniature Benedictine cloister and a Moorish cistern.

Retrace your steps along Via dei Benedettini, cross the road and head up to the inauspicious entrance of the Palazzo dei Normanni, or Palazzo Reale. Once through the gates and then the archway, climb the staircase to reach the

⑨ **Cappella Palatina**. This exquisite chapel was begun in 1130 for Roger II, and his mosaic-encrusted throne sits at the

beginning of the nave. The ceiling is carved in intricate Arab patterns; the Muslim influence is also evident in the geometric tiling and the images of plants and animals. The main theme of the stunning mosaics though is Christian, with *Christ Pantocrator* (Greek for 'all-powerful') dominating the apse and illustrations from the Old and New Testaments lining the walls. The whole space is a magnificent work of combined architecture and artistry.

There is limited access to the rest of the palazzo, which is the seat of the Sicilian parliament. It was originally built by the Saracens in the 9th century and the Normans modified it to create an opulent palace and centre of state affairs. On the floor above the chapel is the Sala di Re Ruggero, or King Roger's Hall, decorated with 12th-century mosaics of hunting scenes.

Outside the palazzo gates, continue up to Piazza Indipendenza to catch one of the frequent buses (#389 and #105) 8 km southwest to the elevated town of Monreale. Leave the bus in the centre of the town at Piazza Vittorio Emanuele opposite the modest porticoed entrance to ⑩ the **Cattedrale di Monreale**. This is yet another brilliant fusion of Arab, Byzantine and Romanesque artistry and is one of the greatest achievements of the Italian Middle Ages. It was founded by William II in 1174, who was spurred to it by his political rivalry with the Archbishop of Palermo. It was completed in a mere decade and has remained largely unchanged.

The main façade fronts onto a larger piazza to the right and it is worth viewing it and the large bronze doors created in 1179 by Bonanno Pisano before you enter the cathedral. Little, though, can prepare you for the scale and complexity of the interior. Some 6,340 square metres of mosaics—primarily in gold—adorn the walls of apses, sanctuary and aisles. The central apse is dominated by the half-figure of Christ; saints and martyrs abound. Scenes from the beginning of the Bible line the central nave and those depicting the creation and the flood are particularly wonderful.

A small fee allows you to climb to the cathedral roof for a superb view over Palermo and over the adjoining cloisters. To reach these (and they shouldn't be missed) exit the cathedral and head past the main façade. The cloisters were part of

< A serious game of *scopa*

the Benedictine monastery that was built in the late 12th century. The Arab-style arches are supported by 228 twinned columns, some with elaborate mosaic intarsias and others carved in intricate detail. The south corner features a small enclosure with a fountain.

You may be reluctant to leave. When the time does come, you'll find the bus back to Palermo waits for passengers around the corner from where you alighted.

## OTHER EXCURSIONS

West of Palermo's historic heart, but well worth the effort of the detour, is the **Castello della Zisa**. Zisa is one of the several Arab-Norman castles built in a huge 12th-century park: another is **La Cuba**, further south. Once a sumptuous palace, Zisa now stands incongruously among urban clutter. It holds a collection of Arabic artefacts including some beautifully carved screens, but the building alone is sufficiently evocative. From Piazza Verdi, walk along Via Volturno, then Corso C. Finocchiaro Aprile. Turn left along Via Normanni to reach Zisa. *Allow 1 hour.*

**Monte Pellegrino** offers a view over Palermo and has the added interest of the Santuario di Rosalia. Rosalia was a Norman princess who chose a life of meditation on the mountain. Her bones, when brought back to the city, saved Palermo from plague

Monreale's celebrated mosaics

and she was made one of its patron saints. The cave where she washed (and which drips holy water) became a shrine in the 17th century; it is still visited by devout Palermitans and bedecked with amulets and trophies. A track beyond the cave leads to the mountain top, a walk of 20 minutes. The summit is occupied by a military installation but there are views to be had nearby. The bus ride from Palermo (#812 from beside the Politeama) also provides views over the pretty bay of Mondello.

---

OPENING HOURS

| | |
|---|---|
| La Martorana | Mon-Sat 8-1, 3.30-5.30; Sun 8.30-1 |
| Cattedrale | Mon-Sat 7-7; Sun 8-1.30, 4-7 |
| S.Giovanni degli Eremiti | Mon-Sat 9-7; Sun 9-1 |
| Cappella Palatina | M-F 9-noon, 3-5; Sat 9-noon; Sun 9-10, noon-1 |
| Palazzo Reale | Mon, Fri & Sat 9-noon (except when Parliament meets) |
| Cattedrale di Monreale | daily 8-6 (treasury and terrace 9.30-12.30, 3.30-5.30) |
| Monreale Cloisters | Mon-Sat 9-7; Sun 9-1 |
| outdoor markets | Mon-Sat 7am-8pm; until 1pm Wed; Vucciria Mon-Sat 7-1 |
| Castello della Zisa | Mon-Sat 9-7; Sun 9-1 |

# TEMPLES OF SICILIA

There is a claim that to see the best of Hellenistic architecture, you need only to go to Sicilia (Sicily). The Greeks would undoubtedly dispute this, but Sicilia does have a wealth of well-preserved Greek temples and theatres, set in beautiful landscapes and ideal for viewing on foot.

Sicilia's strategic position made it a valuable prize for those powers that wished to control the trading arena of the Mediterranean. Waves of colonists—Sicanians, Elymians, Siculians and Phoenicians—arrived to settle on the island, usually establishing their own towns afresh. This continued when various Greek city-states sent colonists, establishing such cities as Syrakousai, Ghela, Selinunte and Akragas.

The Greeks brought architectural prowess and a great tradition of public building. Many of their efforts were destroyed by ensuing wars, either with each other or new invaders. Those buildings that survived were subject to earthquakes and the disdain of the early Christian church for heathen places of

NOTES
Tourist information: Segesta & Selinunte
Via S.Francesco d'Assisi 27,
91100 Trapani,
Tel: 0923 545511 Fax: 0923 29430
www.tiscali.it/trapani/attp.htm
open: daily 9- one hour before sunset

Tourist information: Valle dei Templi
Via C. Battisti 5, 92100 Agrigento,
Tel: 0922 20454 Fax: 0922 20246
open: daily 9- one hour before sunset

worship. More recently, their environment has been endangered by poor planning and corrupt constructors. What remains deserves our full appreciation.

The beautiful towns of Taormina and Siracusa each warrant a leisurely visit and their own chapter, so here we look at some of Sicilia's other ancient sites. Segesta, set 50 km (31 miles) southwest of Palermo within sight of an *autostrada*, is worth the effort of a detour. Though the city has crumbled somewhat over time, the colony's temple still adorns a low hill on Monte Bàrbaro. More remains of the city of Akragas, near modern Agrigento and you will need a full day to take in all that the remarkable Valley of the Temples has to offer. Selinunte, further west along the coast from Agrigento, is only touched on briefly here but also warrants a visit.

Segesta's wonderful setting >

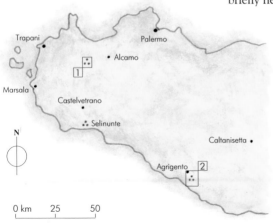

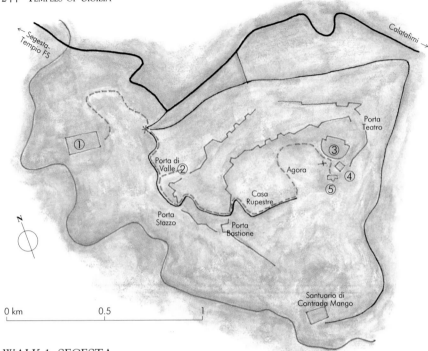

## WALK 1: SEGESTA

*The people of Segesta had an eye for a view and built their temple and theatre to take full advantage of it. Today, the site of the city makes for a wonderful short stroll.*

| | |
|---|---|
| Distance | 4 km (2.5 miles) |
| Time | 3 hours (including stops) |
| Difficulty | easy |
| Start/Finish | entrance gate |
| Transport | bus or train |

AST buses that stop at the Segesta site depart from Trapani and Palermo. Alternatively, the very occasional train stops at the Segesta-Tempio railway siding, from where it is a 2 km (1.25 miles) walk left uphill to the site. More frequent trains stop at Calatafimi station which is 4 km (2.5 miles) from the Segesta site (and some distance from the town of Calatafimi): to walk to the site, turn left from the station and then right onto the side road. Whatever your mode of transport, try to get there when the gate opens at 9 am, so you might have it to yourself briefly before the tour buses arrive.

Segesta dates back to the 12th century BC. Its founders, the Elymians, are of uncertain origin; Thucydides claimed they were refugees from Troy. They settled on Monte Bàrbaro and controlled extensive lands around. The city became Hellenised and established an alliance with Athens in 426 BC. Its arch rival was Selinunte to the south and Segesta engaged the aid of Carthage to defeat the southern neighbours.

After a skirmish with Syrakousai, the people of Segesta jilted the Carthaginians and embraced Roma, benefiting from trade through the port of Castellammare. The city fell into decline and was later occupied by Vandals, Moors, and finally by Normans who deserted it in the 13th century.

A short distance from the gate is the cafe and ticket office window. A shuttle bus runs up and down the hill to the theatre but don't buy a ticket for it as the walk offers changing views. First take the path north to pass a carpark and then climb a short distance to the magnificent

① **Tempio di Segesta** set on a small hill.

Begun about 430 BC, it is unroofed, a state that probably helped its preservation: it has withstood several earthquakes. There has been some conjecture that it was designed this way but certain clues—stone studs in the stylobate or base were always removed on completion—suggest otherwise. Its construction was possibly interrupted by war with Selinunte. It was built in imposing Doric style at a time when mainland Greeks were moving on to more elaborate designs. Stroll around the temple to enjoy it from all angles: the view up the Vallone della Fusa from behind the temple is also lovely.

When you have had your fill of the temple, return down the hill and head past the café and along the wide track. A short detour left brings you close to the

② **Porta di Valle** in the lower city walls which have been excavated. The city was well fortified with another line of defence higher up. Return to the main path and wind uphill, passing through what was once the Porta Stazzo and then through the Porta Bastione in the upper walls.

The jeep track ends at the location of the *agora* or marketplace where you pick

Segesta's Doric temple

up a footpath, passing ruins of the medieval village. The path takes you to the

③ **Teatro**, which, unusually for such structures, faces northeast, presumably to enjoy the wonderful view of hills and distant coast towards Castellammare. The raised motorway now snakes across the scene as well. When the *teatro* was built some time in the middle of the 3rd century BC, it would have had a *scaena* or backdrop but is otherwise well-preserved: you can still see the backrests of seats in the last row. Greek plays are performed here every second summer; the alternate year belongs to the theatre at Siracusa.

No doubt many of the earlier buildings were cannibalised to build later structures. Beside the theatre are the ruins of a

④ **Norman-Swabian castello**, which are worth walking through, as the floorplan is still evident. Little, however, remains of the

⑤ **mosque**, built by the Saracens who settled here before the Normans. There is also a medieval church in this cluster. Retrace your steps down the hillside, covered in fennel and marigolds.

On the southern slope of the hill is the **Santuario di Contrada Mango**, dating back to the 5th or 4th century BC. A long track around to this starts from the café, should you wish to stretch your legs further. Alternatively, consider a restorative *gelato*.

< Segesta's theatre

# WALK 2: VALLEY OF THE TEMPLES

*The Valle dei Templi is not strictly a valley, but it does have temples, and lots of them. This trove of ancient treasures lies just a short walk below the city of Agrigento.*

| | |
|---|---|
| Distance | 10 km (6.2 miles) |
| Time | at least 5 hours |
| Difficulty | easy |
| Start/Finish | Agrigento |
| Transport | bus or train to Agrigento |

Myth would have it that the artisan Daedalus founded the city of Akragas, but the truth is that it was colonists from Ghela and Greece who arrived in 581 BC to secure the Sicilian coast from attack by Carthage. Most of the public works were carried out in the 5th century BC when Akragas was a large and prosperous city, contained in a fortified area on the ridge overlooking the sea. It wasn't until the 7th century AD that the city was relocated to the top of the Girgenti hill, at the site of present-day Agrigento. This may have been to protect the inhabitants from invasion by the Saracens but if so the ploy failed.

Today's city of Agrigento, then, has an old centre with an Arab feel, complete with narrow, winding alleys. Our route doesn't visit this part of town but you should stroll through it and visit the church of S. Maria dei Greci, built over a Doric temple. Outside the *centro storico*, the city suffers from unchecked building which got especially out of hand following a 1966 landslide.

The Valle dei Templi is one of Sicily's most visited attractions and there will be the inevitable coach tours. It is most pleasant at the beginning or the end of the day, when the crowds thin. There is a bar/restaurant on the site, but you would do well to take provisions.

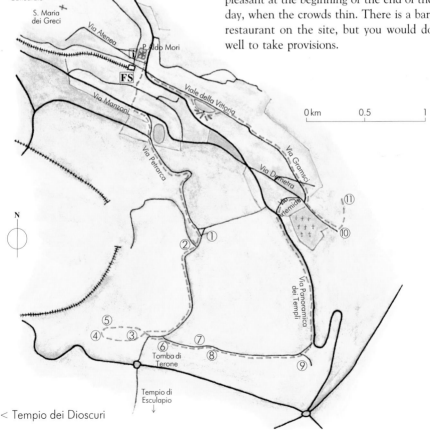

< Tempio dei Dioscuri

The colossal telemon

Our route begins at Piazzale Aldo Mori, near the train station. Leave the planted *piazzale* by the southeast corner to cross beneath Piazza Marconi (via a pedestrian tunnel) and descend several flights of steps. At the broad Via Manzoni, turn left then right into Via Petrarca, before the stadium. This winds downhill to pass through lovely groves of olive and almond trees.

After a sharp loop, the road passes above the Ipogeo Giacatello, a vault that held the city's water supply. Ahead on the left is
① the **Quartiere Ellenistico-Romano**, the urban grid that developed in the 2nd century BC. When the Romans arrived in 210 BC they renamed the city Agrigentum and added drainage and sewage, as well as many floor mosaics, the remains of which are protected. Cross the road again to the
② **Museo Archeologico** complex. The grounds contain the Hellenistic ruins of a tiered assembly space and a small 1st-century-BC temple which was adapted into an oratory during the Middle Ages. The 13th-century Cistercian church of San Nicola forms part of the museum, which holds many artefacts found in and near Akragas, organised chronologically.

Keep on along the road to the junction between the site's two zones: the western zone which requires a ticket for entry and the eastern, which is freely visited. Buy a ticket and head west to encounter the remains of the immense
③ **Tempio di Giove** or Temple of Jupiter. This was planned to be the largest Doric temple ever, with columns 17 metres tall, but construction was interrupted in 406 BC by a Carthaginian raid on the city. What had been built (by Carthaginian prisoners from the earlier Battle of Himera) was later razed by an earthquake. An extraordinary *telemon*, a weight-bearing colossus, lies flat amid the rubble. Nearby are four picturesque columns of the
④ **Tempio dei Dioscuri**: the Dioscuri were Castor and Pollux, sons of the god Zeus. Built near the end of the 5th century BC, the temple was damaged by Carthaginians, erected again and then flattened by earthquake. What now stands is actually a bit of reconstruction work from the 19th century. Like all of the temples it was built with local yellow limestone and probably coated with a plaster of powdered marble.

Just beyond this lies the ruins of the early
⑤ **Santuario di Demetra e Kore**, dedicated to the Chthonic or underground deities Demeter and her daughter Kore, also known as Persephone. Here are altars where

Tempio di Ercole

animals were sacrificed and their blood offered to these deities.

Leave the western zone and cross the road to the Porta Aurea and the broad Via Sacra. A path soon veers off right to the ⑥ **Tempio di Ercole** or Hercules, built at the end of the 6th century BC and possibly the oldest of the temples. It sported 38 tapered columns, a row of which stand resurrected. Just south of the city wall and visible from here is the Tomba di Terone, a solid plain structure erected half a century after the tyrant Theron's death.

Further along the avenue, on your left, lie the evocative cavities of the ⑦ **catacombs** where early Christians sought burial; steps lead down to a gated tunnel extending underground. On the right is the ⑧ **Tempio della Concordia**, a graceful Doric temple built around 430 BC. It is the best preserved of all, as it was converted to a Christian basilica in the 6th century with walls built between the columns. It was restored to its original form in 1748 and given the name 'Temple of Concord' for lack of any other. Further on you pass distinctive Byzantine *arcosols*, funeral niches carved into the rock. At the top of the hill, with a large sacrificial altar in front, lies the ⑨ **Tempio di Giunone Lacinia**. Built just prior to its neighbour, this temple dedicated to Juno was damaged during an earthquake in the Middle Ages: the walls of the *cella* (the inner sanctuary) are completely ruined.

Leave this amazing string of wonders by the gate below and continue along the road known as Panoramica dei Templi. For some distance there is no footpath, so watch for traffic. The road climbs to skirt below the modern cemetery. Turn right into Via Artemide and then right again into Via Demetra. Detour to the end of this road to visit a sanctuary only discovered in 1926: ⑩ **Santuario Rupestre di Demetra**, which predates the founding of Akragas. The sanctuary consists of three galleries carved out of the rocky crag and fed by a spring. Votive statuettes of Demeter and Kore were found in niches here.

A little further is the Romanesque church ⑪ **San Biagio**, built by the Normans over the ruins of a temple to Demeter and Kore.

Return to Via Demetra but soon take Via Gramsci right uphill; it eventually joins the broad Viale della Vittoria, with excellent views out over the Valle dei Templi, and brings you back to Piazza Marconi.

Tempio di Giunone Lacinia

## SELINUNTE

Another ancient site that shouldn't be overlooked is Selinunte or Selinus on the south of Sicilia's western arm. This Greek colony was established around 650 BC and thrived until it was destroyed by its rival Segesta in 409 BC in a terrible massacre.

Selinunte is a little more difficult to reach by public transport: catch a Lumia bus from Trapani or Agrigento to Castelvetrano (or a train from Palermo or Trapani), then an AST bus to Marinella Selinunte.

The site is divided into four zones: the ancient city, the eastern temples, the acropolis and the Sanctuary of Malophorus. A tourist kiosk (closed Sunday) by the east gate can provide a plan. *Allow 5 hours.*

# SIRACUSA

NOTES
Population: 126,000
Getting there: bus from Palermo or
airport at Catania; rail from mainland
via Catania
Tourist Office: Via Maestranza, 33
Tel: 0931 65201 Fax: 0931 60204
email: info@apt-siracusa.it
www.apt-siracusa.it
Market: Piazza della Posta, Mon-Sat am

If you're thinking of making Siracusa (or Syracuse) a quick stop on your grand tour, think again. This city may not be large but it overflows with history and charm. The narrow alleys of Ortigia are rich with fine palazzi. Neapolis, despite its name, is thick with ancient Greek wonders. Even the intervening modern district is enlivened by vendors hawking live snails or by the mobile *salumeria* which does good business day and night in the Foro Siracusano. By the time you leave, Siracusa will undoubtedly have won your affection.

Much of its attraction is the natural setting: a ledge of limestone backs fertile land which culminates in the isle of Ortigia, shaped like a fist with thumb downturned, jutting into the Ionian Sea. The strategic position, complete with a safe harbour and a stream, the Syrakò, drew the attention of Greek colonists from Corinth who seized the small island from Siculian people in 734 BC. They quickly established another centre, Akradina, on the main-land and linked the two with a causeway and then a bridge.

The city flourished as a trading centre and was targeted (and seized) by Gelon, the tyrant of nearby Gela, who transferred the populus of other colonies here in the 5th century BC. This influx created the new districts of Tyche and Neapolis. A series of tyrants ruled the city, at times brutally, bringing prosperity and cultural glory: temples and theatres were constructed, poets and dramatists were patronised in court. Together with Gela and Akragas (now Agrigento), Siracusa dealt Carthage a major blow in 480 BC. Athens, concerned at Siracusa's rise to power, sent a large fleet to capture the city in 415 BC, but the Siracusans outwitted

them and destroyed the fleet, setting those prisoners who escaped execution to labour for seven years in the city's quarries.

Inevitably, after two years of siege, the city fell to the might of the Roman Empire in 212 BC. Christianity came early to Siracusa and left a series of catacombs underneath it. After another long siege, the Moors ransacked the city in AD 878; their influence is clear in the alleyways of Ortigia. They were followed by Normans and the Spanish, but the population had dwindled to occupy only Ortigia and the city suffered plague and famine. The earthquake of 1693 did not cause terrible damage but was the pivot for a programme of restoration, giving the island its baroque flavour. In 1865 it was made a provincial capital and its fortunes began to change, with the mainland being resettled.

< Orecchio di Dionisio

Ortigia's eastern point

Siracusa was bombed heavily in WWII and large sections have a bland post-war feel to them: fortunately, Neapolis and Ortigia survived intact. Industry developed nearby and today Siracusa is once again a prosperous city.

Two itineraries are necessary to take in the sights of Siracusa: the first on the picturesque island and the second to view the monuments on the mainland.

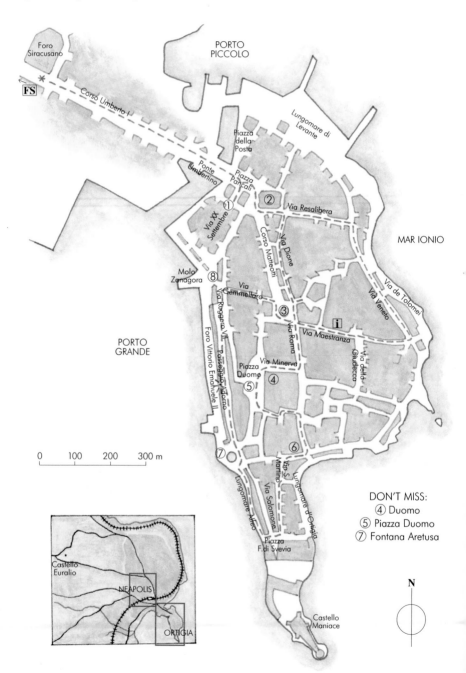

# WALK 1: ORTIGIA

*The Siracusans are great believers in the passeggiata; join them for a stroll around their beautiful island replete with Greek remains and baroque glories.*

Our route starts in the Foro Siracusano on the mainland, a popular meeting place now and in ancient Siracusa, when it was the marketplace or *agora*. Walk southeast down the broad Corso Umberto I and cross the bridge onto the island of Ortigia. Outdoor markets are held in the area just on the left. A short detour down Via XX Settembre on the right takes you to
① **Porta Urbica** or what remains of this ancient gateway to the city. Walk back up to the top of Piazza Pancali to view the ruins of the Doric
② **Tempio di Apollo**, one of the first to be built by the Greek colonists around 570 BC. Little remains of this temple, which later served as Byzantine church, Arab mosque, Norman church and Spanish barracks.

Skirt around the temple site to pass the church of San Paolo. Turn right down Via Dione, the main thoroughfare before Corso Matteotti was constructed in the Fascist era. Continue past Chiesa di San Cristoforo to

Papyrus growing in Apollo's temple

reach the island's heart:
③ **Piazza Archimede**, which honours the greatest scientific mind of the Greek age. Achimedes was born in Siracusa in 287 BC, returned here after his studies and aided the city with his practical theories and defensive mechanisms, only to die here at the hands of a Roman soldier. Today a 20th-century fountain featuring Artemis the Huntress adorns the piazza which is edged by Spanish-Gothic palazzi.

Fishing boats by the Ponte Umbertino >

Make a quick detour left down Via dei Montalto where you'll find the dilapidated Palazzo Montalto, a 14th-century mansion with lovely mullioned windows. Afterwards, continue south up Via Roma past the church of Santa Maria. Turn right into Via Minerva to walk along the side of the ④ **Duomo**, an amazing structure which incorporates the shell of a 5th-century temple dedicated to Athena; you can see the columns in the side wall. The richly adorned temple was much admired by Cicero who visited Ortigia. In the 7th century it was adapted as a Byzantine church when the columns were enclosed with walls. Mosaics were later added by the Normans but these have sadly disappeared. Near the entrance, however, is a much older vestige: an ancient altar created by the Siculi, the first people to settle Sicilia.

The façade of the church was seriously damaged in the earthquakes of 1545 and 1693 and was then rebuilt in its present baroque style. The duomo fronts onto the ⑤ **Piazza Duomo**, one of the most beautiful

Ortigia's temple-duomo

in all of Italy. The piazza's elliptical space is lined with attractive baroque façades, including (clockwise from the duomo) the 17th-century Palazzo Arcivescovile or Archbishop's Palace, the Chiesa di Santa Lucia alla Badia dedicated to the city's patron saint, Palazzo Borgia, the 18th-century Palazzo Benevantano del Bosco and the Palazzo Municipale. The latter was built in 1629 over an unfinished Ionic temple recently unearthed. The façade features, high up at the left corner of the cornice, a motif signature of the architect Juan Vermexio, nicknamed 'the lizard'.

Leave the piazza at its southeast corner, walking past the church of Montevergini. Continue in this direction and then turn right on Via Roma, then right again to the austere 13th-century ⑥ **Palazzo Bellomo** which houses a fine collection of medieval art, including an *Annunciation* by Antonello da Messina and *The Burial of St Lucy* by Caravaggio.

Turn right out of the gallery and then left into Via San Martino, passing on your left the 6th-century basilica of San Martino. Head straight on Via Salomone to Piazza Federico di Svevia. This is the southernmost accessible point of Ortigia; beyond lies the 13th-century Castello Maniace, erected by Frederick II in 1239 and still used by the military. Turn right to reach the water's edge and then follow Lungomare Alfeo along the sheltered (and therefore ideal for promenading) side to the pretty ⑦ **Fontana Aretusa**. This once freshwater spring was, according to ancient myth, the incarnation of the nymph Aretusa. The handmaid was transformed by the goddess Artemis so she might escape the attentions of the river god Alpheus, who found her nonetheless and joins her here in this pool, along with the ducks and papyrus reeds.

From the top corner of the spring continue north along Passegio Adorno. Locals prefer to promenade along the broad boulevard below but this raised street along the ramparts offers wonderful views over the Porto Grande, the location of many great

The baroque Piazza Duomo

sea battles. Continue on Via Ruggero VII to reach the 15th-century gate of ⑧ **Porta Marina**, built in limestone as part of the Spanish defences. After admiring the detail on the outside of the arch, take Via Gemmellaro back up the hill and then Via Scina, passing through a district once inhabited by coopers, to re-enter Piazza Archimede. This time, head east down Via Maestranza, lined with finely decorated baroque palazzi. A small tourist office is located in Palazzo Bonnano at #33. Further along on the left is the Palazzo Impellizzeri, embellished with carved faces.

Turn left down Via Veneto, which was the favoured location for the Spanish nobility and is lined with large palazzi, then left into Via Resalibera to return, through the old Moorish quarter, to the Tempio di Apollo and then to Piazza Pancali.

The other way to see the island is of course by sea, a viewpoint that allows you the sight of Castello Maniace. In season, a boat departs regularly from Molo Zanagora for short trips around Ortigia.

## WALK 2: TYCHE & NEAPOLIS

*The mainland may be less picturesque than Ortigia but it has a wealth of ancient treasures to amaze you, all within a short walk of each other and not far from the city centre.*

Once again we start from the Foro Siracusano. Leave this old *agora* by the northwest corner and walk past the ugly 1936 Pantheon to walk up Corso Gelone. Turn right into Via Testaferrata, then left into Via del Santuario to enter Siracusa's latest monument, the tear-shaped ① **Santuario della Madonna delle Lacrime**. Built to house a statue of the Virgin claimed to have shed tears in 1953, the 90-metre-high project caused much controversy and was not completed until 1994. From the church's terrace you can view an area of **Greek and Roman housing**, currently under excavation.

Continue along Via del Santuario and cross Viale Teocrito to reach the ② **Museo Archeologico Paolo Orsi**, set in the Villa Landolina, a large park filled with historic relics. The museum's superb

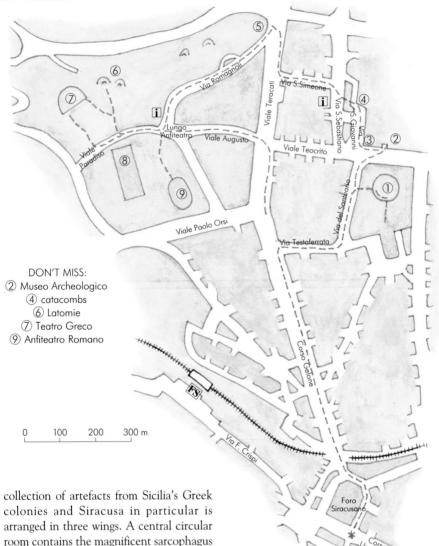

DON'T MISS:
② Museo Archeologico
④ catacombs
⑥ Latomie
⑦ Teatro Greco
⑨ Anfiteatro Romano

0    100    200    300 m

collection of artefacts from Sicilia's Greek colonies and Siracusa in particular is arranged in three wings. A central circular room contains the magnificent sarcophagus found in the catacombs of San Giovanni.

Next door, up a lane, is the small but interesting

③ **Museo del Papiro**, which presents artefacts and information on the use of papyrus. The plant grows along the Ciane river near Siracusa, the only place in Europe where it grows freely. Turn west out of the museum then turn first right onto Via San Giovanni to arrive at the

④ **Catacombe di San Giovanni**. Siracusa's first bishop, St Marcian, was beaten to death on this site and the 6th-century basilica

which stood here once served as the city's first duomo. It now lies in ruins, wrecked by the earthquake of 1693, although its Byzantine crypt is still intact. Further underground lie the extensive catacombs which date back to the 4th century. Here the early Christians buried their dead, enlarging an old Greek aqueduct and tunnelling out long galleries with large niches and adding round chapels for prayer.

The catacombs are now a gloomy place, with all artefacts long removed by grave-robbers, but traces of paint suggest it was once well decorated. There are two other major catacombs under Siracusa, though neither are open to the public at this point.

Walk across the grassy area below a lovely rose window belonging to a small 14th-century church, then cross Via San Sebastiano and head down Via San Simeone. At Viale Teracati, turn right and cross the road at lights. On the corner, beyond the fence, lies the Necropolis Grotticelle. One of the two clearly visible tombs is said to be the ⑤ **tomb of Archimedes**, the great mathematician and scientific thinker whose genius helped hold off the Roman invasion.

Walk along Via Romagnoli, skirting the edge of the Parco Archeologico of Neapolis, with views down to the Greek quarries, the Latomia di Santa Venera and the Latomie Intagliatelle. Here blocks of white limestone were hewn out for building the city, often by prisoners of war held in terrible conditions. Earthquakes have caused the earth ceiling to collapse, so that what were caves are now opened to the light and rich in vegetation. Near the fence is an ancient fig tree known as the Secular Fig.

Turn right after the tourist kiosk and head down the trinket-strewn Viale Paradiso to the entrance of the Parco Archeologico. From the *biglietteria* or ticket office, take the footpath right to wind down to the ⑥ **Latomia del Paradiso**. A pillar of rock which once supported the roof of this quarry still stands; the rest has collapsed and has been planted with a grove of citrus trees that gives the former prison its somewhat ironic name. Still intact is the **Grotta dei Cordari** (the Cordmakers' Cave), a curious grotto hewn into the rock and once used by the city's makers of ropes because its humid air was conducive to plaiting hemp.

Another fascinating sight (and sound) is the **Orecchio di Dionisio**, or the 'ear of Dionysius' a tall narrow cavity with smooth walls. The name was suggested by the artist Caravaggio who believed the tyrant

Teatro Greco with Madonna delle Lacrime on the horizon

Anfiteatro Romano

Dionysius must have used the acoustics to eavesdrop on his prisoners' conversations. It may have been used to rehearse plays for the nearby theatre.

Retrace your steps a short distance and take the path for the wonderful
⑦ **Teatro Greco**, carved into the rock of the hill. A theatre existed here from the 5th century BC, but in the 3rd century BC Hieron II had it expanded to its present size to seat 15,000 people. It was used for popular assemblies but also for staging plays, notably the later tragedies of Aeschylus. The Romans modified it to stage gladiatorial combat and it was later abandoned and even plundered for stone at the order of Charles V in 1526 during the Spanish fortification of Siracusa. These days, a season of Greek dramas are performed here every second summer.

Overlooking the theatre is a manmade grotto with a fountain fed by a Roman aqueduct. Nearby are niches for votive images. On the other side of Viale Paradiso are the remains of
⑧ **Ara di Ierone II** or the altar of Hieron II, dating back to the 3rd century BC. This huge sacrificial altar, of which only the plinth remains, was large enough for hundreds of oxen to be slaughtered here in a single ceremony. It would once have featured a statue of Zeus.

Votive niches for the *pinakis* cult >

Further along on the right is a path lined with sarcophagi and votive niches, leading to the

⑨ **Anfiteatro Romano**. This elliptical arena was built during the Roman occupation, much of it carved out of living rock, though much of the masonry was plundered by the Spanish. It was used for horse races and gladiator fights, and could be flooded for staging naval battles.

Leave the park, passing on the left the little church of San Nicolò ai Cordari and, underneath it, the *piscina* or pool which was used to flood the amphitheatre. To return to the centre of town, walk along Via Augusto and turn right into Corso Gelone, which can be followed back south.

## OTHER EXCURSIONS

Yet another quarry-prison is to be seen at the **Latomia dei Cappuccini**, set beside the Cappuchin convent on the eastern edge of Siracusa. It's unsafe to enter but you can view it from above. To get there from Foro Siracusano, head northeast along Via dell'Arsenale, passing the Greek arsenal, and continue on Riviera Dionisio il Grande, through Largo Latomia, and up Via Puglia to Largo Campania.

**Castello Euralio**, almost 9 km (6 miles) to the northwest, is one of the greatest fortresses of the Greek period. It was built at the turn of the 4th century BC to defend Siracusa from land attack. The extensive fortifications also offer an excellent

Siracusans enjoying a Sunday stroll

panorama over the city. To reach the *castello*, catch bus #9 or 11 from outside the hospital on Corso Gelone near Viale Paolo Orsi.

Further afield, some 40 km (25 miles) west of Siracusa and a little difficult to reach without a car is the site of **Pantàlica**, a vast necropolis of over 5,000 tombs carved into the rocky hillside by the Siculi. To reach it, you could catch a bus from Piazza della Posta to Sortino and follow the signs for a 5 km (just over 3 miles) walk to Pantàlica. Take food and plenty of water!

OPENING HOURS

| | |
|---|---|
| Palazzo Bellomo | Mon-Sat 9am-1.30; Sun 9-12.30; Wed & Fri 3-7 |
| Duomo | daily 8-noon; 4-7 |
| Madonna delle Lacrime | daily 7-12.30; 4-7 |
| Museo Archeologico | Tue-Sun 9-1; 3.20-6.30 |
| Museo del Papiro | Tue-Sun 9-1.30 |
| Catacombe di San Giovanni | Wed-Mon 9-1; 2.30-5 |
| Parco Archeologico Neapolis | daily 9-2 hours before sunset |
| Castello Euralio | daily from 9 till 1.5 hours before sunset |

# TAORMINA

Legend would have it that Taormina was founded by a shipwrecked Greek sailor named Teocle in the 8th century BC. This seems unlikely but if you were going to be tossed into the sea by a peeved Neptune, Taormina would certainly be the place to come ashore. Nestling on a terrace of Monte Tauro overlooking the Ionian Sea, from here you can sip *vino alla mandorla* while eyeing Etna from a safe distance. The weary need only walk short distances; the more energetic can consider steep inclines.

This ledge of land was most likely occupied by Siculi tribes long before any Greek colonists arrived. When Dionysius of Siracusa destroyed nearby Naxos in 403 BC the survivors moved here, calling it Tauromenion. The settlement, sited on the route between Messina and Siracusa prospered from trade. Hellenistic housing was centred north of the Porta Messina and ruins of their homes can still be seen in this area.

The Romans duly arrived and modified the town, which flourished and became particularly powerful during the Byzantine period. After much resistance, Saracens occupied Taormina in the 10th and 11th centuries, improving the farming methods for the surrounding land and moving the

**NOTES**
Population: 10,000
Getting there: bus or rail from Catania or Messina; local bus from rail station up to town or a steep 30-minute walk
Tourist Office: Palazzo Corvaja
Tel: 0942 23243  Fax: 0942 24941
email: aast@taormina-ol.it
www.taormina-ol.it
Markets: each morning, Via Cappuccini

urban centre to around the present duomo. The Normans and the Spanish continued this development and *palazzi* sprang up along the present Corso Umberto I, which followed the ancient consular road, the Consulare Valeria.

Taormina remained loyal to the Spanish during the Sicilian Vespers and, in 1410, it was made the seat of the Sicilian parliament. Later it was occupied by the French and then the Bourbons, before Italy was finally united.

During the Middle Ages, a number of convents and monasteries were established in his region to stave off the danger of Muslim conversion. When tourism developed in the 19th century, there were spacious buildings—monasteries empty as a result of religious suppression—ready to hold the stream of visitors which started to flow.

Taormina, with its flower-lined alleys and classical theatre, has long been a mecca for the tourist-pilgrim: Goethe was seriously impressed and D.H. Lawrence stopped by for several years. These days, Taormina's renowned beauty means you'll inevitably encounter tour groups: to minimise their impact, come in spring, autumn or even winter. You'll also find it an expensive place to sojourn, a factor which may help you to tear yourself away!

The view over Taormina

Piazza Duomo >

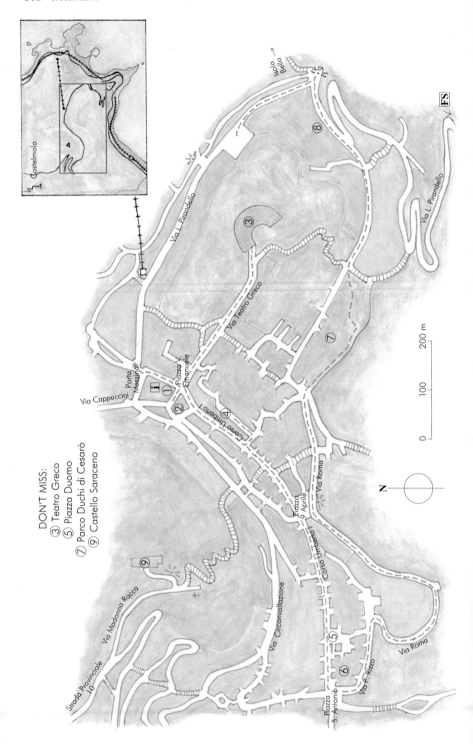

DON'T MISS:
③ Teatro Greco
⑤ Piazza Duomo
⑦ Parco Duchi di Cesarò
⑨ Castello Saraceno

# A WALK IN TAORMINA

*This pleasant walk takes you through the compact town and a little away from the tourist throng to some stunning viewpoints.*

Our itinerary starts at Porta Messina, the northeastern gate in the old fortifications. A short distance south is Piazza Vittorio Emanuele, on which stands the ① **Palazzo Corvaja**. The core of this mansion is an 11th-century Arab tower with battlements; in the early 15th century the right wing with mullioned Gothic windows was added to house the Sicilian parliament. A newer wing houses the tourist office.

Turn right to detour a few steps west to ② the **Odeon**. This small Roman theatre would have hosted music recitals for the town's elite. It was built in the 1st century AD atop a Greek construction (possibly a temple) and was in turn partly covered by the church of Santa Caterina. Although much damaged, sections of the brick-and-lime *cavea* or seating are still visible. It was only unearthed in 1892.

Detour now up a souvenir-lined road to the deservedly famous ③ **Teatro Greco**, which stands in a spectacular site below Mt Tauro. The theatre was probably built by the Greeks in the 3rd century BC and heavily modified by the Romans for displays of combat; they replaced the Greek semicircular *orchestra* with a circular *arena* and added a pit for animals and gladiators. The *cavea* has mostly been hewn out of the rock to seat an estimated 5,400 spectators. The dramatic backdrop of the Bay of Schisò and Monte Etna would have been partly obscured from the Roman audience by a *scaena* wall, which has since collapsed. Further changes were made by the Spanish in the 12th century, who built a residence here. Today it is still a place which combines architectural elegance and natural beauty.

Just south of the theatre is an archaeological area which is due to open to the public and may be worth investigating. Return to Piazza Vittorio Emanuele and begin your walk down the traffic-free Corso Umberto I but soon make a brief detour at

Teatro Greco and a smoke-veiled Etna

< Along the Naumachiae

the first alley left to inspect the curious
④ **Naumachiae**, strangely named because
this is Greek for 'sea-battles'. There are
claims this was the site of a gymnasium, a
place where young men were educated and
trained, and that the base of the high wall
is a remnant of this. The rest of the wall,
which features high niches, was built by the
Romans as an embankment for a reservoir.

Continue on to Piazza 9 Aprile where the
deconsecrated 15th-century church of Sant'
Agostino now houses the town library.
There are excellent views to be enjoyed.
Head through the Porto di Mezzo or the
'halfway gate'; the 12th-century clock tower
above the gate was reconstructed in 1679
after French troops had destroyed it. On
the right, some 150 m further on, at the
top of broad steps stands the Palazzo
Ciampoli, built in 1412 in Catalan style.
Continue along Corso Umberto I to
⑤ **Piazza Duomo**, which features the
fortress-like duomo dedicated to San
Nicolò. It was built around the year 1400
but has a Renaissance portal. Also adorning

Palazzo San Stefano >

the piazza is a baroque marble fountain built
in 1635 and topped by an unusual two-
legged female centaur, the town symbol.

Continue on to walk through Porta
Catania at the western edge and turn left
down Via Pietro Rizzo. On your left is the
⑥ **Palazzo Duca di San Stefano**, a masterpiece of Sicilian-Gothic architecture. This
13th-century mansion, set in a lovely
garden, is of Norman construction but
shows a strong Arab influence, particularly
in the geometric frieze at the top. It houses
the work of sculptor Giuseppe Mazzullo.

Turn right just before the old monastery
of San Domenico (now a luxury hotel) into
Via Roma. There is no footpath here so
take care. The road winds above a lovely
wooded gully and then leads to the side
gates of the
⑦ **Parco Duchi di Cesarò**. These charming
formal gardens were donated to the public
by the Trevelyan family in the 1920s. The
park is filled with Mediterranean plants plus
a few relics from world wars. This is a good
spot to picnic and enjoy the wonderful view
over the bay.

Leave the park at its eastern end and walk along Via Bagnoli Croce and join the hairpin Via Pirandello to pass, on your left, the symmetrical cavities of the ⑧ **Tombe Bizantine**. These cells cut into the hillside are actually thought to be 10th-11th-century Arab rather than Byzantine. This is a small section of what would have been an extensive necropolis.

Further along, the road turns sharply to the left and there is a dramatic *belvedere* or lookout over the Baia dell'Isola Bella.

Follow the road uphill to the bus terminal. From here you can catch a local bus up the winding road and disembark at Via Madonna Rocca (or stay on board to continue up to Castelmola: see 'Other Excursions'). Near the end of Via Madonna Rocca, steps lead up to ⑨ **Castello Saraceno**. This ruined medieval castle sits atop Monte Tauro (398 m), surrounded by prickly pear. It is currently closed for restoration work.

A view from Castelmola

A little further along the road is a small sanctuary built in 1640 and a terrace with a lovely view over Taormina and its theatre. From here, steps zigzag down the hill on Via Crucis, passing the stations of the cross. On reaching Taormina's outskirts, cross Via Circonvallazione and take the stepped alleys south to reach Corso Umberto I near the central Piazza 9 Aprile.

## OTHER EXCURSIONS

If you catch the bus up to the tiny town of **Castelmola**, 5 km (3 miles) of winding road and 325 m above Taormina, you will be rewarded with spectacular coastal views, particularly good from the ruined medieval *castello* perched above the town. For even better views, you could take the path behind Castelmola's cemetery to climb Monte Veneretta, some two hours of walking. The return walk to Taormina via Castello Saraceno is all downhill. Head out of Castelmola but before the road loops, turn right onto the minor Via Dazio. (If you miss this, just follow the winding road downhill.) Via Dazio descends steeply southeast. Where it rejoins the road, turn right. Soon veer left on Via Madonna Rocca and follow directions for the end of the main walk.

To reach the pretty **Isola Bella** below Taormina you can either catch the funivia from near the top of Via Pirandello or descend the steps from the *belvedere* below the bus terminal on that road.

OPENING HOURS

| | |
|---|---|
| Odeon | daily 9-5 |
| Teatro Greco | daily 9-4, in summer till 6.30 |
| Palazzo San Stefano | Mon-Sat 8.30-12.30; 3-5, in summer till 7 |
| Parco Duchi di Cesarò | daily 9-4, in summer till 6.30 |

# SARDEGNAN WILDS

NOTES
Suggested base: Dorgali
Getting there: bus from Olbia ferry
    terminal; airports at Olbia & Cagliari
Tourist Office: Pro Loco, Via La Mar-
    mora 181, Dorgali Tel: 0784 96243
www.regione.sardegna.it
Maps: IGM Dorgali & Oliena 1:25000
Best Timing: avoid July-August

The island of Sardegna or Sardinia remains a mystery to most. Large tracts of land, too rugged to be cultivated, are frequented only by herders and intrepid walkers, climbers or speliologists. The wild beauty of its coast and mountainous interior amply rewards any efforts you make to see them.

There are signs of human settlement from the Paleolithic era and waves of Roman, Arab and Spanish settlers have made their mark but unique to Sardegna were the warrior Nuraghic people who flourished here in the 2nd century BC and built circular towers all over the island.

Recently, tourism has reached Sardegna: in summer Italians flock to resorts along the northern Costa Smeralda. Elsewhere, tourist facilities are less developed but Sards are discovering the value of eco-tourism and many groups now offer guided treks. One of the best regions for walking is the Gennargentu national park, in the east. This comprises various massifs, including the Supramonti which spill to the sea. The limestone

landscape has been carved by water into deep gorges and coastal gullies known as *codule*. The vegetation on the coast is maquis, thick with oleanders, juniper and myrtles. Inland, bare rocky areas are interspersed with patches of ancient forest.

Dorgali, high on a ridge on the northern Supramonte, is an attractive base. Public transport is infrequent in this area and use of a car would increase flexibility. The walks outlined are all possible regardless but include a fair amount of road walking that could be avoided with a car.

The three walks detailed in this chapter are quite varied. The first gives you a flavour of the stunning wilderness coast along the Golfo di Orosei, the second takes you to the startling gorge of Gorropu, and the third is a more ambitious ramble to the hidden Nuraghic village of Tiscali.

Gola di Gorropu >

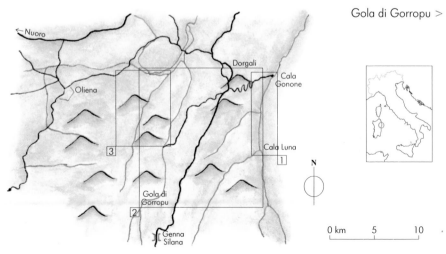

Monte
Chessaruia

Cala
Gonone ①

← Dorgali

△
Monte
Doschele

GOLFO
DI
OROSEI

CODULA FUILI
④
Cala Fuili

③

N

Caletta di
Oddoana

Fruncu
Nieddu △ Cala Luna
CODULA LUNA ②

△
Punta
Is Giroves

0        1        2 km

## WALK 1: CALA LUNA

*This excursion begins with a boat ride to what may be Italy's most beautiful beach then leads over uninhabited coastline above deep grottoes. The path is stony and sometimes muddy but quite clear; take plenty of water.*

| | |
|---|---|
| Distance | 8.7 km (5.4 miles) |
| Time | 3.5 to 4.5 hours |
| Difficulty | easy |
| Start | Cala Luna |
| Finish | Cala Gonone |
| Transport | bus from Dorgali and return |

If you are staying at Dorgali catch an ARST bus through the nearby limestone mountain tunnel and down the zigzagging road to the coastal town of
① **Cala Gonone**. This settlement, isolated until the tunnel was completed in the 1920s, is now a popular resort town with a pretty marina and a small beach.

A mid-morning boat departs from the marina at Cala Gonone; the schedule varies so ask at the ticket kiosk. The boat stops at Bue Marino, a sea cave where the rare monk seal has been sighted: *bue marino* translates as 'sea ox'. You can visit the caves for a surcharge. The boat continues on past numerous caverns to the secluded beach at
② **Cala Luna**. Many summer visitors find their way here by boat or on foot, but you may well have the white sands to yourself. Explore the vast caverns north of beach.

Leave the beach heading inland past the small lake and through pink oleanders and mastic trees to pass the simple seasonal restaurant. The path heads up the codula but soon veers off to the right on a steep stony path ascending the hill of Fruncu Nieddu. The waymark, an inscribed arrow with a circle, is soon augmented with painted green arrows, so there's little danger of losing the way. Shortly you gain an excellent view back over the beach.

The stony path descends somewhat and then rises again to reach the Grotto Oddoana, a shallow cave. Another descent takes you into a small gorge, the Gola di

Oddoana, and then a longer uphill stretch heads inland, a little away from the cliffline. A level plateau offers sweeping views back south along the cliffs and nearby rocks make a possible spot for a picnic lunch.

Further on, a left-branching path leads to ruins at Nuraghe Toddeitto: this is a steep detour inland, offering dramatic views. Otherwise, continue north to soon reach a fork in the path, from where the road is visible across the Codula Fuili.

We recommend a detour (taking about an hour) to the northern entrance of the ③ **Grotto del Bue Marino**. To get there, take the right forking path, which climbs steeply up and down. The final leg is on boardwalk over the sea: very dramatic but not one for those with height anxieties! There is a locked gate at the end of the path which prevents you going very deep inside the grotto. Return along the same path to the junction.

Back at the junction, descend the *codula*. At the floor of the gully, a short detour right takes you along a level path to ④ **Cala Fuili**, a small and pebbly but nonetheless pretty beach. Return to climb the

A woman of the Supramonte

steps to the parking area at the end of the coast road. From here it is a pleasant walk of just over 3 km (almost 2 miles) along the broad Viale Bue Marina, back to Cala Gonone.

The view north from Cala Luna

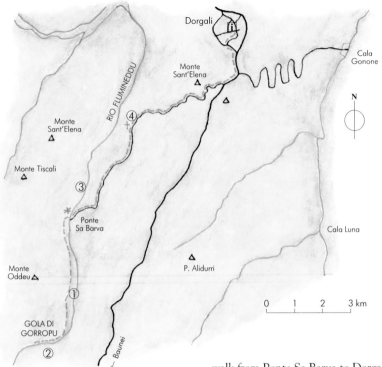

## WALK 2: THE GORGE OF GORROPU

*This pleasant walk follows the course of the Rio Flumineddu to the amazing canyon of Gorropu, with its steep limestone walls. Take lunch provisions and water.*

| | |
|---|---|
| Distance | 20 km (12.5 miles) |
| Time | 4 or 8 hours |
| Difficulty | easy until the gorge, but long |
| Start/Finish | Ponte Sa Barva |
| Transport | need a car or taxi to avoid a long road walk |

If you don't have a car, arrange a taxi to drop you at Ponte Sa Barva, 13 km (8 miles) southwest of Dorgali. This is a picturesque valley road to walk along, but to walk it twice would make the day's journey too long and leave insufficient time to explore the canyon. Walking times are as follows: from Ponte Sa Barva to the gorge entrance and return takes 3 hours or so; allow at least an hour to explore part of the gorge; the road

walk from Ponte Sa Barva to Dorgali would take about 3 hours.

Ponte Sa Barva crosses Rio Flumineddu under the imposing heights of Monte Oddeu. From the bridge a track forks right to Tiscali (reaching the destination point of Walk 3 from the south); you take the left fork, signed to Gorropu. At another fork, the track left descends to a pleasant riverside camping area; take the right track up to a gate.

From here a broad jeep track undulates through beech woods alongside or above the river. Look out for arbutus trees, bearing red berry-like fruit known to Sards as *lidone* or to other Italians as *corbezzolo*. At various points you can scramble down to ① the **bank of the Rio Flumineddu** where a swim would be refreshing in summer. High above to your left you catch glimpses of the Orientale Sarda, the precipitous coast road cut by immigrant woodcutters, which you should make time to traverse either by car or by public bus: the views down to Gorropu and surroundings are amazing.

Vines along the road to Gorropu

Eventually your track descends and narrows to reach the entrance to the ② **Gola di Gorropu**. This is the deepest canyon in Italy, with sheer rock walls some 450 metres (1470 ft) high. The river actually runs underground in the gorge, making it a strangely silent place. The huge smooth limestone boulders make exploration of the canyon a slow affair; you will generally make faster progress if you keep to the right hand side. Eventually the gorge narrows even more—you can almost touch both sides at once—and the scramble gets even more difficult. There is supposedly a route up and out at the southern end (taking you on to the high Orientale Sarda road) but you need to be either extremely proficient or foolhardy to attempt it. Retrace your way to the gorge entrance and return along the track to the Ponte Sa Barva.

To return to Dorgali on foot, cross the bridge and, after a concreted section of road, keep left at a junction to wind up the river valley. The road passes to the right of a ③ **domus de janus**, literally 'a house of the fairies', a prehistoric tomb which predates the Nuraghic civilisation. The site is marked by a sign and is visible across the river: a dirt track leads off to it. Some distance on, you pass the ruined ④ **Chiesa Campestre Buon Cammino**, again on your left.

The gradual ascent continues past terraced slopes of olive trees and vines, some of which produce the local full-bodied red known as *Cannonau*. The land is divided into small plots, most tended by residents of Dorgali. On the slope of Monte Sant' Elena, near a hotel of that name, keep straight on a minor road which dips and then climbs to the outskirts of Dorgali.

Rio Flumineddu >

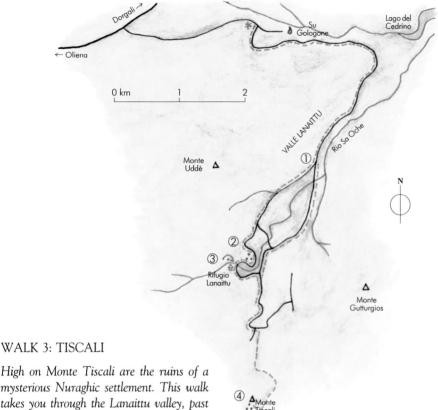

## WALK 3: TISCALI

*High on Monte Tiscali are the ruins of a mysterious Nuraghic settlement. This walk takes you through the Lanaittu valley, past several fascinating sites and up to Tiscali.*

| | |
|---|---|
| Distance | 19 km (11.8 miles) |
| Time | 7 to 9 hours without transport |
| Difficulty | moderate but long |
| Start/Finish | Su Gologone |
| Transport | need a car or taxi to avoid a long road walk |

This fascinating walk is complicated by the lack of signage in the Valle Lanaittu: our map is schematic and you should refer closely to the notes! Another factor is the distance to be covered but it's possible to reach Tiscali and return in a long day-walk if you stay two nights at the wonderful Hotel Su Gologone (tel 0784 287512; fax 0784 287668) which is 2 km off the Dorgali/ Oliena road; a local bus stops at the turnoff. The hotel can arrange a jeep to the end of the road in the Lanaittu valley, from where

< Nuraghe at Sos Carros

you could walk back; they also offer guided treks. If you have a car, you could do an abbreviated loop walk just in the valley.

Estimated walking times are: from Hotel Su Gologone to Rifugio Lanaittu via Sos Carros takes 3 hours; from there to Tiscali allow 1.5 hours; for the more direct return route from Tiscali to the hotel allow 3 hours. Start early, taking water and food!

Just beyond the hotel, turn right onto a concrete road signposted to Tiscali. This winds uphill, around a spur of Monte Uddè and passing hydro-electricity works and a quarry. It becomes a stony dirt road and offers dramatic views of the serrated cliffs across the Fiume Cedrino. The road then heads southwest and descends gently into the Valle Lanaittu.

① At a **fork in the road**, keep right. Ignore a right-branching path and then one on the

Fertile ground in Valle Lanaittu

left to reach a junction. Turn right here on an unsigned track uphill past a tin sheepfold to the fenced compound of

② **Sos Carros**, the remains of a Nuraghic village. The nearby shepherd may be able to open the gate to the archaeological zone for you; inside are the evocative remains of stone buildings, including a sanctuary that contains a strange circular seat.

Return to the junction and turn right, crossing a low cement bridge to Rifugio

Lanaittu (no accomodation; used as a speliological base). Make the short detour on a footpath right to

③ **Grotta Sa Oche**, which means 'cave of the voice'. The name refers to the sound of the floodwaters which pour forth from it after the rains come. Cavers are still exploring the huge underground lake system deep within the mountain. Venture in a short way: your eyes will adjust to the dark.

Head back to the *rifugio* and continue south on the track. Ignore a right-branching track which leads to a swineherd's hut, but otherwise keep right, continuing to a clearing. Leave southwest on the jeep track right which zigzags steeply uphill.

At a large boulder with markings, divert left onto a footpath (to Tiscali), waymarked with red and white. This climbs steeply to a point where a rock wall obscures your view of the valley. Here the path forks: take the left path, now marked with orange arrows, through a narrow cleft and then contour around the mountainside below a rock wall. You then drop a little way to a notice that asks you to ring for the attendant who,

The view from Monte Tiscali

incredibly, is waiting nearby to accept your entrance fee! The ruins of
④ **Tiscali** have an amazing setting: the limestone crest of the mountain has collapsed, causing a huge *dolina* or depression. At some time a Nuraghic tribe took advantage of this natural concealment to build a village here: it may have been as a refuge from invading Romans. It is unlikely that it was a long-term settlement as water would have been scarce. A loop path around the *dolina* takes you past the rounded ruins by way of various labelled shrubs.

Leave the *dolina* and retrace your steps to the clearing for parking cars. Follow the main track back up the valley, keeping to the right. This track heads more directly back, passing between plantations. Keep straight on to leave the Valle Lanaittu and return to the Su Gologone road.

If you have chosen to stay at Hotel Su Gologone, take a short walk the next morning down to the eponymous *sorgente*. This karst spring, which spouts some 300 litres of water per second from a narrow fissure, is set in a pretty landscape and topped by a chapel.

## OTHER WALKS IN THE REGION

### Cala Gonone cliffs
The coastline north of Cala Gonone is quite dramatic as the Supramonte di Oliena plunges into the Golfo di Orosei. Walk to the end of the seaside road and descend steps to pick up a rough track marked with green arrows. Landslips have damaged the track and necessitate some scrambling but the effort is repaid with views and soaring caves. One hour on, you reach sheer cliffs, popular with rock climbers. More scrambling takes you to another cave. The path becomes too difficult and waymarks vanish, so return to Cala Gonone. *Allow 2.5 hours.*

### Cala Luna to Baunei
For those prepared to camp out, there is a route through uninhabited country along the coast. It begins at Cala Luna which can

Cliffs north of Cala Gonone

be reached by boat or on foot from Cala Gonone (see Walk 1). A rough track then leads from Cala Luna south along the coast to Cala Sisine. It follows the Codula Sisine inland to the remote church of San Pietro. From the church, a track leads down to the small town of Baunei, from where you can catch a bus back north. *Allow 2 days.*

### Monte Novo San Giovanni
This is a relatively easy walk in the Supramonte di Orgosolo which takes you past waterfalls to a limestone peak 1,316 m high. You will need a car to reach the starting point. From Orgosolo, which is southwest of Dorgali and Oliena, follow the southbound minor road (marked to Funtana Bono) for 18 km and leave your car at the Caserma Montes. Follow the track which keeps to the right of the Cedrino valley to pass Funtana Rubia and then the better known Funtana Bona. The track veers north and then east; it then becomes a footpath and climbs to the summit of Monte Novo San Giovanni. Return by the same route. *Allow 2 to 3 hours.*

# CAGLIARI

NOTES
Population: 240,000
Getting there: bus from airport 8 km
  (5 miles) NW; rail in Sardegna;
  ferries from mainland and Sicilia
Tourist Office: Piazza Matteotti, 9
  Tel: 070 669255  Fax: 070 664923
  www.tiscalinet.it/asstca
Markets: Sant'Elia on Sundays

Cagliari, the capital of Sardegna or Sardinia, is a wonderful town for walking. Its sizeable hill is not high enough to leave you exhausted but proffers a superb panorama over the city and its surrounds, so you get a clear picture of the sheltered bay which made Cagliari a safe harbour, and of the lagoons and swampland that threatened its inhabitants with malaria. Today the city is thankfully malaria-free and you will find it a smart, sensuous and charming place to explore.

There are signs, such as the great ruins at Su Nuraxi, of settlement by Nuraghic people, but Cagliari was probably founded by Phoenician traders as a handy stopping point between the Middle East and the Iberian peninsula. In 509 BC the Phoenicians sought help from Carthage to subdue local tribes. Kàralis or 'the rocky city' flourished as a trading centre and was a prize of the Punic Wars for the Romans, who gave it civic amenities and an amphitheatre for entertainment.

Following the fall of Roma, Sardegna fell prey to the Vandals, and was liberated by Byzantine forces, only to endure centuries of Arab raids. The seafaring powers of Genova and Pisa took turns to occupy the city, the Pisans fortifying its hilltop with walls, gates and watchtowers. In 1323 the Aragonese arrived and fought long and hard to control the rest of Sardegna. Their Spanish influence is visible in many of Cagliari's churches. The whole island was bartered in various treaties and given to the House of Savoy who developed the port area and founded the university. In WWII the city suffered heavy Allied bombing, so that old and new are now juxtaposed sharply in Cagliari.

Constrained on two sides by lagoons and marshland frequented by migratory birds, Cagliari's modern sprawl is to the north and you will be little troubled by car traffic. The historic core is mostly contained within the Pisan walls but a few outlying sites will demand your attention.

The warren of alleys behind Via Roma hides numerous places to try the local cuisine. The main shopping street is Largo Carlo Felice which rises from the harbour, but the *passeggiata* is more serious along Via Manno. A longer promenade is made at the beginning of each May when, during the Feast of Sant'Efisio, the saint's statue is carried on foot through the city and then by ox cart to the town of Nora, all to commemorate deliverance from the plague in 1656. There's no need to walk that far to enjoy the sights of Cagliari.

Detail on a Pisan watchtower

Rooftops of Cagliari >

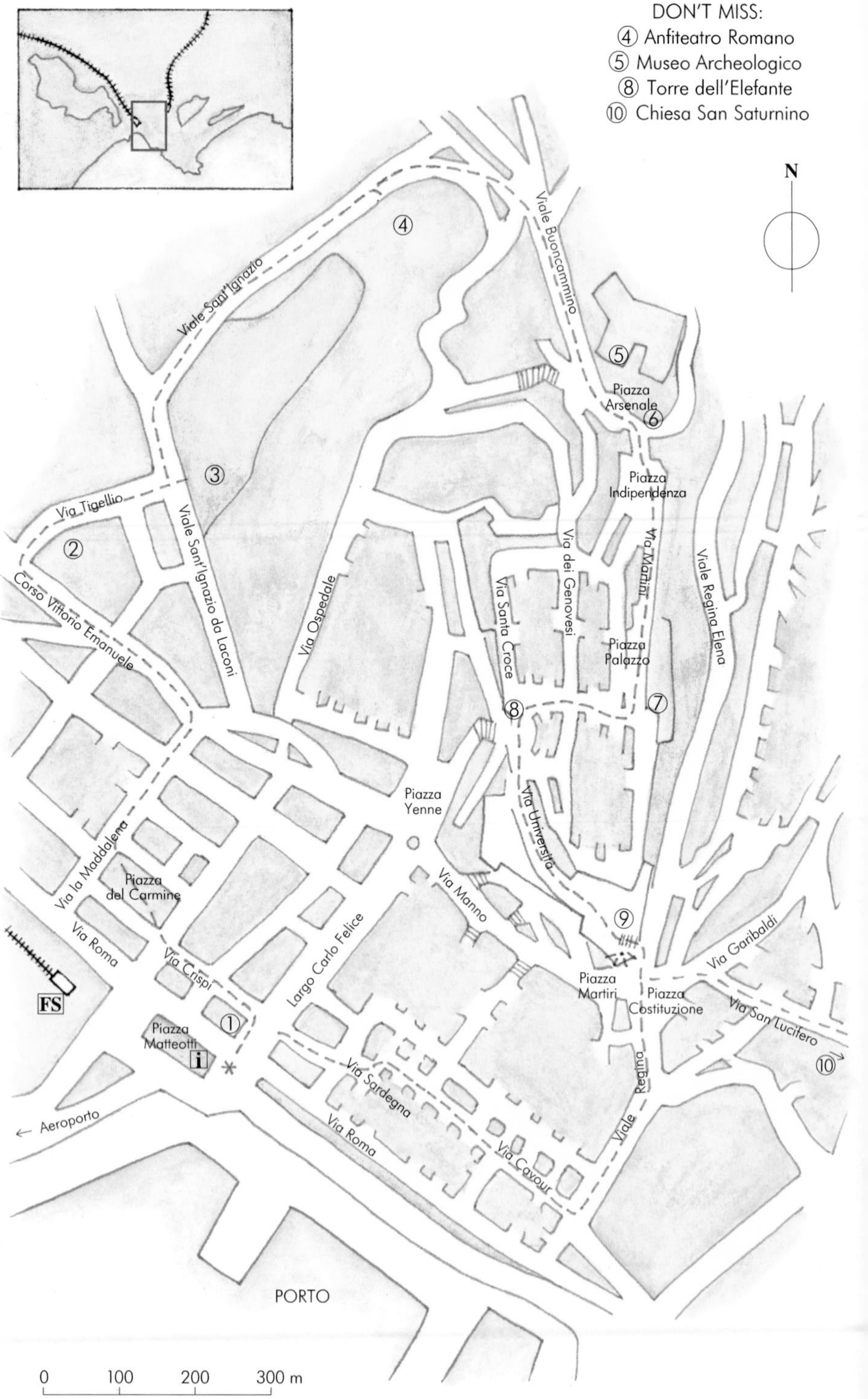

DON'T MISS:
④ Anfiteatro Romano
⑤ Museo Archeologico
⑧ Torre dell'Elefante
⑩ Chiesa San Saturnino

N

④

Viale Sant'Ignazio

Viale Buoncammino

⑤

Piazza
Arsenale
⑥

Piazza
Indipendenza

③

Via Tigellio

Via dei Genovesi

Via Mamiari

Viale Regina Elena

②

Corso Vittorio Emanuele

Viale Sant'Ignazio da Laconi

Via Ospedale

Via Santa Croce

Piazza
Palazzo

⑦

⑧

Piazza
Yenne

Via Università

Via la Maddalena

Via Manno

Via Roma

Piazza
del Carmine

Via Crispi

Largo Carlo Felice

⑨

FS

Via Garibaldi

Piazza
Martiri

Piazza
Costituzione

Via San Lucifero

①

Piazza
Matteotti
ℹ

*

Via Sardegna

Viale Regina

⑩

← Aeroporto

Via Roma

Via Cavour

PORTO

0    100    200    300 m

# A WALK IN CAGLIARI

*This itinerary takes you from the port up to the high Castello district and back down, visiting places marked by Punic, Roman, Pisan and Spanish influence along the way.*

This route starts near the waterfront in Piazza Matteotti where there is a tourist kiosk. Large ferries to Sicilia and the mainland arrive and depart from the nearby wharves. Busy Via Roma is arcaded on the city side with a string of cafés in its shade. Cross Via Roma to the corner building, the ① **Palazzo Civico**, which functions as the town hall. Despite its Gothic appearance, it was built in the early 20th century and restored after WWII bomb damage.

Start walking up the broad Largo Carlo Felice but quickly turn left into Via Crispi. Cut through the pleasant Piazza del Carmine and walk up La Maddalena. Turn left into Corso Vittorio Emanuele and then right into Via Tigellio which skirts the ② **Villa di Tigellio**. Here are the ruins of thermal baths and of three Roman villas, occupied by aristocrats during the 2nd and 3rd century. The site is generally closed to the public but you get a good view from the wire fence. The baths are nearest you, the villas are beyond, divided by an alley which runs parallel to the road. Continue up to the entrance of the lovely ③ **Orto Botanico**. An early botanic collection was relocated here in the 19th century and the gardens contain a diversity of Mediterranean and tropical plants in a shady setting. Most interestingly, the grounds include Punic and Roman wells and cisterns which are worth the viewing.

Turn right when leaving the gardens and then follow Viale Sant'Ignazio right at a fork. This climbs steeply to the entrance of ④ the **Anfiteatro Romano**, the most important Roman building in Sardegna. This vast 2nd-century amphitheatre was hewn into the limestone of a quarry; hence the steepness. A system of canals was used to fill the arena with water for *naumachiae*

Cagliari's Orto Botanico

or water battles and the pit which held wild beasts for fights is still visible. Some of the stone for the tiered seating was cannibalised for buildings in the Castello area.

Continue up the hill and then veer right onto the more level Viale Buoncammino where views reward you for the elevation gained. Walk through the archway to enter the fortified Castello district and arrive at the Piazza Arsenale. On your left is the Citadella dei Musei, converted from the Savoyard arsenal, which includes several art galleries and the ⑤ **Museo Archeologico**. This small but well-presented museum holds artefacts from Sardegna's past, including a unique collection of Nuraghic bronze figurines, stylised but strangely appealing. A visit here is worthwhile to shed more light on what you might see elsewhere in Sardegna.

At the south of the piazza stands the ⑥ **Torre di San Pancrazio**. This watchtower was built by Giovanni Capula in 1305 once the Pisans had won the city from the Genovese. From the top, 130 m (425 ft)

Torre dell'Elefante

interior's two pulpits; all were given to the city by the Pisan overlords. The rest of the marble-filled interior tends to baroque excess. A small door beside the choir leads down to the *santuario* or crypt, hewn out of the rock and decorated with 17th-century embellishments. A chapel holds the tomb of Marie of Savoy, sister to the King of Sardegna, who married Louis XVIII of France.

Descend the steps immediately in front of the cathedral and turn left at Via Santa Croce to reach the second watchtower, ⑧ **Torre dell'Elefante**. This was built by the same architect Capula in 1307 and you can still see the mechanism for opening the gate. Despite their sturdy appearance, the new defences served the Pisans poorly when the Aragonese arrived and took the city from them less than two decades later. The tower overlooks the popular Piazza Yenne, which could be reached by the steps should you feel in need of a refreshing gelato.

Otherwise, walk along Via Università, lined with elegant but dilapidated palazzi, to the imposing structure of the ⑨ **Bastione Saint Remy**, built in the late 19th century over existing Spanish ramparts. From the spacious Terrazza Umberto I you gain a stunning view of the city, the port, distant lagoons and the greater bay, including the Sella del Diavolo (Devil's Saddle) to the southeast. A flea market operates here each Sunday morning.

above the sea, a lookout could view the whole region. Three of its sides are dressed with limestone; the city side was left open, exposing the stairs.

Head down Via Martini, walking past the church of San Lucia and the 1769 palazzi of the Archbishop and the Viceroy which stand in the Piazza Palazzo. In the Middle Ages, the whole of the walled citadel was reserved for administrative and ecclesiastic buildings and for housing aristocracy; common people went home each evening to walled villages further north.

Keep straight on to arrive at the much remodelled ⑦ **Cattedrale**. This was originally built in the 13th century but its Romanesque façade was actually added in the 1930s. The lions guarding the entrance were carved by the same 12th-century sculptor who created the

The Anfiteatro Romano >

Descend the grand stairwell to find yourself in the busy Piazza Costituzione. At this point we strongly recommend that you detour some 500 m down Via San Lucifero to pass **Ex Mà** (the city's old slaughterhouse reopened as a cultural centre) and visit the early church of

⑩ **San Saturnino**. This 5th-century basilica was built in tufa on the site where the saint Saturnius was martyred and is one of the best examples of early Christian architecture to be found in Italy. Glass now protects the spare interior, introducing an oddly modern touch, but the church retains a Byzantine flavour. San Saturnino has limited opening hours but outside are various interesting fragments from the past, including sarcophagi and cannon balls.

Return to Piazza Costituzione and then walk south down Viale Regina. Before you reach Via Roma, turn right into Via Cavour, to cut through a district once the haunt of fishermen, now lined with restaurants and trattorie. At Via Napoli, turn left then right into Via Sardegna which brings you back to Largo Carlo Felice, near Piazza Matteotti.

OTHER EXCURSIONS

The **Necropoli Tuvixeddu** consist of hundreds of underground burial chambers from the Punic-Roman period. The necropolis is in the Sant'Avendrace district to the west of central Cagliari. To get there, head down Corso Vittorio Emanuele then continue along Via Falzarego. At the end, follow the unpaved track for a few hundred metres to reach the site, which is somewhat overgrown with brambles. Funerary

The *stagni* or lagoons beyond Cagliari

paintings are still visible on some of the tombs. What draws most visitors here is the **Grotta della Vipera**, the tomb of exiled Roman woman Atilia Pomptilla, which is decorated with two snakes and Latin inscriptions.

**Poetta** is a long beach and a popular marina east of Cagliari's centre. It lies at the foot of the shapely Sella del Diavolo which is mostly occupied by the military. To get there, take bus PF or PQ from Piazza Matteotti. From the beach you can walk west to the salt lake of Molentargius, a popular resting spot for migratory birds, including the pink flamingo.

---

OPENING HOURS

| | |
|---|---|
| Orto Botanico | daily 9-1; also Mon-Fri 3-7 from April -Sep |
| Anfiteatro Romano | daily 9-1 & 5-8 in summer; daily 8.30-5.30 in winter |
| Museo Archeologico | daily 9-2; also Wed, Fri and Sat 3.30-6.30 |
| Torre di San Pancrazio | Tue-Sun 9-1; 3.30-7.30 |
| San Saturnino | daily 10-noon |

# OTHER AREAS FOR WALKING

Italy has many other country areas perfect for walking. Here are some of them.

## BRENTA DOLOMITI

The wild grandeur of the Brenta Massif, a western outpost of the Dolomiti, is protected by the Parco Naturale Adamello-Brenta and provides magnificent walking at all levels of difficulty. The modern resort town of Madonna di Campiglio is a good base with several cable cars and gondolas.

## VAL GARDENA

With its picture-postcard beauty, the upper Val Gardena in the northwest Dolomiti rivals the Cortina area as a walker's haven. It provides easy walking on the vast, green Alpe di Siusi, the Alps' largest plateau, beneath the sheer outcrop of the Sasso Lungo. Santa Cristina is one possible base.

## PARCO DELLA STELVIO

Italy's largest national park encloses a vast tract of the Rhaetian Alps in central north Italy. Its centrepiece, the Ortler Massif, is nearly impenetrable, but there's excellent walking in its radiating valleys. A possible base is the resort of Santa Caterina Valfurva near Bormio.

## PARCO ALPI MARITTIME

Shared between Italy and France, the Alpi Marittime in Piemonte's south are the Alps' last upsurge before the Mediterranean. If you like peace and out-of-season solitude, you could consider walking here. The park contains the ranges' highest massifs, granite peaks over 3000 m. The spa town of Terme di Valdieri makes a good base.

## SERCHIO VALLEY

In the north of Toscana is a little-known mountainous landscape at odds with its pastoral image. The valley is flanked by the jagged Monti Apuani to the west and the less daunting Orecchiella range, part of the Appennini, to the east. Corfino is a good village base for the latter; tiny Vagli di Sotto for the former.

## PARCO DEI MONTI SIBILLINI

The Monti Sibillini, Umbria's only truly wild mountains, provide superb isolated walking above the Piano Grande, a unique upland prairie which becomes a carpet of wild-flowers in spring and early summer. Lonely Castelluccio, one of Italy's highest villages, is the closest base.

< A break in the Val Gardena

<Pompeii

extensive; Ercolano's wooden structures were all preserved in a mud-slide. You can choose from several short walks around Il Vesuvio's summit crater. Napoli or Ercolano could serve as a base for all three sites.

## PARCO DELLA MADONIE

Inland from Cefalù, on Sicilia's north coast, are the Montagne della Madonie, the island's highest peaks after Etna. This national park allows for the exploration of medieval villages, caves, high plains and peaks. Good bases are Isnello, in the park's north, and Petralia Sottana in its south.

## MONTE ETNA

This smouldering volcano dominates the landscape of eastern Sicilia and is a magnet for adventurous walkers. Its many craters and lava deserts are very surreal, quite unlike other high landscapes. You can reach the summit either by a jeep service and long day walk from Piano Provenzana in the north, or by the southern approach from the Rifugio Sapienza, where a cable car usually runs part way. During active periods, the summit is off-limits.

## PARCO D'ABRUZZO

Protecting the heart of the Abruzzi Massif, the national park shelters the Appennini's rarest fauna within its immense forests. There are 150 marked itineraries providing access to valleys, mountains and cascades. The village of Pescasseroli, the park's administrative centre, is a suitable base.

## GARGANO PROMONTORY

The Gargano is the sparsely populated spur in Italy's heel, a peninsula of flowery limestone terraces, newly protected by a national park. Its ancient Foresta Umbra is Italy's largest original forest. The eastern coastline has rugged cliffs, caves and rock arches; to the north are sandy white beaches. There are numerous coastal towns.

## POMPEII, ERCOLANO & IL VESUVIO

Two fascinating days can be spent traipsing through the extraordinary ruins of Ercolano and Pompeii, each destroyed by Il Vesuvio's AD 79 eruption. Pompeii was the more opulent town and its ruins are more

Monte Etna >

# FURTHER READING

## GENERAL WALKING BOOKS

*The Independent Walker's Guide to Italy* by Frank W. Booth (very short walks)

*Walking in Italy* by Helen Gillman et al (more demanding walks)

## REGIONAL WALKING BOOKS

*100 Hikes in the Alps* by Ira Spring & Harvey Edwards (not just Italian Alps)

*Walking in the Dolomites* by Gillian Price

*Walking in the Central Italian Alps* by Gillian Price

*Walking & Eating in Tuscany & Umbria* by James Lasdun & Pia Davies

*Walking in Italy's Gran Paradiso* by Gillian Price

*Walking in Tuscany* by Gillian Price

*Walking in Sicily* by Gillian Price

## RELATED TOPICS

*A Traveller's History of Italy* by Valerio Lintner

*Wild Italy* by Tim Jepson

# USEFUL CONTACTS

ENIT (Italian State Tourist Board)
www.enit.it

**Australia**
Level 26, 44 Market St, Sydney NSW 2000
Tel: 02 92621666; Fax: 02 92621677
E: enitour@ihug.com.au

**Canada**
175 Bloor St, East Suite 907 South
Tower, M4W3R8 Toronto, Ontario
Tel: 416 9254882  Fax: 416 9254799
E: enit.canada@on.aibn.com

**Great Britain**
1 Princes St, W1R 9AY-1 London
Tel: 20 74081254  Fax: 20 74936695
E: enitlond@globalnet.co.uk

**USA**
630 Fifth Avenue, Suite 1565
New York 10111 NY
Tel: 212 2455618  Fax: 212 5869249
E: enitch@italiantourism.com

CLUB ALPINA ITALIANO (CAI)
Via E. Petrella 19, 20124 Milano
Tel: 02 2057231; Fax: 02 205723201
www.cai.it

MAP SUPPLIERS
Libreria del Viaggiatore, Via del
Pellegrino 78, **Roma**  Tel: 06 68801048

Libreria all'Orologio, Via Governo
Vecchio 7, **Roma**  Tel: 06 68806659

Libreria il Viaggio, Borgo d. Albizi 41r
50122 **Firenze**  Tel: 055 240489

Internet map suppliers:
www.themapshop.co.uk
www.stanfords.co.uk
www.omnimap.com
www.themapcentre.com

< Olives ripening in Toscana

# GLOSSARY

| ITALIAN | ENGLISH |
|---|---|
| acqua | water |
| affittacamere | rooms to let |
| agora | Roman marketplace |
| agriturismo | farm-stays |
| albergo | hotel |
| alpe | high pasture |
| alta via | high-level route |
| alto | high |
| anfiteatro | amphitheatre |
| aperto | open |
| ara | pagan altar |
| autostrada | motorway |
| badia | abbey |
| basso | low |
| battistero | baptistry |
| borgo | hamlet |
| bosco | forest, wood |
| CAI | Italian Alpine Club |
| cala | beach |
| cambio a | change at |
| campanile | bell tower |
| campo | field, piazza |
| canalone | gully |
| cappella | chapel |
| casa | house |
| cascata | waterfall |
| castello | castle |
| cattedrale | cathedral |
| cengia | ledge |
| centro storico | historic centre |
| chiesa | church |
| chiostro | cloister |
| chiuso | closed |
| cima | summit |
| città | town |
| codula | coastal gully |
| colle | hill, pass |
| comune | council |
| condottiere | leader of mercenaries |
| corso | main street |
| cortile | courtyard |
| doge | state leader |
| dolina | a depression |
| duomo | cathedral |
| eremo | hermitage |
| fattoria | farm |
| feriale | Mon to Sat |
| fermata | bus stop |
| festivo | Sun & holidays |
| fiume | river |
| fondamenta | canal path |
| fontana | fountain |
| fonte | spring |
| forcella | pass, saddle |
| foro | meeting place |
| fosso | canal or ditch |
| frazione | district |
| funivia | cable car |
| galleria | gallery, tunnel |
| ghiacciaio | glacier |
| ghiaione | scree |
| giardino | garden |
| giornaliero | daily |
| gola | gorge |
| golfo | gulf |
| grotta | cave |
| ipogeo | burial chamber |
| lago | lake |
| malga | alpine farm |
| mercato | market |
| montagna | mountain |
| mura | wall |
| museo | museum |
| neve | snow |
| nuovo | new |
| orto botanico | botanic garden |
| palazzo | mansion |
| parcheggio | carpark |
| passeggiata | a stroll |
| passo | pass |
| pasticceria | cake shop |
| pedonale | pedestrian |
| pensione | guest house |
| percorso | route |
| pericolo | danger |
| pian, piano | high plateau |
| piazza | public square |
| pieve | parish church |
| pinacoteca | picture gallery |
| podere | farm |
| ponte | bridge |
| porta | door, gates |
| pozzo | well |
| punta | point or peak |
| rifugio | mountain hut |
| rocca | fortress |
| salita | steps |
| santuario | sanctuary |
| seggiovia | chairlift |
| senso unico | one way |
| sentiero | trail |
| sorgente | a spring |
| sottoportego | passageway |
| strada | road |
| tempio | temple |
| torre | tower |
| torrente | high stream |
| trattoria | restaurant |
| val, valle | valley |
| vallone | large valley |
| vecchio | old |
| vendemmia | grape harvest |
| via | route, road |
| via ferrata | steep, cabled route |
| viale | avenue |

## DIRECTIONS

| | |
|---|---|
| a destra | to the right |
| dietro | behind |
| diritto | straight on |
| discesa | descent |
| distanza | distance |
| est | east |
| giù | down |
| in salita | uphill |
| lontano | far |
| nord | north |
| ovest | west |
| ripido | steep |
| sbagliato | wrong |
| a sinistra | to the left |
| sud | south |

## ASKING FOR HELP

| | |
|---|---|
| incidente | accident |
| giusto percorso | correct route |
| direzione | direction |
| medico | doctor |
| emergenza | emergency |
| lontano | far |
| pronto soccorso | first aid |
| aiuto! | help! |
| guida | guide |
| mappa | map |
| a piedi | on foot |
| vicino | near |
| pioggia | rain |
| ferito | wounded |

## CONVERTING DISTANCES

| | |
|---|---|
| 1 metre | 1.09 yards |
| 1 metre | 3.28 feet |
| 1 kilometre | 0.621 miles |

# INDEX